# GRANNY MIDWIVES AND
# BLACK WOMEN WRITERS
*Double-Dutched Readings*

Valerie Lee

Routledge
New York and London

Published in 1996 by
Routledge
29 West 35th Street
New York, NY 10001

Published in Great Britain by
Routledge
11 New Fetter Lane
London EC4P 4EE

Printed in the United States of America on acid-free paper.

FRONTISPIECE: A group of Mississippi granny midwives. Note that some of their bags are more "professional" than others. (Photo courtesy Mississippi Department of Archives and History)

Part of Chapter Three in the present work originally appeared as "Testifying Theory: Womanist Intellectual Thought." (1996) *Women: A Cultural Review*, edited by Isobel Armstrong and Helen Carr, 6:2. Copyright 1996 by Oxford University Press. I use it in this volume by permission of Oxford University Press.

Library of Congress Cataloging-in-Publication Data
Granny midwives and Black women writers: double-dutched readings / by Valerie Lee
p.    cm.
Includes bibliographical references and index.
ISBN 0-415-91507-4 (hc.)  —  ISBN 0-415-91508-2 (pbk.)

1. American prose literature—Afro-American authors—History and criticism. 2. American prose literature—Women authors—History and criticism. 3. Women and literature—United States—History—20th century. 4. Afro-American midwives in literature. 5. Afro-American women in literature. 6. Afro-American midwives—History. 7. Afro-Americans in literature. I. Title.
PS153.N5L43   1996
818'.5099287'08996073—dc20

96-31239
CIP

*To my grandmother, Lydia,*
*who delivered my sister, Patty*

*and*

*To my children, Erica, Jessica, Adam, and Andrew*
*All of whom can jump double-dutch*

# CONTENTS

# ILLUSTRATIONS

# ACKNOWLEDGMENTS

For archival materials, I thank the following: The Penn Center of St. Helena Island and Alfreda Smalls Thompson with whom I walked as a "daughter of the dust"; Waring Historical Library at the Medical University of South Carolina; The South Carolina Historical Society; The Avery Research Center for African American History and Culture at the College of Charleston; The Georgia Department of Archives and History; The Southern Historical Collection at The University of North Carolina, Chapel Hill; The Smithsonian Institute's Office of Folklore Programs; The Mississippi Department of Archives and History; The Amistad Research Center at Tulane University; the Archives, Manuscripts, and Special Collections at the Earl K. Long Library, University of New Orleans (especially Beatrice Rodriquez Owsley for remembering where a discarded picture of an early granny was); The Schomberg Center for Research in Black Culture; and Elizabeth Higgs, cultural anthropologist at the Bureau of Florida Folklife Programs, who took a special interest in my research.

For personal interviews, I thank the following great storytellers: Lavella Crawford, Maggie Moore, Jessie Mae Newsome, Bertha Parker, and Carver Parker.

For academic support, I thank: The Ohio State University Seed Grant Program and The Elizabeth Gee Fund for Research on Women; The Robert C. Good Fund at Denison University; my colleagues for their support and critical conversations; all of my Summer Research Opportunities Program (SROP) students (Vernell Bristow, Angela French, Kochobie Gibson, Leslie Higbee, Tonya West, Wesley Williams, Jr.) and the many graduate students in my English and Women's Studies classes, especially Kim Sanders for all her tedious work with midwifery registration records and a computer program that will remain unmentioned, Jodi Lastman for the creativity and joy she brought to the project, Bennis Blue and Tonya Briggs for their vigilance in looking out for me, and Linda Stingily for introducing me to her family.

For invaluable support, I thank: M.C. Adams and Mary Stingley Wesley for their help in Mississippi; my research assistants: Rosemary Hathaway, who believed in the project from its inception, Antonia MacDonald-Smythe, to whom I am forever indebted, and Susan Yadlon, who in a room full of black women, turned out to be the only person who really knew how to jump double-dutch, showing that if white men can't jump, white women certainly can.

For personal and family support, I thank: the Ephesians and other saints who prayed for me; my reading group, Womanist Readers, who share my passion for speakerly/sisterly texts; my children who missed choir rehearsals, soccer games, and sit-down meals so mommy could finish her book; my sister Patty and my mother-in-law, Ernestine Lee, for becoming my children's *othermothers*; my mother, Ann Gray, for sharing with me her love for archival work and for cleaning my house while I was cleaning my manuscript. And I thank my husband James for his love and encouragement in the midnight hour.

Young girls, Jessica, Erica, Nyika, and Kara, warming
themselves on a wintry day by jumping double-dutch.
(Photos by Valerie Lee)

INTRODUCTION

# *Sistah* Conjurer
## *Text and Context*

*So I'm lettin out one a my secrets. I don't want to bury em.*
*There's so much that I don't want to die with. Not sharin it with*
*somebody....*

—Midwife Onnie Lee Logan, *Motherwit: An Alabama*
   *Midwife's Story*


*Jump Shamador, my darling. Jump Shamador my dear.*

—West Indian and African-American Jump Rope Song

HAVING DELIVERED HUNDREDS OF BABIES IN A CAREER SPANNING almost forty years, Onnie Lee Logan in *Motherwit*, the first book devoted to the life of a granny midwife, expresses her desire and impetus for telling her story. Because so many of her fellow grannies already had died by the time she narrated her story to Katherine Clark, and others were well beyond eighty years old, Onnie Lee Logan worried about the necessity and expediency of speaking her story. That story is an oral autobiography of a woman who, delivering babies, dispensing medicines from nature's pharmacopeia, and maintaining age-old traditions, saw her role in the community as God's servant and woman's agent. Before her death, Logan, in the spirit of what black feminist critic Patricia Hill Collins calls "an ethic of caring and accountability,"[1] shares some of her secrets.

Perhaps Onnie Lee Logan would have been less worried had she known that in the absence of sustained historical accounts of grannies, twentieth-century African American women writers were resuscitating the representation of the granny, breathing new life into a woman stooped with age, and thereby creating complementary, but alternative literary texts to the grannies' lived texts. Logan might have been less worried had she known that African American women writers—"culture bearers,"[2] Toni Morrison calls them—were participating in the reconstruction of the granny[3] and her cultural matrix. In the folkloristics of African American women writers, healing, rootworking, and midwifery are important activities, and the characters who practice these skills are central to their narratives. As such, the granny's life is not depicted as a past historical occurrence, but as an evolving cultural icon. The writers recognize that the granny's story is contested terrain, a story constantly being rewritten on a number of different social registers. In response, these writers offer their own rewriting and reformulation of the granny midwife. Critic Athena Vrettos calls the attention which African American women writers give to black women healers "the first step in the healing of ancestral wounds" (456).

This volume is interested in both texts—the historical grannies' life stories and the literary artists' re-creation of those stories. In preserving the spirit and substance of the two types of culturally grounded texts, I discuss ways in which each speaks to the other by using methods that are themselves culturally grounded. The need for more culturally grounded frameworks for the reading and teaching of African American literature has long been apparent. From Henry Louis Gates's early work on speakerly texts[4] and Elsa Barkley Brown's creative use of reading as quilting[5] to bell hooks's and Cornel West's concepts of breaking bread,[6] there has been a desire on the part of African Americanist critics to provide what Karla Holloway calls a "cultural mooring place."[7]

I call my cultural mooring narrative method "reading double-dutch," a reference to jumping double-dutch, a folk activity on playgrounds across America. Although both white and black girls and boys jump double-dutch, traditionally double-dutch has been associated especially with the lives of African American girls,[8] who have been instrumental in artistically crafting and culturally transforming this folk activity into a sophisticated performance. Unlike skipping rope, jumping double-dutch requires two ropes and a company or community of jumpers, no fewer than three. The hands turn the ropes in the same direction, but with a different timing. Only by listening to the sounds of both ropes and concentrating on the rope closest to them do the jumpers know when to enter the interlocking space that each rope provides. It is from that space that they chant their lore. The divergent timing of the turning of the ropes is as important as the interlocking space that beckons the jumpers to enter. While chanting, the girls must keep complementary rhythms or else they become entangled in the ropes. They must be sure that one rope is above their heads and one is at their feet.

There are two ropes to my analysis—the lives of the historical grannies and the writings of African American women writers. What does narrative double-dutch mean? Deliberately eschewing a "lore-in-literature" approach,[9] I am less interested in proving authenticity and one-to-one correspondences between the cultural and literary "granny texts" than I am in suggesting dual cultural performances—the grannies as performers; the literary texts as performances, two sets of meanings interacting with each other. Therefore my procedure will be to move easily between the two performances, much like young black girls do when jumping double-dutch. To separate one rope from the other is not to jump double-dutch at all, but merely to skip rope, mimetic representation. Jumping double-dutch requires the jumpers to multiply locate themselves between ropes. The greater sophistication and creativity demanded by jumping and reading double-dutch result in a more integrated performance. Anyone can skip rope. Double-dutch, however, has attained sportslike status.[10] After my beginning chapters develop the historical and literary tradition, I use Toni Morrison's *Song of Solomon* and Gloria Naylor's *Mama Day* to show how both histories come together. Rather than privileging either folklore methodology or literary methodology, I read double-dutch.

Why is it that with the history of the grannies and their representation in African American women's literature, it is particularly important for critics to read double-dutch? How does the process change the way readers perceive text and context? Reading double-dutch allows readers to hear more readily the orality of these texts. It also permits readers to see how the writers use the figure of the granny midwife for multiple purposes: to place in the foreground the politics of race, gender, and class; to affirm a history of resistance; and to offer a counter discursive practice that problematizes notions of health, healing, and wholeness. Further, it allows the reader to notice the intertextuality of each story, how the turning of several narrative ropes simultaneously creates intertwining cultural performances. As someone who teaches women's studies, black studies, literary studies, and folklore, reading double-dutch gives me the interdisciplinary freedom I cherish.

Through oral autobiographies, archival data, ethnographic materials, and personal interviews, I explore how the writers transform the granny's "text" into narrative myth. Yet I am not as interested in one-to-one correspondences as I am in interplay, which my trope of a double-dutched reading highlights. I combine the writers' mythologizing of the midwife/woman healer character with the many different voices of historical grannies in order to re-create a polyphonic range of black women's voices, jumping in the space between orality and literacy. As such, I share Hazel Carby's insight regarding the relationship between literary stereotypes and culture. In *Reconstructing Womanhood: The Emergence of the Afro-American Novelist* she argues:

> Any analysis that measures literary stereotypes against an empirically proven
> 'reality' is motivated by the desire to find correspondences or non-
> correspondences between literary figurations and actual social behavior and
> assumes that literary forms are mere reflections of reality. . . . (22)

As a contrast to what is routinely done, Carby explores literary stereotypes as reconstructions rather than mere reflections, as expressions that "function as a disguise, or mystification, of objective social relations" (22). When black women authors write about the grannies, they reconstruct and mystify the representations. Consequently, the grannies' oral histories, the ethnographic data, and fictional narratives taken together provide an amazing interplay of storytelling rituals that become a means for both the historical and literary grannies to transcend oppression through each of their respective brands of resistance tales. The stories the historical grannies recount and the stories the fictional narratives reconstruct create a larger meta-narrative wherein the oral histories of the grannies read as cultural fictions, and the writers' fictions read as cultural performances.

## WHO ARE THE HISTORICAL GRANNIES?

> I call her "Mama" because at that time you couldn't help but say, "that's my
> mama." She's the one that really brought you onto the world, even though
> your bloodmother had a part with it.
> —Minister in video, "Delivered with Love"

Because Chapter One details a fuller history, what I want to stress in this preview of the granny is the way society socially constructed her, beginning with her very name, "granny," a contested term. Lay midwives, indigenous midwives, traditional birth attendants, and folk or common midwives are alternative names for the granny (Doughtery, "Southern Midwifery" 125; Davis and Ingram 198). Almost exclusively associated with black women's lay midwifery practices and experiences, "granny" has been both a burdensome label as well as handy nomenclature. Although rooted in the fact that most of these women were older women, hence "grannies," there is no escaping the patronizing and servile echoes of the term. When other older black women were "aunties," simply by virtue of a monolithic racial categorization, the grannies, as women too old for their masters' fields or sexual advances, at least enjoyed the distinction of a grouping by vocation. Sometimes called "cotton dollies," the grannies were not necessarily the same as the plantation's mammies. Edna Roberts, Director of Public Health Nursing for the Mississippi State Department of Health, using information from Mississippi State Archives, makes a subtle but important distinction between the two groups of women, a distinction that fiction writers sometimes erase:

> The granny midwives or cotton dollies were women who delivered the slave population. Mammies delivered plantation owners' women and raised their children. After the Civil War the mammies usually remained on plantations to care for the owners' children, whereas the granny midwives or cotton dollies assumed the role of itinerant midwife for local African-American communities. . . . It is the latter group that eventually came under the supervision of the state health department. (57)

"Granny" was a label that never let the women forget they were black lay midwives. By the early decades of the twentieth century, "granny" had become a term so associated with ignorant, southern, black women that one would have thought its usefulness irrecoverable. But as members of a group known for taking names thrust upon them [11] and reinvesting those names with their own sets of meanings, the grannies, as if assured of their place in history, have themselves in past decades embraced "granny," not as a racial epithet, but as a derivative of *grand*—wise women who stand tall in their communities. It is in the spirit of this recovery of the term that I use it in my study.

Sharon Robinson, critic and professor of midwifery and black health-care systems, argues in her 1984 study for the *Journal of Nurse-Midwifery* that the first black lay midwife came to America in 1619, bringing with her a knowledge of health and healing based on her African background. With the growth of slave communities in America and slavery's emphasis on the breeding of human chattel, black lay midwives performed important roles. They were everything from herbal to ritual specialists. Delivering babies was respectful, ancient work, and African American lay midwives, as well as the early midwives of most cultures, earned respect for their skills. From Reconstruction to the end of the nineteenth century, black lay midwives continued to deliver babies of both black and white women, particularly in rural, southern communities.

It was common for grannies to practice for thirty to fifty years, delivering several generations of a family. Usually, they worked a particular area of a county, respecting the boundary lines of other grannies. Noted for their attention to the needs of the whole family, grannies customarily moved in with the family several weeks or days before birth and stayed at least nine days and sometimes several weeks afterward. Most gave nine days of postnatal attention because, as so many grannies said, "If it takes nine months to have a baby, the least I could do was to stay nine days." During the time spent prenatally and postnatally, the grannies assisted in doing whatever the household needed:  cooking, mending, babysitting, washing, any task that in the long run would help the mother. For those families for whom the midwife could not come early or who did not solicit her in advance, a selected family member would walk to fetch her before labor started. Oftentimes, an apprentice would be present at the birth. Unlike apprentices in other vocations, the apprentice to the granny had to have more than a willingness to learn a particular skill; she, too, needed some sign that she had been "called":

> Because the passing on of the tradition to either a female relative or a young woman who had received a special calling from God was a matter of grave importance, the lines of authority and transmission of midwifery skills and lore were tightly controlled. (Mathews 63)

The greatest numbers of practicing grannies were from the turn of the century through the mid 1920s. A federal public health survey in the early 1920s estimated a total of 43,627 practicing lay midwives, most of whom were black, serving primarily black communities (Kalisch and Kalisch in Edna Roberts 58). As late as the 1940s the percentages, although declining, were still very high with grannies assisting "more than 60 percent of childbirths by black women in Alabama, Arkansas, Florida, Georgia, Mississippi, and South Carolina (Blackburn in Davis and Ingram 192). Licensure procedures, repeal of federally funded midwife-training programs,[12] mandatory retirement ages, and changes in notions of what constituted good health care were among the major factors affecting the decline in numbers.

State by state analyses follow the larger pattern. In Mississippi in 1921, there were 5,000 registered grannies; in 1941, roughly 3,000; in 1961, barely 1,000; in 1980, there were 20 and in 1985 only one granny was listed as still practicing with a permit (Edna Roberts 61). In Alabama in 1942, there were 2,200 registered grannies; by 1980, there were only 70 (*American Journal of Obstetrics and Gynecology* 691–93). In 1910, in St. Louis, Missouri 76 percent of births were attended by lay midwives, but by 1955 only six lay midwives were listed in the city directory, from a number of 340 listings in the early part of the century (Perry 21).

According to the many surveys that Holly Mathews of the Southern Anthropological Society analyzed to study midwifery populations in North Carolina, in 1925 there were 6,500 lay midwives, representing one-third of all babies born in North Carolina. Of the 6,500, 80 percent were black. A later survey in 1931 indicated midwife-assisted births at 31 percent, 23,234 of the 74,743 babies born. By 1940, only 24.6 percent of the births were attended by midwives, by 1950 only 10.9 percent, by 1970, only fifty registered lay midwives were still in practice, by 1980, only ten were practicing, "and in 1988 there were no official records of any deliveries in North Carolina by lay midwives" (Mathews 61). "Killing the Medical Self-Help Tradition Among African Americans," the title of Mathews's article places her among an increasing number of scholars who are now asking what has been lost with the demise of a strong granny tradition. In states such as North Carolina the "unapproved practice of midwifery was named a misdemeanor, and a grace period was declared from the law's effective date of 1 October 1983 until April 1984, for midwives authorized under the repealed law to leave the field of practice" (Mathews 76), accounting for decline in numbers from the early 1980s to the late 1980s.

Over the past decades, it has been very difficult to tabulate the number of grannies. Many practiced and a few continue to practice despite lack of registration with the respective county boards of health. When I asked one informant whether her grandmother, a well-known, Huntsville, Alabama, midwife, had been properly registered, she replied, "When Big Mom heard the officials were coming, she left and went fishing, not wanting to be bothered with the paper work" (Crawford Interview 1995). Forms used to gather occupational information, such as income tax forms, have not been useful, for many did not file income taxes and "only where lay midwives are licensed does a register of their names exist" (Reid 225).

These grannies did not have the same status as midwives today do. Contemporary midwives are nurse-midwives, credentialed nurse specialists, rather than the "ritual and ceremonial specialists,"[13] which the grannies were. In speaking of southern lay midwifery, Molly C. Dougherty notes:

> Midwives, holding positions at the lowest level of the health hierarchy, are deprecated, their skills and abilities rarely appreciated by those above them. Within their own communities they provide needed services, and their supernatural and technical abilities are respected. Lay midwifery in the South exemplifies women in conflict, competition, and cooperation, often manipulated and controlled by institutions over which they have little control. (163)

Although respected in their communities, the grannies had to juggle their communities' needs with state requirements. States have never been uniform in their position on lay midwifery. Even today, some allow lay midwifery if the grannies have passed a state qualifying examination; some require that they be registered; others are silent on the whole issue; and many prohibit lay midwifery altogether (Reid 220). As far back as 1961, Beatrice Mongeau argued that grannies were surviving through their "power and prestige in the Negro community" (Mongeau et al. 497). I would add that today the grannies survive because of the rescue operations of black women writers. Grannies often expressed their desire for someone to carry on after them with their willingness to help those who would be their apprentices. As granny Mary Lee Jones said in an interview, "Anyone who want to come up, they can come on under me" (Susie 169). It is as if the writers, would-be aprrentices, have accepted the invitation to come up under the grannies.

### WHO ARE THE LITERARY GRANNIES?

*Everybody's mama now.*
—Gloria Naylor, *Mama Day*

Midwives, root workers, and traditional women healers dominate and transform the narratives of a significant number of black women writers, including Toni Morrison, Alice Walker, Gloria Naylor, Toni Cade Bambara, Julie Dash, Ntozake Shange, Tina Ansa, and Paule Marshall, to name a few. These authors invest women healers with magical, ancient, life-affirming powers that rise out of their characters' folkloric pasts and persist as part of their functioning present. Despite the early efforts of science and history to silence the grannies, the writers continue to bring to voice Pilate, Circe, Marie-Thérèse, Ajax's Mom, Indigo, Minnie Ransom, Aunt Cuney, Nana Pezant, and a host of other women healers and midwives.

Called everything from swamp hag and snake to "everybody's mama now" (*Mama Day* 89), these characters rise tall in their respective works, so much so that Morrison speaks of not wanting Pilate "to loom too large."[14] In her multiple roles as midwife, herbalist, and traditional healer, the literary granny is a character with an eclectic profession and an electric presence. It is often through the literary grannies' multiple roles that the writers place in the foreground the politics of identity, race, and class. As black women catering to mostly poor neighborhoods, the grannies are apt subjects for theorizing difference. Unfortunately, the medical establishment began to see their roles as regressive, even transgressive.

It has remained the task of the women writers, along with a very active black women's health movement,[15] to bring renewed dignity to the grannies. Writers such as Toni Morrison, whose great-grandmother was a midwife (McKay 416), and Alice Walker, who grew up fed by her mother's stories of women's folk healing, bring to their narratives culturally based health beliefs. It is through these types of collective memories that African American women writers choose lay midwives and women healers as pivotal characters, reaffirming the validity of orality and cultural performance, engaging the complexities of a socio-literary process, contesting categories through African based cultural traditions. The documentation of births, registration records, and other paper work that health officials required, revealing the grannies' "illiteracy," has given way to literary pages that argue that these women, although unlearned, were not ignorant.

What was true of Pilate is true of the granny: "Although she was hampered by huge ignorances, [she was] not in any way unintelligent" (*Song of Solomon* 149). The writers help the grannies speak by re-articulating the relationship between orality and literacy. Through their fictions, the writers try to maintain the spirit and language of oral forms, inviting us to "hear" their novels as well as read them.

The grannies spoke in stories and testimonials, not in the language of health department forms. Misunderstanding the value of African American orature, health officials saw the grannies as ignorant, unable to articulate the concerns and practices of a larger more educated community to the people in their own communities.[16] In an interview with Nellie McKay, Morrison describes the "women in [her] family [as] very articulate," although those such as her great-grandmother, the midwife, could not read (McKay 416). Black women writers, in centering the lives of the grannies, reaffirm an African-centered epistemology by exposing literacy for what it is—"a set of social practices" (Lee, *Signifying as Scaffold* 3). The writers highlight the act of storytelling by choosing a folk character, the granny, whose performance in the literary text speaks to the text of her historical performance. The constructions of the literary and historical grannies become inseparable narrative performances. The historical grannies were involved in the labor of childbirth. The literary grannies are involved in what literary critic Anne Goldman refers to as the painful labor of becoming a speaking subject (322).

The black women authors who create the literary grannies are ethnographers interested in the larger issues of socio-literary constructions of health.[17] As Butler Evans points out in speaking of Morrison's canon, "fictional narratives . . . are an ethnographic enterprise" (7). Part of the literary ethnography is to show that health and healing are related to the total worldview of a person. There are many works within African American women's literature that ask readers to recognize their views of wholeness and balance as culturally specific. As early as 1927, Georgia Douglas Johnson, the well-known Harlem Renaissance writer who wrote over thirty plays, gives us Charity Brown, a precursor of the literary women in my study in terms of how knowledge about healing is socially constructed, reflecting the values of its culture.

Charity Brown is one of four characters in Johnson's award-winning play, *Plumes.*[18] The play opens with Charity heating a poultice to use to cure her sick daughter. At the same time she is working on finishing a dress for her daughter. Her friend, Tildy, volunteers to help her finish the dress. They baste the hem, allowing for the flexibility of having a short dress if the daughter lives, but a longer one if she dies. Almost fourteen, the daughter is suffering, and Charity is trying to improve the poultice. The doctor is supposed to be on his way, although Tildy observes, "doctors is mighty onconcerned here lately" (25). As the girl gets sicker, Charity "braces" herself and puts the coffee on the stove. She is worried because

> "The doctor said last time he was here he might have to operate—said she mought have a chance then. But I tell you the truth, I've got no faith a-tall in 'em. They takes all your money for nothing." (25)

Tildy agrees with Charity's view of modern doctors: "They takes all you got and then you dies jest the same. It ain't like they was sure" (26). The two women begin to talk about funerals and the audience learns that they live in a community that values how one puts away a loved one, no matter how poor. They believe in "a shore nuff funeral, everything grand,—with plumes!" (26). Charity asks Tildy to foretell the future by reading coffee grounds. Tildy looks in the cup and sees a procession, and then an actual funeral procession passes by the house. It is the funeral of a woman for whom death ends intense suffering. Charity and Tildy are impressed with the plumes on the horses' heads. This funeral is a "fine sight" and they praise the woman's husband for "putting her away grand." Finally the doctor comes and orders the mother out of the daughter's room, telling her, "You can't possibly be of any service." The doctor wants to operate and the women are faced with a choice. They have money for an operation or for a funeral. Their hesitancy to make an immediate decision causes the doctor to question their love for the child. What kind of mother is Charity? Certainly, her mother's love ought to make her choose the operation.

Yet Charity does not see the issue as one of love. Of course, she loves her daughter, but as Tildy reminds her, the doctor is "promising nothing and ten to one killing her to boot. . . . Don't you trus' him. Coffee grounds don't lie" (29). The failure of modern medicine to promise recovery with certainty disturbs Charity. She is caught between the inexactness of science and the "coffee grounds [that] don't lie." The doctor tells her to throw out the "senseless" coffee grounds. To misread the story is to conclude that the mother does not want to place money on the daughter. She does, but she wants to do it in a way that is both medically and culturally responsible. I am reminded of two Hausa proverbs that reflect her dilemma: "*Magani da ku'di, shi ne da wuyar sha*": Expensive medicine is difficult to drink; and "*Wanda zai mutu magani ba ya tsaishe shi ba*":

Medicine will not revive one who is doomed to die (Wall 279; 284).

Charity's feelings, the air, the coffee grounds, all tell her what to do. Just then, the two women hear a strangling noise and running into the daughter's room, Charity decisively gives the final lines of the play, "Rip the hem out, sister Tildy" (30). The daughter is dead and one can read the ending in divergent ways. The women were right all along; the daughter was too far gone and the money would be best spent on her funeral. Or perhaps Charity and Tildy waited too long and should have without hesitation given the doctor permission to operate, not that he had brought his tools with him.

The dilemma of the ending is not nearly as important as the message this early story in the African American women's literary tradition gives: attitudes about health are rooted in the larger cosmology of one's views on life and death, and all perspectives are culturally mediated. The white doctor fails to see his science as a cultural system.[19] Although state-sanctioned, he is not more informed or more sensitive than the women. As ethnographers, black women writers create a literary text that both comments upon and changes the social text.

## WHO ARE *SISTAH* CONJURERS?

> We *live in* conjure.
> —Houston Baker, Jr., *Workings of the Spirit*

To use the collective term *"sistah* conjurer" is to recognize the multiple roles, the versatility, and the African heritage of the grannies and writers who are engaged in a curative transformation of reality, a process so complex as to require a double-dutched reading. Historically, conjuring has been a pejorative label used to explain the inexplicable power of the Other, most notably the racial other who was thought to be steeped in African superstitions. In *Playing in the Dark*, Morrison speaks of an American need for a "brew of darkness":

> What rose up out of our collective needs to allay internal fears and to rationalize external exploitation was an American Africanism—a fabricated brew of darkness, otherness, alarm, and desire that is uniquely American. (38)

As long as there is a "brew of darkness," the magic and power of black women who mix concoctions for childbirth and general healing will always be reduced to a narrow, outsider's definition of conjuring. Often, physicians feared that dissatisfied grannies would place death hexes on them (Freedman 102–3). Despite the fact that most grannies, as Christians, eschewed any alliances with the devil, many doctors nevertheless reductively labeled their activities as witchcraft.

Rather than the negative associations of witchcraft, conjuring has been an empowering concept for many black women. Conjuring pays homage to an African past, while providing a present day idiom for magic, power, and ancient wisdom within a pan-African cultural context. My use of conjurer as a collective term for the historical and literary grannies, for the authors, and for me as critic builds upon the meanings of the word as outlined in Houston Baker's "Conjure and the Space of Black Women's Creativity" in *Workings of the Spirit: The Poetics of Afro-American Women's Writings* and Marjorie Pryse's introduction to *Conjuring: Black Women, Fiction, and Literary Tradition.*

By speaking of "conjure space" and "living in conjure," Baker widens our understanding of the poetics of African American women's writing, as his subtitle promises. Baker asserts:

> I believe the Afro-American cultural sign that appropriately unites mythomania as classical cultural performance, notions of the classical medium's space, and useful notions of the poetic image is the sign 'conjure'. (77)

Baker proceeds to point out that the conjure doctor in African American communities was commonly called a two-headed doctor, a reference to double wisdom (77). Certainly, having double wisdom was an aid to people forced to live with a double-consciousness.[20] Baker moves from what he terms a "'colonist' history of conjure" with its "stupidly condescending description" to conjure's "connection to ancient African sources syncretized by a community of diasporic believers with Christian scriptures..." (79–89). Although Charles Chesnutt has been a common source for a discussion on literary women conjurers, Baker grounds his discussion in Hurston's *Mules and Men*, for "Chestnutt, unlike Hurston, never puts forward a truly scintillating image of the woman prophet, magician, or healer herself as a figure irradiant in the magnificence of her specific powers" (78). The contemporary writers of my study and the grannies themselves put forth such an image and as such are conjurers in Baker's sense of the word.

It is only in recent years that African Americanist critics have begun speaking of conjure as a discourse to explain some of the phenomena of African American literature as well as other fields, such as African American religion. In *Conjuring Culture*, Theophus H. Smith interprets the Bible from the perspective of "descendants of Africans in North America" who saw the Bible as "the great conjure book in the world," as Zora Neale Hurston records in *Mules and Men* (280). Smith notes the "conjurational performances of black culture itself" and argues that "conjure is a magical means of transforming reality"(4). Smith is careful, however, to distinguish between American society's general notion of a magician and a differently nuanced African American conjurer: ". . . when we turn to the black American conjuror we find not only a magician but also a kind of doctor" (5). Smith's emphasis on the linkage between conjure and curative transformation holds true for my study:

> This African American meaning, conjure as folk pharmacy, appears prominently in the traditional designation of the expert practitioner as a "conjure doctor." This prominence sharply differentiates black American usage from popular use of the word to mean only imagination on the one hand, or only sorcery, witchcraft, or occultism on the other. It also indicates a point of differentiation between African American and English or European conjure traditions. (5)

The term "*sistah* conjurer," when placed within an African-based legacy, speaks to the multiple and converging positionings of the grannies and writers. *Sistah* conjurer is a term that rather than dismissing the women as superstitious or incompetent gives them historical and personal agency.

Equally useful to my study is Pryse's interpretation of conjuring. Pryse notes that Alice Walker, and I would add other black women writers, follow in Hurston's footsteps by viewing the writing of fiction as a type of conjuring (2). The magic of black women's writing is "in combining folk and female material, transforming the power of the root-doctor's conjure" (15). A *sistah* conjurer is a woman who, through ancient wisdom, can do what Pryse points out is Walker's definition of conjure in Walker's story, "The Revenge of Hannah Kemhuff": "The story defines conjure as the power to reassert the self and one's heritage in the face of overwhelming injustice" (16). In an interview in *Black Women Writers at Work*, Alice Walker informs us that she based her story, "The Revenge of Hannah Kemhuff," on one of her mother's stories, carrying around the germ of that story with her for years, waiting to use it (186). Walker dedicates the story to Hurston, from whom many of the folk cures and curse-prayers in the story are drawn.

In the story, Mrs. Kemhuff, an old black woman, visits a conjure woman, a community rootworker named Tante Rosie. Tante Rosie's apprentice narrates the story. When Kemhuff walks in the room, Tante Rosie impresses her by guessing her name out of thin air. We learn from the apprentice, however, that Tante Rosie's prescience was based on the extensive files she kept of everyone in the country in cardboard boxes under her bed. Tante Rosie begins by showing her knowledge of human psychology, rather than her knowledge of roots. From the very beginning, she tries to build Kemhuff's self-esteem and says whatever good common-sense dictates. As Kemhuff rambles on with her life story, Tante Rosie tries to act the part of being all knowing, remembering that Kemhuff's sister, Carrie Mae, was killed by a gangster, but failing to realize that the gangster was Carrie's husband. When she wants Kemhuff to speed up her story and get to the point, Tante Rosie simply announces, "I see a pale and evil shadow looming ahead of you in this journey."

This prompts Kemhuff to get to the point. During the Depression Miss Sadler, a "little white moppet," a "little slip of a woman, all big blue eyes and yellow hair, [a] little *girl*. . ." (65) had the power to decide that Kemhuff and her family were not worthy to receive food stamps. Dressed with pride but not in luxury, Kemhuff's family did not look poor or hungry enough to merit assistance. Kemhuff is incensed that this young white woman, a girl compared to her, could look her in the face, calling her "Hannah Lou" as if she were the girl and Miss Sadler were the older woman, and tell her that her family was not needy. The snowballing effect of this incident was that Kemhuff's husband leaves her and all her children die. Kemhuff almost starves to death, her body suffers, and her "spirit never recovered from that insult" (66). Her story reads as a black woman's Job story—Why do the righteous suffer? Where is God in the midst of suffering? Should I curse God and die?

Kemhuff decides to go and see Tante Rosie because it does not appear that God is on the side of the oppressed. Miss Sadler married in the spring after the incident and has been living a happy life. Kemhuff goes to Tante Rosie for retribution and justice. Tante Rosie uses some of Hurston's curse-prayers from *Mules and Men*, which make the curse prayers in David's Psalms read benevolent.[21] One representative line deals with motherhood. Instead of simply asking that the wombs of the women who are their enemies be closed, Rosie asks that the women bear children, but only for strangers, and that those children have weak minds. After the ceremony, Kemhuff leaves feeling physically and emotionally empowered.

Tante Rosie instructs her apprentice to go and tell Miss Sadler (who is now Mrs. Holley and fifty-three years old) that a hex has been placed on her. The strength of the rest of the story is that it reveals hoodoo as a signified form of psychotherapy. Decrying her nonbelief in "colored foolishness" and "nigger magic," Mrs. Holley protests too loudly, inevitably bringing about through her own fears the power of the hex. Eating her nail parings and placing all of her feces in plastic bags so that these items could not be used in the hoodoo, Mrs. Holley brings about her own demise. Tante Rosie has demonstrated that she has murderous insight into human nature,[22] and "achieves her real 'power' by affirming Hannah Kemhuff's perception of injustice" (Pryse 16).

What needs to be noted, however, is that the power of hoodoo in the story is verbal power. Baker argues that "the poetry of *conjure* as an image resides in the secrecy and mysteriousness of its sources of power. . ." (89). In "The Revenge of Hannah Kemhuff," I would argue that Walker deconstructs the idea that the power of hoodoo is in its secrecy. The threat of power, the news itself of the possibility of power, a sort of rhetorical magic, brings about the extraordinary from the ordinary.

Therefore, it is not that *sistah* conjurers exercise institutional power or corporate power, but that they "live in conjure," speak a "conjure discourse,"[23] conjuring up stories necessary for their psychic survival. Baker lists "dynamic conjuring" as one of the elements of African American women's expressive production (9). The stories that the grannies tell, the stories that the writers create, and this volume's story are all a part of a dynamic conjuring process. In *Fiction and Folklore*, Trudier Harris speaks of novelists and narrators as tradition bearers, spinning stories that pacify and provide life blood (166–67). This volume is not simply about health and healing; it spins a story as a healing event. Critic Athena Vrettos's observation is meaningful in this regard: "By taking healing as a metaphor for spiritual power, black women emphasize the restorative potential of their own narrative acts . . . locating in language a new curative domain" (456). A *sistah* conjurer uses storytelling as a curative domain. After Mrs. Kemhuff shares her story and hears all that Tante Rosie can do, she remarks, "You are a true sister" (68). A *sistah* conjurer is a true sister.

CONJURING CHAPTERS

> *Black women must speak in a plurality of voices as well as in a multiplicity of discourses.*

—Mae Henderson, "Speaking in Tongues"

Chapter One, "Western Science and Folk Medicine: White Men's Forceps and Black Women's Forces," gives a brief history of lay midwifery, concentrating on the historical moments when the grannies' histories intersect the larger history of midwifery. The literal histories of the grannies are as fascinating as the fictional narratives within which African American writers embed them. Although very much a part of a larger story, the grannies' stories, infused with their own complex nexus of racial and gender politics, are a part of, yet remain apart from, the larger story. Chapter One begins by tracing some general trends and shifts in early European and American lay midwifery: shifts from home deliveries where women encouraged each other to be active participants in their own deliveries to hospitals where babies were delivered unto women; shifts from birth as a natural process to one where birth became a medical event; shifts from midwifery as a gendered activity to one where race, gender, and class become divisive.

In this chapter I argue that of all the lay midwives practicing in America during the early twentieth century, it was the granny midwife who was most affected by changes in medicine and state regulations. It was she who had the most to lose with the movement from folklore to forceps, asafoetida to anesthesia, home to hospital, licensing from God to licensing by the State. I push this argument further by suggesting that the campaign to discredit the granny focused on more than vocational competence. The granny midwife's very body, the physical body of an elderly, black woman, was seen as unclean and deviant. Additionally, the material culture with which the granny midwife had practiced her craft, most notably her midwife's bag, became a trickster's bag for subversive practices. Prior to beginning Chapter Two, a chapter that focuses on literature, I end Chapter One with a transitional short story, illustrating how a wide range of issues in the histories of the grannies are rooted in a cultural matrix with different definitions of what constitutes health and well-being.

Chapter Two, "Literary Recovery of the Granny: The Body, the Mind, the Material," focuses on the womanist[24] reclamation of the grannies' histories. It has a call-and-response relationship to Chapter One. African

American history calls and African American literature responds. By reframing the problems outlined in Chapter One, the literary writers posit a counter-discourse on hygiene, the body, science and medicine, socio-relational politics, and material culture. Although feminist health workers and women patients in general have been able to effect a renewed interest in midwifery in general, it has taken a long list of womanist writers to come to the aid of the grannies. Literature written by black women as early as the Harlem Renaissance subverts notions of patriarchal authority by reinscribing power to the grannies and the other black women healers in the community. Although most grannies no longer practice, the literary writers refuse to concede the victory to science, using their narratives to interrogate patriarchal discourses of power that muted the grannies' powers.

In Chapter Three, "God and the Grannies: Testifying Theory," I develop the notion of the grannies as women committed as much to a spiritual tradition as to a medical one. Propelled by their sense of a divine mandate, both the fictional and historical grannies voice an ethic of caring and activism that is anchored in their self-defined spirituality. Noting the many spiritual frameworks that black critics have suggested for analysis, from Audre Lorde's definition of the erotic to Cornel West's "politics of conversion," to bell hooks's "sisters of the yam," I contend that the grannies testify theory and as such are womanist theologians. Chapter Three moves from the literal testimonies of grannies who testify to how God directed their lives to testimony as a theoretical trope. Testifying theory resonates with Mae Henderson's "speaking in tongues,"[25] and like Henderson, I "signify a deliberate intervention by black women writers into the canonical tradition of sacred/literary texts"(*Changing Our Own Words* 24). Always working within paradigms that are indigenous to my subjects, I offer at the end of this chapter, which is heavily dependent upon black church liturgies, my own "altar call"—a call for the scholar to be as much a womanist critic as the granny midwife was a womanist theologian.

Whereas Chapters One through Three demonstrate the need and lay the groundwork for a study that links ethnic literatures with indigenous medical systems by showing the topic's breadth, Chapters Four and Five demonstrate how readings of both the medical history and literature change when one uses an integrative, comprehensive approach to the canon of African American women's writings, contextualizing texts within their contexts. Chapter Four, "Women Who Work Magic: Literary and Cultural Icons," moves from a general discussion of how the writings of many African American women writers inform and reform the grannies' histories to a discussion of the earliest, most sustained example of a work that exemplifies my thesis and way of reading double-dutch: Toni Morrison's *Song of Solomon*. Through narrative and character alchemy, Morrison mythologizes her women healers. Curiously, the historical grannies constructed and re-constructed their identities in ways that made it easy for their communities and the literary writers to see them as larger than life. Indeed, by examining the information in hundreds of granny registration records, I saw a pattern emerging, a pattern that this chapter discusses. The grannies' stories are formulaic enough to be neo-slave narratives and incredible enough to be cultural romances. Thus, this chapter argues that healers as literary icons exist in tandem with the historical grannies as cultural icons, each construction playing off the other.

It is in Chapter Four where I provide a working example of my double-dutch trope for understanding my volume's interplay, an interplay that is both tight and tense. I read double-dutch between the ropes of both of my foci, not subsuming either to the other. Those proficient with double-dutch wait until they hear each rope hitting the ground before they jump in, thereby maintaining rhythm and voice. I turn both ropes, that of the grannies and that of Morrison's text, inviting all readers who have been listening to the grounding of the ropes to jump in the discourse, moving towards a more central space.

Following Chapter Four is a chapter on "Conjure Discourse in Conjuring Communities: *Mama Day* and Fieldwork in Paradise." Using the same double-dutch technique as in Chapter Four, I explore Gloria Naylor's *Mama Day* as cultural performance. The most comprehensive representative of my topic in terms of the constructions of character and a community totally immersed in a culture of healing, *Mama Day* becomes another work that profits from being read alongside the lives of historical grannies. History through the eyes of *Mama Day*'s Miranda or the historical grannies might seem a marginal viewpoint to some. However, in their respective communities, from the sea islands off the Carolina coasts to rural Alabama hamlets, these women were known for their social and political activism. Perhaps, the ordinary lives of the historical grannies become extraordinary in fictional narratives because they have always been such in their communities. For her Willow Springs community, *Mama Day*'s Miranda is both grandmother and *grand* mother.

Chapter Five ends with a narrative of my fieldwork in Mississippi. By the time readers reach this point, I hope they will be empowered with enough historical and literary rope to read double-dutch with the final narrative, without my orchestrating the ropes and without them hanging themselves. As folklorist Jack Santino points out, folklorists are "so often accused of unskeptical romanticism" (165). If there are places where I have been tempted to engage in romance, I hope the final narrative, where praxis meets practice, undermines the tendency as I walk dusty southern roads, encountering some subjects who were all too eager to talk and others who gave me their own private tests to measure my ability to hear their stories. I am humbled that some of them reflected the attitude of folklorist Rayna Green's grandmother: "Granny used to say that what I did, after asking lots of seemingly senseless questions, was 'just to lay up and write,' the equivalent in her terms of 'laying up drunk'" (7). The final narrative is a self-reflexive dialogue of a scholar who had both the audacity and temerity to "lay up and write."

In its totality, my research, far from being what James Clifford calls a "vanishing primitive" study,[26] emphasizes the vitality of the grannies' stories and the growing body of African American women's fiction that sustains and energizes the stories. Although the authors write works that present a full range of African American folklore, including proverbs, myths, superstitions, folk language, folktales, folk customs and customary behavior, dance, and music, the figure of the granny midwife/woman healer provides a pivotal structural and thematic framework. By exploring the relationship between a literary folk figure and her complementary ethnomedical framework, I follow in the footsteps of those African American artists who, resisting dichotomous categorizations of art and life as distinct, emphasize a way of coming to know that runs counter to many Western discursive practices.

In the end, I hope to have written a volume that is as useful to the communities that generate the lore as to those that study the lore. I do not wish to fall prey to the same weaknesses as characters I later discuss: *Beloved*'s schoolteacher, *Dessa Rose*'s historian, or *Mama Day*'s Reema Boy. Schoolteacher, the man of learning in *Beloved*, was surreptitiously writing a book about Sethe and the other slaves: "It was a book about us but we didn't know that right away" (37). Adam Nehemiah, the historian in *Dessa Rose*, is so obsessed with his subject that he becomes the animal he accuses Dessa of being. Schoolteacher and Adam, white men of learning writing black women's lives, separate themselves from their subjects. I most fear becoming a Reema's boy—someone whose distance from his subjects has been a matter of crossing certain bridges. After reading the scholarship of Reema's boy, who was born and bred in their all black community, the residents of Willow Springs feel that modern educators have made him a "raving lunatic." They complain that the educators went so far as to "put his picture on the back of the book so we couldn't even deny it was him—didn't mean us a speck of good" (*Mama Day* 8). I hope that those in whose communities I have lived will not question my mind nor my motive. I do mean more than "a speck of good."

# ONE

# Western Science and Folk Medicine

## White Men's Forceps and Black Women's Forces

*For black women, history is a bridge defined along motherlines. It begins with a woman's particular genealogy and fans out to include all the female culture heroes, like the folk curers and shamans known as root workers and Obeah women. . . .*

—Susan Willis, *Specifying: Black Women Writing the American Experience*

*You uncompetent nigra woman. You don't know what you're doin. If you want to deliver any mo' babies go back to Africa where you come from.*

—Doctor in *Motherwit: An Alabama's Midwife Story*

GRANNY MIDWIVES ARE THE FOREMOTHERS AND HISTORICAL counterparts of Pilate (*Song of Solomon*), Marie-Thérèse, (*Tar Baby*), Minnie Ransom (*The Salt Eaters*), Indigo (*sassafras, cypress & indigo*), Sapphira Wade and Miranda Day (*Mama Day*), Baby Suggs (*Beloved*), and a host of other literary black women healers and midwives. A study of the early presence and subsequent forced absence of the historical granny midwives helps one to understand what literary recovery entails. The historical grannies were women whose roles, although central to their communities, were distinctly circumscribed by a complex nexus of racial, gender, and class politics. Theirs is a history that is *a part of* the longer history of women as healers; yet many elements of their history remain *apart from* the history of Anglo-American women healers.

To examine this history, a history that moves from folklore to forceps, from asafoetida to anesthesia, from home to hospital, from license from God to licensing by the State is to begin to understand how these women's lives were entangled in America's politics of cultural interpretations, politics that stereotyped black women as Mammy, Sapphire, Jezebel.[1] Although unique in their myriad functions and revered by their respective communities, the grannies battled a medicalization process that they were destined to lose. Characterized by some doctors as "uncompetent nigra wom[e]n" (Logan 166), they were women who lost their high cultural status, their bodies becoming the terrain where a history of desire and defiance was fought.

In this chapter I situate the historical granny by first summarizing issues from the larger history of midwifery that were to affect the South's grannies. How does one move from a Euro-American worldview that said a man in a birthing chamber should be burned[2] to government publications that describe midwives as "necessary evils"? (Bredesen 23). How did the practice of midwifery become the midwife problem? Or, to raise a question at the heart of American midwifery history: "How did one particular set of healers, who happened to be male, white and middle class, manage to oust all the competing folk healers, midwives and other practitioners who had dominated the American medical scene in the early 1800's"? (Ehrenreich and English 21).[3] Why was it necessary to discredit the women in order to legitimate the doctors?

Second, and more important to this volume's purpose, I show how this history takes a distinctive twist when black women began to dominate rural southern midwifery. This was a time when the grannies' phrase "catching babies" became "studying obstetrics," erupting cultural conflicts over the black female body and psyche. I examine this history so as to lay the foundation for Chapter Two where I argue that the historical and cultural contexts of the grannies' lives inform African American women's literature. Whereas feminist social scientists and medical persons have reclaimed nurse midwifery, it has been left to African American women novelists to preserve the language, lore, and learning of the grannies. This chapter historicizes the lives of the granny midwives and those aspects of African-American women's literature that speak to that history.

Some contend that midwifery is the second oldest profession (Freedman 102). Whatever its ranking in chronological lists of vocational beginnings, one fact is clear: among the many records of midwives, there are records of biblical midwives (Exodus1:15–22), Greek and Roman midwives (Towler and Bramall), and West African midwives (Mbiti). Historical midwives include Socrates' mother. Although many of the women from antiquity, including nuns and ladies of the manor, performed their duties as acts of charity, British history records a tradition of women who delivered babies for pay. Cecilia of Oxford, court surgeon to Queen Philippa, wife of Edward III, was such a midwife (Donnison 2). In America, midwife Bridget Lee Fuller,wife of Deacon Samuel Fuller, came over on the Mayflower and practiced midwifery until her death in 1664.[4] Many other colonial women, including Anne Hutchinson, known more for her religious fervor, worked as midwives. For centuries, women proudly functioned as midwives. Increasingly, however, their lack of educational opportunities distanced them from this vocation. As early as 1792 feminists such as Mary Wollstonecraft were arguing for a continued presence of women in midwifery and for women in general to have greater access to the various branches of knowledge: "Strengthen the female mind by enlarging it, and there will be an end to blind obedience..."(107). Wollstonecraft felt that the sexes should have intellectual exchanges and was against having medicine as a males-only discipline. Preferring female attendants at her births,[5] Wollstonecraft wanted women trained in the anatomy of the mind and the anatomy of the body (305). Her attitude was in response to those who did not feel that women had the brain power to pursue an education beyond the home. Throughout the nineteenth century there were debates on what academic subjects, if any, women should study.

As late as 1847, Dr. Charles Meigs, in his "Lecture on the Distinctive Characteristics of the Female" at the Jefferson Medical College of Philadelphia charged:

> The great administrative faculties are not hers. She plans no sublime campaign, leads no armies to battle, nor fleets to victory.... She discerns not the courses of the planets.... She composes no Iliad, no Aeneid.... Do you think that a woman ... could have developed, in the tender soil of her intellect, the strong idea of a Hamlet, or a Macbeth? Such is not woman's province, nature, power, or mission. She reigns in the heart; her seat and throne are by the hearthstone.... She has a head almost too small for intellect and just big enough for love. (58)

Similar to Dr. Meigs, Dr. Joseph DeLee of the Chicago Lying-in Hospital in 1895 inquired: "Do you wonder that a young man will not adopt this field [obstetrics] as his special work? If a delivery requires so little brains and skill that a midwife can conduct it, there is not the place for him" (qtd. in Susie 4).

As the aforementioned quotes indicate, alongside a tradition in Euro-American communities of using midwives as needed (partial utility), there was a concurrent tradition of dismissing and discrediting women as healers. According to Barbara Ehrenreich and Deidre English, once men entered "the last preserve of female healing—midwifery," they went as far as to burn women healers as witches. The statistical data for the burnings are staggering.[6] Midwives, the "unlicensed doctors and anatomists of western history," carried the dual identity of a wise woman and a witch (Ehrenreich and English 3). Those whose deliveries did not go well were in danger of being associated with the devil. One such example was the case of colonial woman Jane Hawkins, a friend of Anne Hutchinson. Unfortunately, the baby she delivered was

> a stillborn menopausal baby described by contemporaries as a "monstrosity." This birth was the subject of much debate and speculation among New Englanders, and John Winthrop denounced Hawkins as "notorious for familiarity with the devil." (Litoff 4)

Using the results of deliveries as the litmus test for determining which women were good healers and which ones were in cohorts with the devil resulted in suspensions of practices at best and death at worst. Women were caught between restrictions that deemed them too delicate for certain medical tasks and too devilish when those tasks were ill performed. In European history, "the witch-hunts left a lasting effect: an aspect of the female has ever since been associated with the witch, and an aura of contamination has remained—especially around the midwife and other women healers" (Ehrenreich and English 6).

By the late eighteenth century in Britain and America, some factors effected visible changes. Although the issues surrounding the demise of widespread lay midwifery were very complex and no single reason causal (Tom 5), there were several interlocking factors which produced changes. In *Lying-In: A History of Childbirth in America*, Richard and Dorothy Wertz summarize some of these:

> Women ceased to be midwives ... because of a change in the cultural attitudes about the proper place and activity for women in society. It came to

be regarded as unthinkable to confront women with the facts of medicine or to mix men and women in training even for such an event as birth. As a still largely unscientific enterprise, medicine took on the cultural attributes necessary for it to survive, and the Victorian culture found certain roles unsuitable for women. (47)

Other contributory explanations for the decline of midwifery include: 1) weakly organized midwifery organizations compared to aggressively orga- nized professional medical organizations, such as the coalitions that the American Medical Association built; 2) establishment of all-male medical schools, barring women from access to medical knowledge; 3) increasing infant mortality rates, which were always a locus for scapegoating mid- wives and grannies in particular; 4) new surgical childbirth instruments which only doctors could use; 5) doctors' alliances with upper-class white women (Wertz 47); and 6) the growing presence of the black woman as the prototypical midwife. I am most interested in the last three reasons, for they were the ones most problematic for the grannies.

## FORCEPS AND OTHER MEDICAL INSTRUMENTS

When babies began to be delivered into the hands of men, a number of surgical procedures and instruments became popular. Because of their access to medical schools, men learned how and why to use interventive medicine—medicine that had the potential to complicate, complement, or convolute the delivery process:

> In 1808 Dr. John Stearns first used ergot to induce labor. In the 1820's, the stethoscope was used to monitor the fetal heartbeat through the mother's abdomen. With the use of anesthesia in surgery in the 1840's, Dr. Walter Channing encouraged the use of ether in normal as well as difficult births. . . . In the mid-1800's, J. Marion Sims designed a curved vaginal speculum and in the 1870's, silver nitrate for the newborn's eyes were first used. (Susie 3, 4)

As the title of Susie's text implies, such interventions as chloroform, twi- light sleep, stethoscopes, and speculums were not *In the Way of Our Grandmothers*. Poor immigrant midwives and the black grannies had nei- ther the money to purchase the technology nor the access to medical knowledge to benefit from perceived advantages of these interventions.

Some of the interventions assumed that health personnel would be performing caesarian births and/or episiotomies, procedures lay midwives were not supposed to perform.

The most threatening looking intervention was forceps. During the earliest use of forceps, male physicians were very apprehensive about their maternity patients seeing these instruments. Forceps served to further place midwifery under the province of science and surgery. Labeled a surgical instrument, forceps were not for lay use. Peter Chamberlen, the British surgeon, who in the seventeenth century invented forceps, at first kept his invention a family secret (Achterberg 126). Later, he blindfolded his women patients, so that they would not see his obtrusive and intrusive device. Carrying his expensive forceps in a carved gilded box, he, along with many physicians who were privy to "the secret," experimented with this instrument on poor women (Litoff, *American Midwives* 7). To experiment first on poor women was not unusual. It was not the class issue that had changed. Rather, it was that Chamberlen, a male, had a new appendage to insert into females. Only through disguise could he hope to use his invention. Connections between forceps and phallus are not to be ignored. Both are hidden men's tools used to penetrate women's bodies. Science and biology dictated that granny midwives would have neither. In ensuing years, male midwives, already under criticism for their mere presence in the birthing chamber, used various means to hide forceps. Cartoons in eighteenth-century Britain ridiculed William Smellie, spiritual heir of Peter Chamberlen. Smellie, an early male midwife, wore a gown to hide his forceps (Wertz 40–41). Booming business, rather than doctor/patient honesty, brought forceps out in the open:

> The "secret" of forceps, having been sold for profit too many times, finally leaked out. Medical men, who had cleverly commandeered the blueprint for their manufacture, became specialists in their use, and established formal training programs from which women were excluded. (Thurer 200)

Of special interest to male doctors and midwives was whether women could give birth in the new position necessitated by forceps—on their backs. Lying on their backs pre-empted pregnant women from participating in what was historically known by the expression "brought to bed." "Brought to bed" was supposed to happen during the final phase of delivery, after the women had exhausted more active postures. Janet Bogdan notes the distinction between the historical concept of "brought to bed" and the present condition of giving birth in bed. "Brought to bed" implied that most women were doing activities and testing birthing positions right up until the time delivery was imminent; consequently, they were active until others brought them to bed. Their beds were their last recourses. Contrastingly, to plan from the beginning of pregnancy to give birth in bed was a convenience to doctors who could "have better access for internal examination, or touching, and for forceps, should they want to use them" (Bogdan 111). Forceps required that the woman be in bed and on her back.

After entering birthing rooms during the late eighteenth century, doctors were delivering 50 percent of all babies by the early twentieth century (Leavitt 295). Initially, in the history of midwifery, the assistance of a woman in the birthing chamber was thought to be better than a man: "If deprived of midwives, . . . women would rather have amateur assistance from the janitor's wife or the woman across the hall than submit to this outlandish American custom of having a male doctor for a confinement" (Wertz 212). In eighteenth-century America, Dr. William Shippen, Jr., of Philadelphia, did much to change the birthing room to a place where men were comfortable by starting a practice that catered to the urban elite (Leavitt 3). Using drugs such as opium and demonstrating his expertise by using manikins and poor women as specimens, Shippen effected change:

> The transition to male attendants occurred so easily among advantaged urban women that it can only be explained by understanding the women's impression that physicians knew more than midwives about the birth process and about what to do if things went wrong. Women overturned millennia of all-female tradition and invited men into their birthing rooms because they believed that men offered additional security against the potential dangers of childbirth. By their acknowledgement of physician superiority, women changed the fashions of childbearing and made it desirable to be attended by physicians. (Leavitt, 283)

Doctors and male attendants courted upper-class women. Once these women accepted the changes, it was easier to institutionalize the changes.

FEMINIST RECLAMATION OF MIDWIVES

Midwifery has always been embattled in gender and class politics and the birthing chamber a contested site. Dr. Wertt, a German physician who donned women's attire so that he could view the delivery process, was burned to death for his impropriety (Donegan 18). Wertt had mistaken what he considered to be educational for what members of the community thought to be voyeuristic. Although with each decade male doctors continued to increase their presence in birthing chambers and delivery rooms, some scholars argue that women never relinquished the camaraderie surrounding pregnancy and birth, a camaraderie that only women fully shared. During colonial times, many mothers had groaning parties:

> Once mother and baby were settled and well, the appreciative mother would throw a banquet for the women who were present at her birth. The name was reminiscent of the groans of labor as well as the groans of the women who would undoubtedly stuff themselves at the feast. (Susie 17)

Women were used to childbirth as a communal, social experience, a bonding process. To be present at her friend's delivery was accepted and expected, but "as doctors took over, the rooms became literally and psychologically too crowded" (Wertz 5). Women did not know if they should trust attendants who had never and could never birth a baby themselves.

By the 1800s, issues of class and issues of gender became more pronounced. Midwives charged less than doctors, but with doctors one had the benefit of someone sanctioned by newly created medical schools and validated by the American Medical Association, founded in 1848. Although the College of Midwifery of New York City and the Playfair School of Midwifery in Chicago began conferring the diplomas for midwifery in 1883 and 1896 respectively (Litoff 34–5), these schools did not provide the opportunities that institutions such as Johns Hopkins, did, and very few women were admitted to medical schools. Elizabeth Blackwell was denied entrance to twenty-nine medical schools before Geneva Medical College accepted her in 1847 (Wertz 59).

Actively interested in health issues, many first-wave feminists during the 1830s and 1840s were central to the Popular Health Movement, a movement, "usually dismissed in conventional medical histories as the high-tide of quackery and medical cultism" (Ehrenreich and English

24–25). The Popular Health Movement urged women to know their bodies (Wertz 54). In the 1920s other women's reform groups, consisting of
working-class and farm mothers and public health officials, along with
magazines such as *Good Housekeeping*, were the most enthusiastic lobby-
ists for the passage of the Sheppard-Towner Act for mothers and children
(Tom 7). In fact, as activists they were so strong that *The Journal of the
American Medical Association* declared that the women had created "one
of the strongest lobbies that has ever been seen in Washington" (Tom 7).

As part of an educational thrust, Congress passed the Sheppard-Towner
Act in 1921. Congress gave grants to the various states to train their midwives. Opposed by the American Medical Association as too socialistic,
the program, although supported by female reform groups, eventually
died (Devitt, Tom). Just as feminist efforts in the Popular Health
Movement backfired, they did so with the Sheppard-Towner Act, precisely because its advocates did not discern the toll it would take on issues
of race and class. Documenting the North Carolina experience, Mathews
observed that "after almost seventy years of systematic effort, state officials
succeeded in eliminating the only officially sanctioned lay health practitioners in North Carolina—the midwives, most of whom were black
women living in rural areas delivering black babies" (61).

The women who designed and administered the Sheppard-Towner Act
made a serious attempt to defend midwives and to improve the health and
well-being of women and children in every sector of the population and
every part of the country. Yet their cultural insensitivity, reliance on state
authority, and blind faith in modern medicine made it impossible for
them to build a health care system that kept childbirth and maternity care
in women's control. Ironically, Sheppard-Towner administrators—the
chief supporters of midwives in the 1920s—contributed to the decline of
midwifery and the medicalization of birth.

Second Wave feminism has sought to reclaim the values of midwifery,
and significant numbers of women are now welcoming midwives back to
delivery rooms. Cooperation between midwives and physicians, although
not smooth in all places, is certainly much smoother than it was in the
years when the grannies were seen as "necessary evils." Indeed, places
such as The Farm in Tennessee[7] have enjoyed respect since 1971 as a lay
midwifery and birthing center. Yet, with all of the renewed interest, "those
who have benefitted most are certified nurse midwives, registered nurses

with additional training in midwifery" (Griffin 57). Black lay midwifery has not been the focus of the renewal of interest in midwifery. A notable exception is taking place in Boston, where a group promoting home birthing called Traditional Childbearing Group, Inc. (TCB),[8] founded in 1978, combines modern techniques with traditional values. Although some of the women have college degrees, they affirm the grannies' methodology of apprenticeships and the ideology of God's calling. Unlicensed, these women are free to use whatever natural techniques and salves they feel are needed—from olive oil for back aches to raspberry tea for menstrual cramps. As with the Black Women's Health Project, TCB is interested in black women's empowerment through health care services. Co-founder of TCB, Shafia Monroe (Shafia means "healer" in Arabic) often brings up black nation-building aspects of current black lay-midwifery:

> . . . It's the racism. I don't care how well you eat or how many herb teas you drink, you're going to have to fight racism on your job, in your neighborhood, and in your school system on a daily basis, and that's going to affect you. Why do you have higher blood pressure among black women? Because we are angry. (Dula and Goering 212)

Monroe calls her group's type of health care "afrocentric midwifery," arguing that her group's roots are intertwined with the grannies and "are much different from the experience of middle-class white women who became midwives" (Dula and Goering 211). Tensions between black and white women's midwifery and attitudes about health care have been festering for some time. To Ehrenreich and English's earlier question on how could white middle-class healers oust all other healers and midwives, I would add, "How complicit were white women in the process?" Did they misjudge white women's/black women's relational politics? The rest of my chapter looks at how my focus group, the grannies, entered American midwifery history triggering long lasting socio-cultural debates. Yet very few histories of American midwives include comprehensive or corollary histories of black midwives.[9]

## HISTORICAL GRANNIES

*[Midwives] didn't get burned as witches in Africa; we were always honored.*
—Contemporary midwife, Shafia Mawushi Monroe, Traditional Childbearing Group

*In the birth of a child, the whole community is born anew; it is renewed, it is revived and revitalized.*

—John S. Mbiti, *African Religions and Philosophy*

Whereas such countries as Germany, Italy, France, and England burned thousands of women healers, African American women healers come from a tradition more respectful of indigenous medical systems, systems uncomfortable with divisions sharply labeled orthodox/unorthodox, legitimate/illegitimate, healthy/sickly. In many African societies, midwives and women healers have used a pharmacopeia of herbs to maintain balance in the lives of their patients. In such societies, the word or metaphor for health is "balance." [10] Because one of the goals of these indigenous medical systems has been to balance lives, midwives and healers have enjoyed their community role as facilitators of harmony, wholeness, and order. As such they continue to command respect. A Hausa proverb affirms that *zama lafiya ya fi zama sarki* or "being well is better than being chief" (Lewis Wall 334). Such an attitude has given women healers vocational prestige. In conjunction with this attitude, centuries-old views on the importance of birth have helped many African midwives maintain their status:

> Birth is usually considered a significant movement because it provides an entry into life itself. Among the Igbo of Nigeria, birth songs are traditionally sung by women upon the birth of a child. In many cases nowadays, women from the immediate kin of the baby's mother, as well as friends and clubmates, accompany her from the clinic singing these songs. In other cases, the songs are performed on a traditionally appointed "outing" day several days after the birth of the baby. On this occasion, the women (who may come with their children) are entertained with food and drinks as they sing and dance to celebrate the arrival of the new baby. (Okpewho 119)

This type of celebration of birth differs sharply from what Achterberg describes as early European attitudes to birth and the role of midwives before social reformers began arguing on their behalf:

> With the few rare exceptions, midwifery was a less-than-honorable profession. Birthing was regarded as an objectionable, private, and nasty business. That the birth passage was placed between where feces and urine were eliminated was often cited as God's way of showing disgust for the birth of yet another

Granny with two of her "babies." Note sign near door advertising her as a midwife. (Courtesy Archives, Manuscripts, and Special Collections, Earl K. Long Library, University of New Orleans)

sinner. The act of giving birth itself defiled the mother, who could be readmitted to the Church only after rites of purification, called "churching." (119)

When slave ships brought black women to America, these women came with attitudes about health care that were African-based rather than European. They came with a knowledge of midwifery and botanic roots. Today there are still roots that bear the names of those slaves who first identified their medicinal purposes, such as the Samson root.

In eras when many older slaves were expendable commodities, elderly black midwives were thought of as assets in their slave communities. They were fertility specialists, moral counsellors and root workers. In "Empowered Caretakers . . . ," Sheila Davis and Cora Ingram argue that granny midwives

> represented the high point of authority and control—and provided a pivotal empowering element—in plantation communities. They bestowed healing among women. Midwives whose hands linked generations through the miracle of birth were seen in their communities as models of strength, wisdom, and power. At a time when blacks were relegated to the legal status equalling three-fifths of a person, African-American midwives experienced high cultural autonomy and prestige. They also earned stature in the eyes of white owners as they attended a significant number of white births. (195)

There is much evidence that black midwives were central to the structure of a slave economy wherein black women were breeders. The forced fertility of black women gave the midwives plenty of practice and therefore, "they were regularly called upon to attend not only other bondsmen, but also the plantation owner's wife and other local white women" (Bogdan 115).

In the years after slavery, these women still maintained "high cultural autonomy and prestige" within their own communities. Midwives, ministers and morticians formed a trinity. All three enjoyed freedoms and mobility, especially in comparison to other members of what were often isolated communities. Slowly, however, some of the larger changes in Anglo-midwifery began permeating black communities and the image of the grannies suffered. By the early 1900s there was a backlash against all lay midwives and I will address those elements that fed the backlash, especially against the grannies. These are the same elements that have captured the attention of African American women writers.

### HANDS OF IRON AND HANDS OF FLESH

Forceps or "hands of iron"[11] gained prominence just when the grannies' "hands of flesh" became symbols of uncleanliness. I revisit the subtopic of forceps because as instruments they affected the lives and images of the grannies in ways different from the way they affected America's other lay midwives. With the others, forceps were a technological intrusion. With the grannies, forceps were the invention that most mimicked what would be done to them. The reductive gaze of physicians saw the grannies as their bodily parts, especially their hands. Because of infections and fevers, government publications warned the granny: "Keep your hands out of the mother" (Bredesen 7), an ironic admonition given that their hands of flesh did not enter the mother as nearly as much as the hands of iron eventually would.[12] The grannies had prided themselves on the ability of their hands to catch babies. In their oral histories, they speak of catching babies as an art. However, science told them that their hands were dirty, weakening the potency of their primary vocational metaphor. The women were also told that their hands were too manly. When men first entered birthing rooms in England, midwives complained of their horse like hands (Litoff, "The Midwife Through History" 5). As early as 1724, written descriptions of criteria for selection of midwives admonished that "she ought not to be too Fat or Gross, but especially not to have thick or fleshy Hands and Arms, or large Bon'd Wrists; which (of necessity) must occasion racking Pains to the tender labouring Woman. . ." (qtd. in Litoff, "The Midwife Through History" 3).

By the 1920s in America, the black woman, bearing the burden of the stereotype of the large mammy, everybody's mother and nobody's woman, was the one whose hands the medical personnel criticized. Her hands were too large, too ashy, too dirty. It was hard for the granny to believe that hundreds of micro organisms were on her hands. She was unclean.

### HYGIENE AND THE BODY

When the movement to retrain and/or eliminate immigrant midwives and grannies began, the medical establishment used various public relations tools. One advertisement which was especially harmful was a well-circulated poster depicting an Italian woman, an Irish woman, and a granny, all marginalized women who, when framed against a dark background and more sophisticated looking Anglo women, appeared Old Worldish. As poor ethnic women who were responsible for their plights, all three of the women on the poster were to be viewed as sub-human, so that middle- and upper-class women would not choose them to deliver their babies. In *The Politics & Poetics of Transgression* Peter Stallybrass and Allon White remind us that "To the extent that the poor are constituted in terms of bestiality, the bourgeois subject is positioned as the neutral observer of self-willed degradation" (132). The posters contributed to a growing skepticism on the part of bourgeois women for the services of poor women.

Despite the negative images of all three midwives as poor and inept, the circulars were not nearly as scathing of the Anglo immigrant midwife as they were of the granny. The home countries of the immigrant women, Italy and Ireland, did not bear the slurs brought against all of West Africa. Whereas the circular spoke of the "filthy customs and practices" brought by the two immigrant women, the granny was labeled "ignorant and superstitious, a survival of the 'magic doctors' of the West Coast of Africa" (Susie 5; Wertz 216).

The grannies were survivors of these "magic doctors" but not in the dismissive and derogatory ways that perpetrators of the campaign thought. To an uninformed public, Africa was a dark continent where light could not have possibly shone. Viewed by some outsiders as a cross between a superstitious hag and a meddlesome old biddy, the grannies were soon to become the subjects of an attack leveled against their very bodies. Their likenesses distorted and placed on circulars, the grannies had to fight their own bodily representations in a society where only females who were delicate enough to require hospitalization were constructed as women (Susie 7). To be constructed as "ignorant" and "filthy" in the language of educated health personnel, yet as "wise woman" in those communities to whom she renders service had to have taken a toll on the grannies' psyches. Sneja Gunew reminds us that

> . . . if you are constructed in one particular kind of language, what kinds of violence does it do to your subjectivity if one then has to move into another language, and suppress whatever selves or subjectivities were constructed in the first? And of course, some people have to pass through this process several times. (66)

Constructions of the granny are indeed in two different languages—the language of a powerful medical community and, as we shall see in the next chapter, the language of womanist recovery.

For the medical establishment, more so than her white counterpart, the granny midwife became a grotesque body. In *The Myth of Aunt Jemima: Representations of Race and Region*, Diane Roberts, using Bakhtin's model for classical and grotesque bodies, argues that black women's bodies routinely were seen as grotesque. A classical body is "ethereal, sanctioned, and official" (Roberts 3); a grotesque body "low[ers] . . . all that is high, spiritual, ideal, abstract; it is a transfer to the material level, to the sphere of earth and body in their indissoluble unity" (Bakhtin quoted in Roberts 3). My state-by-state study of the *Lesson for Midwives* manuals published by the states' respective Boards of Health and my study of hundreds of midwifery registration records[13] reveal that midwives were never clean enough. To County Health Boards, it appears as if the grannies were black Pilates,[14] continually trying to wash off historical prejudices which had already been inscribed on their bodies.

At the beginning of most of the manuals is "The Midwives' Creed." At the center of the creed is the statement, "We believe that cleanliness is next to godliness, and that cleanliness in body, mind and soul, and obedience to the law of hygiene, faith in God and reverence for Him as the Author of life are the first qualifications of a worthy midwife." To maintain moral authority, medical personnel linked Western hygienic practices to godliness. Because many grannies were religious women (as I will discuss in Chapter 4), they worked very hard to appear and to be clean. Lesson One in South Carolina's manual, *Lesson for Midwives*, sets the tone for the whole document. Centered on the first page of "What a Midwife should be" are the following lines:

> She must also
> —keep her body clean.
> —keep her hair clean.
> —keep her mouth clean.
> —keep her underclothes clean.
> —keep her uniform clean.
> —keep her nails short and clean at all times.
> —keep her mind clean.
> (*Lesson for Midwives* 1)

These manuals reiterate and detail all of these points except how to keep a clean mind. A clean mouth, for example, means no "decayed teeth or bad tonsils." Yet for all of this emphasis on cleanliness, when midwives were required to register, medical personnel were very general and subjective when judging cleanliness. Rather than giving a thorough physical examination, they judged the appearance of cleanliness most often as "good," "fair," and "average," "clean," "ok" (Georgia Registration Records). Proportionately, medical personnel evaluating the grannies gave little attention to actual midwife performance on the certification cards in comparison to the attention they gave to compliance with state regulations and the appearance of cleanliness. They were judged on the cleanliness of their homes, as well as the homes in which they delivered babies. A good midwife showed her patient how to keep everything clean and helped in cleaning everything from soiled linen to dirty kitchen pots.

Stigmas of cleanliness symbolically, as well as literally, fed stigmas of incompetence. During the campaign to discredit the grannies, magazines ran articles alleging that grannies baked rat pies and the caption under the picture of one elderly black midwife read: "A former slave, 98 years old, still actively engages in the work of midwifery! A direct transplantation into a progressive American city of African voodooism!" (Wertz 216). There were, of course, many things the grannies needed to learn, such as the use of silver nitrate to prevent gonorrheal ophthalmia. Although non-degreed, they were never as uneducable as biased health boards thought: "'They [the midwives] are too dumb, I can't waste my time on them,'" complained a Florida County public health nurse (Susie 39). Many doctors contemplated the issue of the educable midwife in very patronizing ways, asserting that "'educated midwives would be aseptic rather than lethal abortionists, and therefore more women would seek them out for a criminal waste of infant life'" (Wertz 214). As late as 1970, a nursing supervisor in a federally sponsored publication reported that some midwives in Texas were using lemon juice for the eyes and wrapping baby cords around rusty nails, causing cord tetanus (Bredesen 23). Other than learning appropriate medical procedures, the grannies also had to learn that family planning and nutrition were important to survival after birth.

LICENSURE AND TRAINING

*I delivered so many, brought 'em in 'fore I knowed anything 'bout de health
department and certificates and all. I was 'bout forty 'fore I knowed anything*

*'bout it but just delivering dem babies. But now it's five hundred or more since I had the authority. But I done so much 'fore I had my authority.*

—Granny midwife, *Ms.*, June 1987

*But I wasn't ready to stop. I was a young woman in my 50's.*

—Granny midwife in video, "Delivered With Love"

Between the years 1900–1930, many states enacted regulatory legislation for midwives. Teaching the grannies to deliver babies after they, as a group, already had delivered thousands, was no easy task, many feeling that they had indeed "done so much 'fore [they] had their authority." The licensing procedures by County Health Boards, referred to as legal authority, came after large numbers of grannies already had received their authority of experience. Because black lay midwives were indeed grannies, in terms of age, significant numbers of them were unable to and/or unwilling to take the newly required courses. Many of the older ones were not licensed; as one explained, "They did ask me if I wanted to further my education. I would have to go to Richmond, but I was sixty-five years old then, so I wasn't thinking about that" (C. Smith 21). The states wanted to recruit those who were still "malleable," young enough to be reshaped. Consequently, the median age of the grannies dropped a whole decade (Doughtery 117).

Nevertheless, doctors did need help. Given their maldistribution, they could not possibly service everyone. A conciliatory attitude developed among physicians as expressed by one physician: "Midwives are a necessary evil; they serve mothers who are economically or culturally barred from the health care system. . . . Midwives must be trained"(Bredesen 23).

### TURF BATTLES: FROM HOME TO HOSPITAL

*"They [white doctors] took so long to come that the baby died. The doctors were too white to apologize."*

—Midwife Onnie Lee Logan, *Motherwit: An Alabama Midwife's Story*

The relationships of grannies to physicians were very complex. Although not the enemy, doctors with their differences in behavior, beliefs, and expectations (Dula 32), were culturally quite different from the grannies. Often, the grannies interpreted these differences as a lack of caring: "They didn't care anything about no big black woman and no lil bitty black babies" (Logan 12). Sometimes, the aforementioned geographic maldistribution of physicians contributed to the grannies' appraisal of them. If doctors were not nearby, but had decided to come upon summons by a granny, they were often too late. For all the negative comments that the grannies expressed about doctors, there was still much goodwill. In their oral narratives, most grannies love to relate stories wherein doctors affirmed their skills: "Onnie you would have made a good doctor"(Logan 104), Onnie Lee Logan recalls a doctor telling her. Grannies loved how the doctor's learning, received through years of schooling, confirmed what their intuition and God-given insight told them all along. They reveled in the validation. Some imagined themselves as doctors. Midwife Sarah Maddux's father had studied medicine but had taken a job as a postmaster, a field much more open to blacks than medicine. Maddux proudly explains, "I went by the [medical] books and what my daddy taught me. I didn't make it up" (Video, "Granny Woman"). She feels that she followed her father's dream. Of course, her medical talent was also assured by having a lay midwifery mother whom she describes as "the smartest woman in the state of Tennessee in obstetrics." The grannies were not opposed to knowledge outside of their experiences. They knew there were advantages that doctors had by virtue of their book learning. However at odds with physicians, the grannies speak of what they learned from physicians: "I know how unprofessional it is to leave a big navel on a baby" (*Ms.* 1987). Constantly striving to be professional, they self-evaluated their performance against the performance of doctors. One granny midwife with a successful clinic commented, "Might expect to see Johns Hopkins, the way I talk" ("Gladys Delivers").

Yet, inevitably, tensions arose. State regulations gave grannies strict orders to call doctors whenever a delivery took a turn for the worse or when they anticipated such a delivery. Because grannies delivered poor white and black babies, their practice interfered with the physicians' access to classroom models (Susie 4). Doctors used the poor to demonstrate their techniques. With the grannies, poor women were not on view for public consumption. Although grannies were formidable forces in the homes of their communities, when doctors moved childbirth from homes to hospitals, the grannies were on alien turf. In *In The Way of Our Grandmothers*, midwife Augusta Wilson explains the difference in turf thusly:

> Cause when a woman have a baby at home, she have more privileges. See, she can walk. Like a pain hit her, she can get up and walk around that chair,

or she can walk around. A woman can move around during her labor. But you see, in the hospital, no quicker than you get there they put you in that bed and let you stay there by yourselves. (77)

The shift from home to hospital marked a shift from neighborly service to lucrative business (Ehrenreich and English 20), from natural process to pathological malady (Susie 5), from noninterventionist to interventionist techniques, from among friends to among strangers. The medicalization of birth was a victory for doctors and a challenge for the grannies. There was a time when maternity hospitals were called "urban asylums"—places for poor women only, for "genteel women had babies at home . . . Women became convinced that there were worse germs in their homes than in hospitals" (Wertz and Wertz 132–33).

By the end of the nineteenth century, some white women were so over-joyed by the changes in how childbirth was being presented and experienced that they named their children after pain killers (Thurer 218). By the early twentieth century, hospitals were the places where upper-middle-class and wealthy women went to have their babies: "[Blacks] didn't go to no clinic to have no baby," reflects Onnie Lee Logan on this era (Logan 12). Magazines carried advertisements with well-to-do white women praising their hospital stay as a "vacation" (Leavitt 297), a passive vacation unencumbered by any vigorous or painful labor. As one of the grannies in a state documentary explains, when a woman calls a midwife to attend her at home, she is saying, " 'You come help me do it.' When someone walks into the hospital, she is saying, 'Here I am—take care of me' " (*Delivered With Love*). Once again, class issues permeate the history of midwifery. Hospitals might have been vacation spas for some women, but they were not recreational for black women who, due to Jim Crow laws, were admitted to basement wards or segregated wings. Nor were they initially desirable for poor women who lost what little autonomy and control they had. Even today, one notes that

Shortly after entry into the hospital, the laboring woman will be symbolically stripped of her individuality, her autonomy, and her sexuality as she is "prepped"—a multistep procedure in which she is separated from her partner, her clothes are removed, she is dressed in a hospital gown and tagged with an ID bracelet, her pubic hair is shaved or clipped (conceptually returning her body to a state of childlessness), and she may be ritually cleansed with an enema. (Robbie Davis-Floyd 304)

Having activities performed upon her, the hospitalized maternity patient loses some of the agency she had when "birth among women was an event of power, not the powerless ordeal of the hospital" (Susie 23). Ironically, "mystification of childbirth deepened as the hospital rather than the home became its normal locus" (Bogdan 119). In *The Technocratic Model of Birth*, Davis-Floyd quotes Diana, a maternity patient, observing that:

> As soon as I got hooked up to the monitor, all everyone did was stare at it. The nurses didn't even look at me anymore when they came into the room—they went straight to the monitor. I got the weirdest feeling that *it* was having the baby, not me. (306)

Lay midwifery associated hospitals with passivity, and not just the patient's passivity. Augusta Wilson's earlier quote condemning hospitals for not allowing women to walk at will is followed by a criticism on the passivity of doctors and nurses: after leaving a woman in the delivery room, doctors and nurses can be found "going about their own business" or the doctor might not even be at the hospital, but at home "laid up with his legs crossed reading a book"(Susie 77).

## MATERIAL CULTURE: THE BAG OF RESISTANCE AND MODEL-T FORDS

> *"Papa's got a brand new bag." [and Momma too]*
> —Singer James Brown, King of Soul

In interviewing and listening to oral histories of the grannies, I was struck by their reference to one item, the midwifery bag, a bag that literally became their bag of tricks, a bag I would call their bag of resistance. During the licensing and certification and state regulations, the various agencies instructed the grannies on the proper care and use of their white uniforms and caps and the contents of their midwifery bags. Pictures of grannies easily attest to their pride in keeping their uniform starched and pressed. As crafts women, they took pride in their dress. Yet, I found case after case where the women, after having their bags checked, would place in those bags items not in accordance with the new medicalization of birth, but carry-overs from their practice of folk medicine. This was not the type of activity they would broadcast, for "noncompliance with bag regulations was considered evidence of midwives being superstitious or overstepping the bounds of practice as defined by the health department" (Doughtery 120).

When I checked hundreds of registration records, I noticed that the categories "bag condition" and "bag contents" were usually marked "satis-factory," "clean," "good." However, in conversations today, decades after their practices have ceased, the grannies show their bags and speak of the "extras" they felt they had to carry. To reconcile these two facts, I am sug-gesting that the grannies successfully used their bags to dupe authorities. As Linda Holmes points out, "So entrenched were many midwives in community-based experiences and values that midwives continued to sup-port a variety of practices that lacked official medical sanction" ("African American Midwives in the South" 286). Holmes identifies some of these items as castor oil, ginger tea, black pepper tea, and May Apple root, all labor stimulants. As with the grannies of the Ozarks, southern black grannies were known to carry camphorated goose grease and a wide range of assorted herbs (Perry 15). Additionally, although doctors were empha-sizing that women should give birth on their backs, some of the grannies continued to carry collapsible birthstools in their bags. With birthstools, the woman could give birth the same way many women, cross-culturally, had done for generations. Many of colonial America's midwives had car-ried such a stool (Litoff, "The Midwife Through History" 4).

Commenting on the practice of lay midwifery in Florida, Doughtery states that "specific items were required and all others were supposed to be eliminated" (120). To be included in her bag were such items as baby scales, basins, five ampules one percent silver nitrate solution, safety razor and new blades, an O.B. Pack No.1, and a compilation of twelve other items (Doughtery 120). Altogether, the Florida bag, representative of other state bags, required seventeen items. One would think there would not be space left in the bag for contraband items. The midwives, never-theless, carried "vaseline, rose water, comb, nail file, smelling salts, cam-phor, toothache drops, aspirin, paregoric, castor oil and many others" (Mongeau qtd. in Doughtery 121). I am with those who suspect that many grannies kept two bags, one for inspection and one for delivery. Ironically, the one carry-over that the states allowed lay midwives to keep, their black satchel bag—a bag meant to give them an air of professionalism, was the very item that the grannies manipulated to do with as they chose. Intended to represent their compliance with professional codes, their bags attested more to her ingenuity and rebellion. The grannies were enlarging the definition of a professional bag. The grannies did not want to be without items that they had tested and tried.[15]

The midwifery bag had always been a source of wonderment to young girls even before entering the vocation. The bag held the mystery of sexuality for children and teenagers who were not in an environment where sexuality was openly discussed. They knew that babies and the bag were somehow connected, and looking in the bag became a furtive act. The bag was therefore a means of learning about the female body, an education that continued as they became midwives themselves.

In addition to the midwife's bag, her transportation vehicle was very important, and, therefore, a significant material change for the historical granny was the invention of the car. Whereas many families had horses, wagons, buggies, or a reliable mule, few black families at the turn of the century had cars. Because the granny needed a car, members of the community were more than willing to help her secure one, albeit an old one. In interviews and written accounts, the grannies love to describe their means of transportation. Mrs. Sarah Maddux, long time granny in Tennessee and subject of the video, "Granny Woman tells how she traveled by foot, buggy, wagon, motorcycle, taxi, car, bus, everything except airplanes. Some sent taxis to pick her up, but as she explains, "They usually sent me back in a Ford. There was no hurry to send me home." After having spent several days with the family, they did not want her to leave. In the video "Delivered with Love," the grannies trade transportation stories. One tells of a Ford that she drove for twelve years; it was her "ambulance," and it did not need to be as fast as an ambulance, for "if the baby came before I got to the hospital, I would just stop along the road and deliver it and then go on back home. I've done did that plenty of times". In my interview with Alfreda Smalls Thompson, one of the granddaughters of Mrs. Maggie Smalls,[16] a very prominent granny midwife of the Sea Islands (St. Helena), the granddaughter attributed her grandmother's popularity to her black 1942 Ford, mentioning it as one of the reasons she was called frequently. When I asked what her grandfather thought of his wife having so much mobility, she replied, "But granddaddy allowed all of that. He allowed her to use the talents God gave her. She used them until she got a letter saying she could no longer do so" (Alfreda Smalls Thompson Interview).

In many of the most isolated communities, the midwife was the only person in the community with a car. Certainly, transportation vehicles gave the grannies some of the "high cultural autonomy and prestige" that Sheila Davis and Cora Ingram (195) point out she had during slavery. It was useful to have a car to travel the many backroads in all kinds of weather. The irony with the midwives literally traveling backroads is that, unbeknownst to them, they were soon to be "travelling the backroads of obstetrics"[17] and that is the journey the literary authors write.

## THE TRANSITION BETWEEN THE HISTORY AND LITERATURE'S REFORMULATION OF THAT HISTORY.

> *Old woman old as that ought to forgit trying to cure other people with her nigger magic . . .*
> —Alice Walker, "Strong Horse Tea"

The campaign to discredit the grannies was so successful that even some poor black women tried to distance themselves from all that the potions and skills of these grannies represented—a misrepresented African past, an embattled present, and a limited future. To go to the doctor or the hospital became a test of modernity for many black maternity patients. One way for them to prove their new-world sophistication was to divorce themselves from their old-world superstitions. The patients were being pulled in various directions. Should they elect the aid of the women who serviced their mothers and grandmothers? Or should they, upon recognizing that there have been advances in the field of obstetrics, go to a hospital? Alice Walker's short story "Strong Horse Tea" in the collection *In Love and Trouble* captures the granny and the conundrum she faced in this transitional stage.

In her interview with Claudia Tate (*Black Women Writers* 186), Walker names "Strong Horse Tea" as yet another of the stories her mother heard while growing up. Full of stories about how poor women had to survive with their own medical concoctions, Walker's mother shared many stories with her: stories on how she corrected her son's stuttering habits, stories on the medicinal benefits of boiled cow hoofs and stories on strong horse tea: "There's always somebody using 'strong horse tea' in the world; this day this minute, there's some poor woman making strong horse tea for a child because she's too poor to get a doctor" (186). "Strong Horse Tea" tells the story of Rannie Toomer, a poor black woman living in the backwoods, whose beloved Baby Snooks is dying. Rannie "was not married. Was not pretty. Was not anybody much. And he [Baby Snooks] was all she had" (88). Hopefully but naively, Rannie is waiting on the white doctor to come to cure her baby. In the house with her is Sarah, "an old neighboring lady who wore magic leaves round her neck sewed up in possumskin next to a dried lizard's foot" (88). Sarah is known for her understanding and practice of "magic"—home remedies. Although Sarah has enjoyed the respect of her community, times are changing and Rannie has heard that the white doctor can give her baby something called "shots." Shots do not grow in a garden. They are formulated in laboratories. Sarah thinks that Snooks has "NEWmonia" and anything new needs the latest technology. At this point in the story Rannie reflects the position of those who view "folk medicine as vestigial and marginal" (Hufford, "Contemporary Folk Medicine" 244).

One of my interests in this story is the way the names that Rannie calls Sarah embody the history and many stereotypes from which the grannies and the larger body of black female healers have suffered. At first, Rannie wants nothing to do with "swamp magic." This label shows how issues of class have always been important, especially in the history of women healers. The second time Rannie describes Sarah's practices she calls them "witch's remedies." Added to the class issue of "swamp magic," we now have the gender issue—female healers inevitably get linked to witches. The final name that Rannie calls Sarah's practices is "nigger magic"—the racialized dismissal of knowledge from Africa.

When the white doctor does not show up, Rannie tries to give a message to the white mailman to deliver to the doctor. Sarah sees the doctor and the mailman as "spirits," but spirits from a different tradition. Sarah wants to heal Snooks with "arrowroot or sassyfras and cloves, or a sugar tit soaked in cat's blood" (89). When the mailman arrives with advertising circulars that Rannie cannot even read, she asks him, as a favor to a mother with a dying baby, to go tell the doctor to hurry. Rannie's ignorance, poverty, and desperation repel the mailman—"Why did colored folks always want you to do something for them?" (92). He tells her to just let *Aunt* Sarah cure the baby, for "he half believed with everybody else in the county that the old blue-eyed black woman possessed magic. Magic that if it didn't work on whites probably would on blacks" (92). Although the mailman has sent for Sarah instead of the doctor, I do not read this as respect for her. He seems to be saying that she might be of some value if she caters to her own. The mailman's body language and thoughts tell us that he sees blacks as animals, and he dispatches Sarah to Rannie's much as one would call a veterinarian for a sick animal. Additionally, in calling Sarah, "aunt," the mailman is placing Sarah in the context of elderly slave women, a patronizing position at best.

When Rannie realizes that the doctor will not be coming, she turns to Sarah who announces, "I's the doctor, child" (94). Rannie had not realized "that there mailman didn't git no further with that message than the road in front of my [Sarah's] house" (94). With time running out, Sarah sends Rannie outside to the pasture to collect some "strong horse tea," a euphemism for horse urine. The same Rannie who earlier did not want to have anything to do with folk medicine is now ready to do whatever it takes to cure her baby. Folklorist Wayland D. Hand observes that

> After people have tried all kinds of clinical medicine and accepted kinds of alternative medicine without success, they will of necessity move to sterner measures. If teas and tonics brewed from plants grown organically and tenderly cared for fall short of expectations, then what is to stop one from going naked or barefoot into sequestered glens, walking backward and stumbling almost providentially, to the very spot where the precious plant at last might be found. (250)

It is raining hard. Rannie, now realizing that she does not have a container, tries to catch horse's "tea" in her plastic shoe, which has a hole in it. When the story ends, Rannie is running home to give warm horse tea to her baby.[18] Knowing the child was too far gone to live, the midwife gives the mother an activity to do wherein she can participate in efforts to save her child. Having been forbidden earlier to help the child, the midwife astutely ministers to the mother's needs. Rannie needs Sarah's mothering and, as with the grannies when they were summoned, Sarah could never minister her services in such a narrow way as to consider only the needs of the child.

Certainly, "Strong Horse Tea" contains so many of the elements that historically have shaped the lives of the grannies—public perceptions, unorthodox practices, culturally mediated priorities. This story is but one representation of a whole canon of stories by black women writers that reclaim the granny. My next chapter posits that there has been a literary recovery of the body and personhood of the granny midwife such that the writers' metaphorical bag of tricks are resistant tools, much as the grannies' material midwifery bags were bags of resistance. The grannies, known for their ability to travel, provide a context for understanding how the authors give us literary grannies who perform what I will term, "diasporic travel," carrying pan-African baggage to readers in all ports of call.

If the doctors thought they were facing formidable odds in trying to lessen the necessity for the grannies, they have certainly been no match for the literary writers who, adding their voices to the grannies, have rallied their support in a concerted effort to meet white men's forceps with black women's forces.

# TWO

# Literary Recovery of the Granny

*The Body, the Mind, the Material*

## HISTORY AND THE DISCOURSE OF THE BODY

*Yonder they do not love your flesh. They despise it.*
—Baby Suggs in *Beloved*

There has been a long history of men viewing women's bodies as defective machines. Accordingly, to have one woman deliver another woman was to have one machine working on another machine. In "The Technocratic Model of Birth," Davis-Floyd argues that

> The demise of the midwife and the rise of the male-attended, mechanically manipulated birth followed close on the heels of the wide cultural acceptance of the metaphor of the body-as-machine in the West and the accompanying acceptance of the metaphor of the female body as a defective machine—a metaphor that eventually formed the philosophical foundation of modern obstetrics. (301)

If women's bodies in general were defective machines, the grannies' bodies were seen as machinery at its worst—unclean parts that could not contribute to a functional whole.

In describing the many skills of black women healers and the grannies, African American women writers approach their texts with Gayatri Spivak's caution: "History cannot be reversed or erased out of nostalgia. The remaking of history involves a negotiation with the structures that have produced the individual agent of history" ("Who Claims Alterity?" 282). In their negotiations with medical structures, African American women writers give back to the grannies their hands. What begins in the grannies' history as a clinical issue—hands carry germs that could be fatal to the health of mother and/or child—become in the literature, part of a larger discourse on race and gender. In her gospel of the body, Baby Suggs preaches, "And O my People they do not love your hands. Those they only use, tie, bind, chop off and leave empty. Love your hands! Love them. Raise them up and kiss them. Touch others with them, pat them together, stroke them on your face 'cause they don't love that either. . ." (88). As an ex-slave whose freedom her son has purchased by working five years of Sundays, Baby Suggs knows that what is most debilitating about the enslaved life is that "anybody white could . . . dirty you so bad you couldn't like yourself anymore. Dirty you so bad you forgot who you were and couldn't think it up" (251). *Beloved* problematizes notions of dirtiness. The unclean hands of a black woman become less of a problem than the unclean hearts of her colonizers.

Similar to *Beloved*, Naylor's *Mama Day* returns to the black woman her hands. Although Miranda, healer and midwife, never had children herself, "she was praised for her gifted hands, folks said" (89). Miranda's hands were gifted because they had caught so many babies. Note that Naylor uses the same verb, the verb "to catch," that the grannies used to describe their delivery technique. At the moment of delivery, to do their jobs well, they had to have their hands positioned correctly, or to use Naylor's phraseology, "hands poised to receive" (59). The hands that deliver both in the literature and real life are serviceable hands. The work's climax centers around using hands. In order to save Cocoa, George needs to link his hand with Mama Day's: "She needs his hand in her— his very hand—so she can connect it up with all the believing that had gone before" (285). The writers reinscribe cultural continuity through the trope of positioned hands. Hands that catch babies, plait hair, and grease legs are the subjects of many narratives and poems in African American literature.[1]

## HYGIENE AND THE BODY: A COUNTER DISCOURSE

*Whenever it erupts, this Funk, they wipe it away.*
—Toni Morrison, *The Bluest Eye*

*. . . and I know you're an animal because I smell you.*
—Toni Morrison, *Tar Baby*

Black women writers have had much to say about black female bodies because their bodies have been dismembered and "disremembered."[2] With the granny, as previously discussed, we see an effort to reduce her to her bodily parts. She becomes her hands. The writers' responses to hands as metonyms for black women's experiences is but a small part of a larger academic and popular conversation to which the writers have responded. The issue of black bodies as never clean enough has not escaped the pens of the novelists. *The Women of Brewster Place* and *Praisesong for the Widow* emphasize cleansing rituals tailored to black women. In what Barbara Christian calls

> one of the most moving scenes in the [*The Women of Brewster Place*], Mattie bathes the numb, grief-stricken Ciel, bringing her from death into life as she reawakens her senses in a ritual or shared womanhood much like Rosalee's bathing of Avey Johnson in Marshall's *Praisesong For the Widow*, a ritual derived from African religions and still practiced in voodoo. (*Reading Black, Reading Feminist* 357)

While Naylor and Marshall enlarge the meanings of cleansing rituals to include the politics of cultural and personal identification, other black women flaunt funk. Rather than reinvesting meaning in a ritual of their own, they start with the primary issue: How have cleanliness and funk been historically constituted? Posited against the mandates for cleanliness to which medicine subjugated the grannies is the counter discourse of "funk" that some novelists propose. Electing to "erupt the funk"[3] rather than sanitize black women's experiences, the writers deconstruct cleanliness.

Black women novelists, especially Morrison, counter hegemonic assumptions about cleanliness with a discourse on funk. In Morrison's hands, funk is a narrative strategy, as well as a state of being. As a narrative strategy, funk is a subversive discursive practice, a destabilizing of what is expected because of an alternative cultural matrix. Funk is in flux, a state ready to disrupt/disobey the rules: *Beloved's* baby ghost can come back with plans, re-entering the narrative to be "treated as familiarly as corn-flakes for breakfast" (Harris,*Callaloo* 388). Funk is the jazzing of narrative until the words become the note that Miles Davis could not reach. Funk is designing *Tar Baby* so that it runs "lickety-split" into folk myth.[4]

As a state of being, funk is what is held in check when trying to assimi-late into mainstream society. Although not termed as "funk," the concept can be found in earlier women writers, such as Zora Neale Hurston and Nella Larsen. Hurston's Mrs. Turner in *Their Eyes Were Watching God* is anti-funk—opposed to any physical feature or mannerism that would link her to Negroes: "Even her buttocks in bas-relief were a source of pride" (208). Larsen's Helga Crane in *Quicksand* is never able to reconcile her education with the funkiness of her life. Efforts to combine the sensual and the cerebral leave her in the quandary of associating the sensual with lower class rural experience. As Hurston's Mrs. Turner would say, funk can "class us off" (210).

Morrison's *The Bluest Eye* best describes how urban northern black women, who no longer grease their hair with Dixie Peach, but "go to land-grant colleges, normal schools, and learn how to do the white man's work with refinement," subdue their funk. Through "the careful development of thrift, patience, high morals, and good manners, . . .[they] get rid of the funkiness" (68). Morrison proceeds to list several types of funkiness: "The dreadful funkiness of passion, the funkiness of nature, the funkiness of the wide range of human emotions" (168). These middle-class black women are so divorced from the sensual that they want the sexual organs "in some more convenient place—like the armpit, for example, or the palm of the hand" (69).[5] These are women who have internalized stereotypes of black people to the point where they see a constructed notion of funk as a sym-bol for a latent primitivism, a beast in the jungle needing to be civilized.

It is funk that Jadine (*Tar Baby*), a black woman who has been a Parisian model eschews. In a work where soap and cleanliness factor heav-ily, the funk of tar and swamps is not easily cleansed. Jadine claims she smelled Son from afar; he counters her claim with his own charge: "'I smell you too,'" he said, and pressed his loins as far as he could into the mute print of her Madeira skirt. 'I smell you too'" (122). Trudier Harris argues that this is the most powerful insult Son lashes at Jadine:

> For a model to smell is perhaps comparable to a debutante loudly expending gas during her formal presentation—just too much for anyone who has eliminated the funkiness from life. No wonder, then, that the insult from Son evokes the fighting response that it does from Jadine. And no wonder that Jadine is able to appreciate natural beauty only when it has been sanitized into the artifice of the hides of ninety baby seals. (*Fiction and Folklore* 142)

Jadine must learn that the stench from the odors of the colonizer is as repugnant as any stench.[6] As Susan Willis points out, "Morrison translates the loss of history and culture into sexual terms and demonstrates the connection between bourgeois society and repression" (87).

ANGLO AND AFRO-CENTRIC AESTHETICS: THE BODY BEAUTIFUL

*. . .they stood together—hands on hips, straight-backed, round-bellied, high behinded women who threw their heads back when they laughed and exposed strong dark gums.*
—Gloria Naylor, *The Women of Brewster Place*

How black women's bodies have been constructed has a direct bearing upon issues of health and obstetrics. Whose body is selected to represent a particular medical procedure and the position that body must assume to illustrate that procedure are all issues that interrelate concepts of self-image and medical culture. In her introduction to the 1992 issue of *The Woman in the Body*, Emily Martin comments:

> Since my book was published I have learned more about how race as a social and cultural category affects reproductive experiences. In the current field of feminist studies we must devote ethnographic attention to the cultural meanings of race, to the meanings of skin color, of phenotypic features, and of moral/physical characteristics such as pain tolerance, as these matters are given cultural significance. (xvi)

For centuries, black women writers have paid attention to the aforementioned cultural meanings. As in life, in literature there has always been a history of the black woman as a marked body. Her color, her features, her hair have served as cultural markers for a racialized body. Black women writers have responded to notions of a monolithic beauty standard and its corollary, the accusation that the black body is not hygienic. In order to place the granny's specific representation into the larger category of representations of black Women's bodies, I will discuss how the black female body has been reconfigured in African American literary history.

The conversation on the black female body begins with a beauty aesthetic inscribing what Western notions of an attractive body should be. In early African American literature the body beautiful was the fair-skinned protagonist, historically called the tragic mulatto, who lives out her life as a confused, alienated person, often committing suicide. Encased within the peculiar position of being both black and white, she is trapped between a patriarchal order and her maternal heritage (Carby, *Iola Leroy* xviii). Slave narratives, as well as fiction from the nineteenth century through the Harlem Renaissance, chronicle her life, the life of the hybrid as "other." Rejecting an essentialized body, black women writers have been making an effort to theorize the multiplicity of black female subjectivities and to write the bodies of all "colored girls" in their canon, remembering that whatever the hue—milky white, brown, tan, cocoa, mahogany, cinnamon, "we was [all] girls together" (*Sula* 149).

It was with the dawning of the "New Negro," the Harlem Renaissance movement, that we first begin to see some changes. In *Their Eyes Were Watching God*, Zora Neale Hurston's Janie is not admirable for her "luxurious hair" that swings down her back (208) nor for her "coffee-and-cream complexion" (208), but because she has learned something about life and love. Indeed, Mrs. Turner, the one woman in the novel who most represents and celebrates the white beauty aesthetic and who in the hands of earlier writers would have been taken seriously as the work's voice of truth, becomes in Hurston's work the object of satire: "Her nose was slightly pointed and she was proud. Her thin lips were an ever delight to her eyes." Because Mrs. Turner has been socialized to respect white bodies only, she feels it is the responsibility of fair skinned blacks to "lighten up de race" and that all blacks who have "flat noses[s] and liver lips" ought to be in a class to themselves (208–11). Janie and her dark skinned lover, Tea Cake, dismiss Mrs. Turner's comments as those of a foolish, misguided woman.

It as also during the Harlem Renaissance that black male writer, Wallace Thurman wrote his satire on the black female body. His work, *The Blacker the Berry*, gives us one of our first dark heroines, and he does so by pushing to the extreme anthropologist Ruth Behar's dictim that "the body in the woman and the story in the woman are inseparable" (270). Emma Lou is left one-dimensional as Thurman makes her more pathetic than perceptive, more color captive than color conscious. She constantly thinks that everyone is staring at her very black skin, a "skin [that] despite bleachings, scourging, and powderings had remained black—fast black—as nature had planned and effected" (4). Although Emma Lou does, indeed, live in a black world where there is a Blue Veins Club whose motto is "whiter and whiter every generation" (12), there is, nonetheless, something pathetic about anyone who eats arsenic wafers to become lighter (120). Thurman gives us a black heroine, but few black females would want Emma Lou as a model for their lives. What Thurman's work successfully does do is raise the color issue and show how much of African American folklore is anti-black skin, especially for women. Constantly hearing folk sayings such as, "Man, you know I don't haul no coal," Emma Lou dislikes mother wit. Although the work's title alludes to the folk saying, "the blacker the berry, the sweeter the juice," another folk saying more accurately describes Emma Lou's journey:

> A yellow gal rides in a limousine,
> A brown-skin rides a Ford,
> A black gal rides on an old jackass,
> But she gets there, yes my Lord. (Thurman 179)

Hurston's and Thurman's works concern themselves with the ways in which African American folklore has been a co-conspirator in denigrating the bodies of black women. Unlike contemporary black literature, which challenges notions of the black female body, African American folklore in previous decades shows evidence of an internalization of black female bodies as deviant.[7] In one scene in *Their Eyes Were Watching God*, the men sit around and joke about the disadvantage of a very dark woman: when her husband hits her, her welts do not show (219). How is a man to show his control over a woman if she is too dark for the physical evidence to be seen? In her essay, "My People! My People!" Hurston comments on these self-negating concepts.

> I found the Negro, and always the blackest Negro, being made the butt of all jokes—particularly black women. They brought bad luck for a week if they came to your house on a Monday morning. They were evil. They slept with their fists balled up ready to fight and squabble even while they were asleep.

They even had evil dreams. White, yellow and brown girls dreamed about roses and perfume and kisses. Black gals dreamed about guns, razors, ice-picks, hatchets and hot lye. I heard men swear they had seen women dreaming and know these things to be true. (*Dust Tracks* 225)

A little over a decade after *Their Eyes Were Watching God* came out, Gwendolyn Brooks published *Maud Martha*, another novel focusing on the construction of black women's bodies. Because of her dark complex-ion, Maud knows that her future husband will not consider her attractive: "Pretty would be a little cream-colored thing with curly hair" (53). An important chapter in *Maud Martha* is the one entitled, "If you're light and have long hair." Born with neither fair skin nor "good hair," Maud feels that her husband will have a very high wall to scale before he will be able to allow himself to appreciate any of her inner qualities: "But he keeps looking at my color, which is like a wall. He has to jump over it in order to meet and touch what I've got for him. He has to jump away up high in order to see it. He gets awful tired of all that jumping" (87–88). Given the negative reactions of the rest of black society to dark skin and to black features, the Emma Lous and Maud Marthas have difficulties. They measure themselves against a white beauty aesthetic and find themselves lacking. This too is the case in Toni Morrison's first novel, *The Bluest Eye*.

In *The Bluest Eye* the young black female character, Pecola, lives in a world where Shirley Temple, Betty Grable, and Hedy Lamarr define beauty. In such a world Pecola sees herself as ugly. Unlike her friend Claudia who "was physically revolted by and secretly frightened" of white doll babies, such as Raggedy Ann with their "moronic eyes, the pancake face, and the orangeworms hair," Pecola sees white doll babies as the epit-ome of beauty. In this respect, Pecola is reminiscent of all those black chil-dren who participated in the white-doll/black-doll psychological test that Dr. Kenneth Clark conducted in the 1950s wherein when given the choice, black children repeatedly selected white dolls over black dolls as their preference. Susan Bordo cites the responses of black children to this doll test as one of many examples of "the hegemonic power of normaliz-ing imagery" and of the continued need to understand "a cultural history of racist body-discriminations" (119–20). Pecola's cultural history tells her that she is not the "high-yellow dream child" that another black girl, Maureen, is. On the contrary, she is very dark and lacks Maureen's long brown braids. Her ugliness affects the way others treat her in her home and at school. A product of parents who themselves have no self-esteem, Pecola's life is doomed. She starts off life much like the new sofa her parents have bought: "the fabric had split straight across the back by the time it was delivered" (32).

The turning point in Pecola's life is when she goes to see the supposedly gifted folk healer, Soaphead Church, to ask for blue eyes, the traditional symbol of white beauty. Soaphead muses over Pecola's unusual and extraordinary request and then in an act of Faustian power gives it to her. By the end of the narrative, blue eyes are no longer the symbol of beauty but of Pecola's descent into madness.

It is with *Sula* and *The Color Purple* we see our best portraits of black women who are comfortable with their blackness and bodies. In *Sula* Toni Morrison gives us a portrait of how a friendship between two women, Sula and Nel, grows and sustains itself despite the departure of lovers and the disintegration of a whole community. Each woman brings something to the personality of the other. Thus, both complete themselves. Sula is the one who is secure in her identity, who helps Nel to perceive and to see. That is why when Sula returns to the town after having gone away to college, Nel remarks that "it was like getting the use of an eye back, having a cataract removed. Her old friend had come home, Sula. Who made her laugh, who made her see old things with new eyes" (82). One "old thing" that Sula had helped Nel see anew was her blackness. Born the daughter of a custard-colored Creole whore, Nel's mother, Helene, had a high standard of lightness and fine features against which to measure herself. By Nel's generation, the custard colored skin of Helene had already been diminished to Nel's skin color—that of "wet sandpaper"(52). Also, unlike Helene, Nel's nose was a "broad flat" one and her lips were "generous lips." Therefore, Helene required that Nel use all her spare time to improve herself: "While you sittin' there, honey, go 'head and pull your nose" (47). Into a world made color-conscious by Nel's mother, Sula, a "heavy brown," comes. When Sula is around, hotcombs, skin color, sharp features decrease in significance:

> After she met Sula, Nel slid the clothespin under the blanket as soon as she got in the bed. And although there was still the hateful hotcomb to suffer through each Saturday evening, its consequences—smooth hair—no longer interested her. (47)

Helene has lost control over Nel's life. In fact, many women who feel that only a white beauty aesthetic is acceptable seem doomed in modern black literature. They either end up the object of satire as Hurston's Mrs. Turner, the object of scorn as the mother and daughters in Baldwin's *If Beale Street Could Talk* or the symbol of sterility as the daughters First Corinthians and Magdalene are in Morrison's *Song of Solomon*. These latter daughters with their "buttery complexions," end up in their forties still "sitting like big baby dolls before a table heaped with scraps of red velvet," making artificial roses (10). Weak and confused, First Corinthians and Magdalene are fair damsels, who heretofore would have been worshiped, but in *Song of Solomon* they languish, having none of the spunk/funk and vitality of the other women in the work—Pilate, Hagar, and Reba.

The best example of a truly black complexioned female as a credible voice, as the work's center, is that of Shug in Alice Walker's *The Color Purple*. Shug, the "Queen Honeybee" of the novel, is "black as [Celie's] shoe." Celie's finds Shug's "long black body with it black plum nipples" extremely attractive. And Shug doesn't have "good hair" to atone for her skin color. Celie remarks: "She [Shug] got the nattiest, shortest, kinkiest hair I ever saw, and I loves every strand of it" (53, 57). Because Shug is the most powerful and respected woman in the work, she marks a turning point in black literature. Unapologetically she stands, a black nappy-haired woman. Celie and none of the other women characters in the work are color-struck. In fact when Harpo proudly announces that Sophia, his wife-to-be, is bright, Celie thinks that surely he means intelligent, for no one would place a premium on sheer skin color. Harpo, however, is so dark that he has inaccurately described Sophia's color. We find out later that Sophia is actually a "clear medium brown" like the "gleam . . . on good furniture" The only fair-skinned woman in the work is Squeak. The black men like her traits, her yellowish skin and her "teenouncy voice," but Squeak herself makes it clear in one of her songs that if blackness cannot be an affirmation of female beauty, then she does not want "yellow to be an affirmation either." *The Color Purple* is a work where black is synonymous with positive terms—"shining," "luminous," "dazzling," the way many black Africans look (131).

Positively connecting African American physical traits with African traits is the direction that the most recent works by black female authors is taking. One such example is Gloria Naylor's *Mama Day* (1988). Because Willow Springs is an isolated community with air that is pure, even primal, it has maintained an Afro-centric view point when it comes to the beauty aesthetic. The people in Willow Springs feel that slavery diluted the blackness of skin in black people, and they yearn for the days of "18 & 23 blackness," a term used to signify a number of things including the years of Sapphira Wade, the legendary presence that dominates the work:

> We ain't seen 18 & 23 black from that time till now. The black that can soak up all the light in the universe, can even swallow the sun. Them silly children didn't know that it's the white in us that reflects all these shades of brown running around Willow Springs. But pure black woulda sucked it all in— and it's only an ancient mother of pure black that one day spits out this kinda gold. (48)

In Willow Springs, Cocoa, the young black woman whose name betrays her diluted skin is at a disadvantage. Her lightness makes her feel like a leper. The African American tradition seems to have come full circle, as Cocoa has the exact opposite problem of someone like Thurman's Emmy Lou:

> Who could possibly want the leper? It was awful growing up, looking the way I did, on an island of soft brown girls, or burnished ebony girls with their flashing teeth against that deep satin skin. Girls who could summon all the beauty of midnight by standing, arms akimbo, in the full sun. It was torture competing with girls like that. And if some brave soul wanted to take me out, they would tell him that I had some rare disease that was catching. (232–33)

Once Cocoa leaves Willow Springs and crosses the bridge into eurocentric communities, people treat her differently: "I was treated very differently beyond the bridge—my physical features were an asset at times" (233). Cocoa is caught in the web of too many essentialized notions of what coloring she must be. In her first novel, *The Women of Brewster Place*, Naylor laid the foundation for a wide spectrum: "nutmeg arms," "gnarled ebony legs," "saffron hands," any shade engaged in the same activities of "leaning over window sills . . . carrying groceries up double flights of steps, . . . string[ing] out wet laundry on back-yard lines" (4).

The writers also protest the notion that black hair is unclean and unkempt. They take the slavery-generated concept of nappy-haired pickaninnies and turn it on its head. My pun signifies upon Gwendolyn Brooks's pun in her poem on black hair: "To Those of My Sisters Who Kept Their Naturals, Never Again to Look a Hot Comb in the Teeth" (*Primer for Blacks* 12, 13). To have nappy hair is to have hair that does not flow in tresses. Not only do the writers challenge this notion, but some, such as Ntozake Shange have gone as far as name a volume of poetry, *Nappy Edges*. After Audre Lorde dreaded her hair, that is, placed it in dreadlocks, she was denied permission to enter a Caribbean country, because her hair was deemed political. In retrospection, she wrote an article, "Is Your Hair Still Political?" with the emphasis that it should be. Alice Walker speaks of having had to dread her hair before writing *Possessing the Secret of Joy* and in *Living by the Word*, she has an essay entitled, "Oppressed Hair Puts a Ceiling on the Brain!" Lucille Clifton's poem, "Homage to My Hair," links nappy hair to tasty greens, acknowledging that nappy hair has the ability to "jump up and dance" (167). *Song of Solomon*'s Hagar thinks she is losing Milkman, her black lover, because she is no Goldilocks. However, as her mother/midwife/healer Pilate points out, "How can he not love your hair? It's the same hair that grows out of his own armpits. The same hair that crawls up out his crotch on up his stomach. . . . It's his hair too. He's got to love it" (315). In "I Shop Therefore I Am," Susan Willis comments that

> If Hagar had indeed achieved the "look" she so desperately sought, she would have been a black mimicry of a white cultural model. Instead, as the sodden, pitiful child who finally sees how grotesque she has made herself look, Hagar is the sublime manifestation of the contradiction between the ideology of consumer society that would have everyone believe we all trade equally in commodities, and the reality of all marginalized people for whom translation into the dominant white model is impossible. (179)

Running around in a limited period of time to acquire things that will make her look better, Hagar becomes a post-modern black Cinderella, untransformed by Madison Avenue, and as Willis argues, "the living articulation of consumer society's solution to racism and sexism" (178).

Morrison's *Tar Baby* celebrates Son's identifiably black hair as "living hair," as "foliage [that] from a distance . . . looked like nothing less than the crown of a deciduous tree" (132). Rather than the "sunset hair" of Margaret (112) or Jadine's short "shaggy-dog" coiffure (64), Son is a veritable Samson whose hair, from a Eurocentric perspective is "wild, aggressive, vicious hair that needed to be put in jail. Uncivilized, reform-school hair. Mau, Attica, chain-gang hair" (113). Unlike the biblical Delilah who cuts Samson's hair in order to destroy him, Son is lured by Marie-Thérèse, the healer, rootworker, midwife who burns his uncut hair to protect him.

Perhaps more viciously assaulted than brown skin tones or nappy edges have been the constructions of black hip size. The historical antecedents can be seen in the pornographic treatment on the exhibition block of Sarah Bartmann. In his-well known essay, "Black Bodies, White Bodies: Toward an Iconography of Female Sexuality in Late Nineteenth-Century Art, Medicine, and Literature," critic Sander Gilman asserts that the most "riveting" part of the black woman's body to her European audience "was the steatopygia, or protruding buttocks" (213). Europeans paid to view Bartmann's buttocks, an act that equated bodily orifices and colonialism.[8] Large hips constituted the deviant other. In "Theorizing Deviant Historiography," Jennifer Terry lists excessive size as one of the traits that discourses that pathologizing "deviant" bodies highlight (61). Instead of debunking the myth of large hips, Lucille Clifton in "Homage to my Hips," praises hips that "don't fit into little petty places," and hips that despite slavery, "have never been enslaved" (6). In this same spirit of freedom, when Paule Marshall's Avey in *Praisesong for the Widow* leaves the white, upper-class cruise ship, she takes off her girdle, releasing her hips to freely explore her Caribbean legacies.

## THE MIND: MEN OF SCIENCE IN WOMANIST NARRATIVES

*And we done learned that anything coming from beyond the bridge gotta be viewed real, real careful. Look what happened [to] Reema's boy . . .*
—Gloria Naylor, *Mama Day*

*I know this darky, I tell you; I know her well. . .you understand. Science. Research. The mind of the darky.*
—Adam Nehemiah in *Dessa Rose*

Many of the writers critique notions of objectivity and principles of empiricism by giving us portraits of men of science and learning whose paradigms and methodologies are culturally biased at best and inhumanely dangerous at worst. Through an oppositional discourse, the writers show what happens when empirical analytic styles devalue other interpretive frameworks. Repeatedly, black women's narratives demonstrate what happens when men of science meet women of faith on landscapes that still bear what Patricia Hill Collins would term the contours of an African centered feminist epistemology: concrete experience can and does contribute to meaning; knowledge comes through dialogue and

is governed by an ethic of care; the community expects personal accountability.[9] By violating these principles, men of science and learning,
whether black or white, become targets of critique and ridicule in the narratives. Through narrative, the writers disempower men of science with
means the grannies never had. They use their stories to validate knowledge claims in the non-linear, polyrhythmic discourse of many black
communities. It takes a different type of listening ear. Therefore, *Mama
Day* warns us to

> Really listen this time. . . . You done heard it the way we know it, sitting on
> our porches and shelling June peas, quieting the midnight cough of a baby,
> taking apart the engine of a car—you done heard it without a single living
> soul really saying a word. (10)

There are paradigms of knowledge not to be subsumed under western
logocentric epistemology and useful, if we but listen to them—"really listen this time."

*Mama Day's* Reema's Boy, in what is sure to become the classic case of
book learning that negates and falsifies communal knowledge, thinks that
he is able to solve a problem that only becomes a problem when he learns
how to do scholarship. When Reema's boy, "the one with the pear-shaped
head—came hauling himself back from one of those fancy colleges mainside, dragging his notebooks and tape recorder. . ." (7), he made a terrible
mistake. Because Willow Springs was such an out-of-the way place, he
thought it would profit from becoming the object of his scholarship—a
kind of native-son-as-ethnographer approach. Reema's boy's focus is on
the folk expression, "18 & 23." Through acts of word play, the inhabitants
of Willow Springs use the expression liberally, fluidly: there's 18 & 23
black women's history; 18 & 23 black women's beauty; 18 & 23 black
women's rites of passage; 18 & 23 black women's trickery, and other phenomena and activities.

As a trained ethnographer, Reema's boy comes home to research "18 &
23." In Willow Springs, he has returned to do "extensive field work,"
although the inhabitants, upon hearing the word "field," point out that he
"ain't never picked a boll of cotton or head of lettuce in his life" (7).
Reema's boy translates the expression, which the inhabitants repeatedly
told him "was just [their] way of saying something" into academic jar-
gon—18 & 23 is about "inverting hostile social and political parameters";
the expression should really be reversed, "81 & 32" to denote the lines of

longitude and latitude of Willow Springs. The folks of Willow Springs felt that Reema's boy was taking them for a fool, assuming that they were "ass-backwards" (8). If he had wanted to know the truth, he needed to listen in a different way, with moss in his shoes, the way that the work's folklore instructs. If he had tried to understand 18 & 23 in its cultural context, he would have realized its double-voicedness[10] and accepted it for the float-ing signifier that it is.

Throughout *Mama Day* there is an emphasis on culturally mediated knowledge. George, a New York engineer, plans to analyze the use of hydro-electric power and solar energy while in Willow Springs. He knows that he has a rational and analytical mind. When he watches football, he is "fascinated with the mechanics of the game, the mixture of science, raw strength, and a touch of human unpredictability" (124). When he plays poker with the men in Willow Springs, he relies on what he has learned in his Columbia University mathematics course, "infinite numbers," "matrix charts" and the "axis of maximizing a minimum result and minimizing a maximum result" (210). Once again, the home folks are no fools. They did not need game theory to teach them how to play poker. They were playing the way they wanted to play and did not need the man of science to step in and define what was cheating and who was cheating. One of the poker players, Parris, sums up the havoc that George's rationality has brought to the game: "This mess is becoming a mess" (211). George's argument that "only the present has potential" is lost upon ears where the past has power. Toward the work's end and faced with the task of doing something to save Cocoa, George is compelled to ask himself "What good was all that math and logic now?" (263)

Reema's boy and George function as warnings to the other black char-acters not to sell their souls to science. Mama Day, as healer and midwife, has authority because she lives in a community where science is an act of faith with even less power than communal faith acts. Such is the case also with Minnie Ransom, Bambara's healer. Critic Elliott Butler-Evans notes that "Minnie represents a triumph of folk wisdom over scientific knowl-edge, of women's culture over patriarchal dominance." Butler-Evans speaks of the way Minnie and other women in black women's narratives valorize their culture (182) and traces the "undermin[ing of] scientific knowledge by emphasizing subjugated forms of knowledge" as far back as Zora Neale Hurston (43).

Unfortunately, when the historical grannies were asked to step aside for science, their oral narratives were dismissed as superstitions. They had to work with doctors and health boards, complying with regulations and licensing that would eventually signal their decline. The response of the midwives can be seen in the framework that Jennifer Terry uses to discuss the production of deviant subjectivity in "those who come to be called lesbians and gay men":

> Through a process of what I call *vengeful counter-surveillance*, I am interested in exposing the ways we have been constituted as deviant subjects, and most importantly in locating how we have spoken back against the terms of a pathologizing discourse which has relied upon us parasitically to establish its own authority. By *deviant subjectivity* I mean the process by which a position or identity-space is constructed discursively by sexology and medicine and strategically seized upon by its objects of study, who, in their processes of self-inquiry, are at moments compliant and at other moments resistant to pejorative or pathologizing characterizations of them by doctors. (59–60)

The grannies were in such a position, helping to train their replacements, trying to obey regulations that would seek to erase or diminish their presence. What Terry speaks of as vengeful countersurveillance, I would call, to use a trope from *Beloved*, the "I-made-the-Ink" syndrome—the complicity on the part of some in the participation of their own destruction.

Perhaps the greatest injustice that the men of learning commit in black women's narratives is the way their violation of female bodies parallels their control over textual production. Anne Goldman's cogent analysis in "'I Made the Ink': (Literary) Production and Reproduction in *Beloved* and *Dessa Rose*" is useful in understanding how black women's bodies and narrative production interrelate. Goldman develops the notion that with Sethe and Dessa Rose "both the body and the word become commodified; texts upon which the white man makes his mark" (314). Very aware that "the production of texts occurs within a context of political inequality" (Goldman 314), Morrison and Williams give us learned men who, by virtue of their powers over black women's bodies, seize the right to write their narratives. I would make the same claims for "the story that is writ in Dessa's privates" that Jean Wyatt makes for the story on Sethe's back: both privates and back have "been appropriated and reified as a tablet on which the slave masters have inscribed their code" (478).

Schoolteacher, the scholar in *Beloved*, keeps a ledger of the animal characteristics of all of the slaves on the Sweet Home Plantation. Because he wants to see what the "nature of the beast" is like, his text reads like a dairy management text or an animal sciences treatise. Morrison refers to him as a "scientific racist," someone who, although part of a culture that speaks of the "rights of man," knows just enough to devalue others. In a touch of irony, Sethe explains that Schoolteacher "liked the ink I made." It is with this ink that he was able to construct a narrative that, as Sethe explains, could "dirty you so bad you couldn't like yourself anymore. Dirty you so bad you forgot who you were and couldn't think it up" (251). As Susan Bowers points out, in *Beloved*, "remembering is part of reversing the 'dirtying' process that robbed slaves of self-esteem" (63). What the work calls "rememorying" serves to relocate the dirt on places other than the black woman's body.

Learned men who would desecrate black women's bodies fare no better in *Dessa Rose*. Dessa is a member of a slave community rich in its knowledge of healing roots. Roots can stop mouths from talking, seeds from impregnating (11) and jail doors from imprisoning. Adam Nehemiah is a historian who is planning to write a book for slaveholders on the management of slaves. Because Dessa is a woman who has led a slave rebellion, who kills "white mens [for] the same reason Massa kill Kaine. Cause [she] can" (13), Adam is particularly interested in her; she is a good case study—a "darky and a female at that" (16). He could not have hoped for a better specimen. With pen in hand, he tries to write her story with the linearity of Western rhetoric rather than the circularity of her rhetoric, dismissing her remarks about her black lover, Kaine, as tangential to the point of his story: "this was hardly germane"(33), he thinks. Adam's summary of the slave rebellion purports to be concise and objective:

> The master smashed the young buck's banjo.
> The young buck attacked the master.
> The master killed the young buck.
> The darky attacked the master—and was sold to the Wilson slave coffle. (35)

For Dessa, Kaine represented laughter and love; when he called for her in the slave quarters , she felt that "no one . . . said her name so sweet" (43). When Kaine and others die in the rebellion, Dessa stands alone before Adam Nehemiah. They offer competing histories. Adam's story is the history of the colonizer; Dessa's history is "writ about her privates," where she has been delicately whipped. Unlike Kaine, Adam calls Dessa "out of her name."[11] As Mae Henderson points out, Adam Nehemiah is the "archetypal white male namer" who wants to capture Dessa literally and linguistically, his pen the patriarchal whip; her skin the colonized parchment (25–26). Adam's physical world collides with Dessa's metaphysical world. As female trickster in a community that used its speech patterns, spirituals, folk beliefs, and all of its folkways as survival strategies for "fooling massa," Dessa escapes her cellar dungeon, aided by the community of slave-women folk healers, rootworkers. Emotionally, "they sat with her in the cellar" and when the time came, they liberated her. From Adam's perspective, these women are "she devils" (15). In writing this text on authorship and history, the author herself, Sherley Anne Williams, becomes the "she devil," who, like Dessa, now "kills white mens because she can." Ultimately, it is she who alerts her readers that she is writing a text that challenges or as Henderson and others note "signifies" upon William Styron's *The Confessions of Nat Turner*.

Rather than the perspective of scholar, the narrative privileges Dessa's memories by placing those memories at the beginning and end of the novel. At the work's end, Adam Nehemiah also offers his "text"—field notes, the result of his ethnographic encounter with Dessa. Yet, in a racist frenzy, he drops all of his notes. The narrative critiques the production of texts and raises the issue of what types of research are emancipatory. Dessa deconstructs Adam's subject position. She repeatedly refers to him as a "trifling white man." Adam both fears this female of the species who "kills white mens" and desires her text, which is inseparable from her body, given that it is "writ upon her privates." The work's final act of subversion is when Adam is denied the right to "read" Dessa's body. Instead an older black woman reads Dessa's body/text differently from Adam, thus freeing her.

As the narrative ends, it is Adam Nehemiah whose name loses syllables and meanings. He is "Nemi." Contrastingly, Dessa affirms, "my name Dessa, Dessa Rose. Ain't no O to it." Nehemiah had "othered" her by calling her Odessa. Dessa refuses to accept the marginalization process. Mary Kemp Davis asserts that Dessa "transforms herself into the Dessa Rose Anti-Defamation League. By the time of the action in the novel's Epilogue, she has begun to inscribe her own history in her own hand for her descendants and others who might peruse her tale." Davis points out that *Dessa Rose* answers Baldwin's lament: "Nobody knows my name" with its own assertion: "everybody will know her name" (Davis 544–55).

Adam's beginning and ending claims that he "knows this darky" because of his science and research (255) become the ravings of a mad man. Although Davis points out that Adam's other biblical name "Nehemiah" connects him to a man on a heroic enterprise, it is worth noting that Williams takes the biblical Nehemiah's phrase, "I am doing a great work, so that I cannot come down" (Nehemiah 6:3), a phrase representing his fidelity to the restoration of Jerusalem's walls, and turns the attitude it represents into an obsession. Adam Nehemiah will not come down from the walls of the ivy tower; he mistakes his maxims for groundbreaking research.

African American women's narratives discuss science and scholarly pursuits as grounds of appropriation and power. In contrast to the men of science in the texts discussed who feel they have all knowledge, the black women are much more cautious about knowledge claims: "onliest mind I be knowing is mines" (*Dessa Rose* 36); "Look like to me only a fool would want you to talk in a way that feel peculiar to your mind" (*The Color Purple* 184). Yet, such caution does not prevent them from reconfiguring power relationships. Mama Day, Sethe, Baby Suggs, and Dessa all disrupt hegemonic assumptions that constitute patriarchal logic. Although not having the type of power that is predicated upon white Western masculinist ideology, they bring with them alternative conceptions of both power and knowledge.

## LITERARY RECOVERY OF RELATIONAL POLITICS

> Her [the white woman's] freedom is shackled in chains to mine, and she realizes for the first time that she is not free until I am free.
> —Civil Rights Activist Fannie Lou Hamer, in Lerner

> White women and women of colour not only live different lives but white women live the lives they do in large part because women of colour live the ones they do.
> —Elsa Barkley Brown, "Polyrhythms and Improvisation"

The grannies were proud that they "caught" black as well as white babies. Despite Jim Crow laws, which were prevalent in the South during their heyday, the grannies experienced some freedoms not accorded to others. Poor women, white and black, needed the services of the grannies. Viewing childbirth as an equalizing activity, the grannies responded to the call of mothers, all mothers. In *Motherwit*, Onnie Lee Logan repeatedly affirms that she gave food, clothing, whatever was necessary to any of her patients in need: "I did that all through the times with both my white and colored families. Whatever they needed and whatever had to be done I did it" (Logan 96). Often when the grannies give their count of number of babies delivered, they add that the number represents both black and white births: " . . . I don't know how many babies I caught; must have been more than 1,000, both black and white babies. . ." (Susie 16). The grannies also speak of white and black women nursing each other's babies.

Although the historical grannies in their recollections of their lives as midwives speak of a relationship with white mothers that seems to have "transcend[ed] racial, cultural, environmental, and oppressive forces to do the Lord's work: deliver babies" (Davis and Ingram 195), there is little evidence that those white women who did have power used that power in ways that would benefit the grannies. When middle-class white women's child mortality decreased, there was a corresponding decrease in funding available for training lay midwives. Most histories of American lay midwifery barely mention the grannies and even when feminists sought to come to their aid, as previously discussed, their efforts backfired.

The cross-culturally embracing attitude of the grannies was probably due to several reasons. First, the women saw themselves as professional and as such they were honor bound to give medical help wherever needed. Second, as to be discussed in Chapter Four, they were very religious women who believed in the ethic of doing for others as one would have others do for them. Third, as pointed out in Chapter One, their historical place in the hierarchies of plantation culture gave them the opportunity to be more than the three-fifths of a person that many other slaves were (Davis and Ingram 195).

As a contrast to the assimilationist mother-stories of the historical grannies, the literary writers give us the stories of their grannies embedded in metanarratives of problematized relationships between black and white women. Even as early as Harriet Jacobs's [pseudonym, Linda Brent] *Incidents in the Life of a Slave Girl: Written By Herself* (1861), we have an account of a black woman who is a mother and not a mammy. As Jean Fagan Yellin observes, "Linda Brent is a black mother committed to the welfare of her own children, not a 'mammy' devoted to her mistress' white babies" (in *The Slave's Narrative* 274). The writers are more interested in the ways in which black women, at large, were excluded from definitions of womanhood and in the ways in which this exclusion intricately shaped both black and white women's lives such that we all become "racialized subjects of our political imagination" as Hazel Carby argues in "The Multicultural Wars" (193). In her pivotal work, *Reconstructing Womanhood*, Carby documents the way black women were forced to function outside the cult of true womanhood. Although acknowledging the role of contemporary women historians who have noted that few white women ever achieved "true womanhood," Carby rightly points out that the traits needed to market a female slave were not the same traits desirable for the wife of the plantation patriarch; therefore the slave woman was "excluded from the parameters of virtuous possibilities" (27).

Contemporary black women's writings frame themselves in the paradox of oppositional relational politics. The construction of one is predicated upon the construction of the other. Similarly, Carby speaks of "a nexus of configurations which can be explained only in relation to each other" (*Reconstructing Womanhood*, 20). When critic Diane Roberts explores the Aunt Jemima stereotype in American history and literature, she argues that this construction has significance to white women also: ". . . the understanding of what it means to be a white woman in the United States, is still largely predicated on what it means to be black" (9). Roberts speaks of "America's racial background noise" (1), a noise that is heard so often in black/white women's relationships that even when white women writers dared to sympathize with their black women characters, they were accused of what amounted to "literary miscegenation"—their pens soiled by the black women they created. Patricia Hill Collins' dictum that "black 'whores' make white 'virgins' possible" (176) is an insight shaped by the uneasy alliances that black women and white women have shared with each other, rather than emancipatory alliances. In *Scattered Hegemonies*, Inderpal Grewal and Caren Kaplan speak of the need for "Western feminists or elite women in other world locations, . . . to acknowledge that one's privileges in the world-system are always linked to another woman's oppression or exploitation" (19).

Given the dialectical relationship between white and black women, why do so few of the autobiographical granny stories critique white women's roles in their plights? How does one explain the granny's penchant for emphasizing the bond she had with black *and* white women, a bond that she does not conceptualize in a framework of the subjugation of one by the other? The grannies had to receive their licenses from white nurses and doctors employed by health agencies. They truly wanted to do their best and realized that an eclectic approach to healing, the best of the clinic's way and the best of their way, would insure success. This attitude might also explain why they as a group have not been as vocal as, let us say, black domestics in criticizing the complicity of white women in their devaluation by society. Perhaps because the historical grannies literally held the life and legacy of white women in their hands, white women were more solicitous of them than they were of other hired black help. Black domestics in the privacy of their homes, at beauty parlors, churches, and other gatherings have passed down a lore of "Ms. Ann" stories,[12] whereas the grannies' silences have given the fiction writers opportunities to respond, as slave narratives once did, to the peculiar situation when persons from positions of power ask their subordinates how well they like the working dynamics. I do not want to imply that the grannies did not want to deliver white babies. They relate doing so, as if it were a badge of honor. However, by the time we read the novelists of the post-Civil Rights and Black Power movements, cultural politics have changed. To have delivered and cared for white babies is no longer viewed as the honor it once was. African American novels, which emerge from cultural politics, also shape those politics and as such change the discourse. Cultural codes shift, making novels possible, and at the same time the novels affect cultural codes.

Accordingly, there is a scene in Walker's *The Color Purple* wherein Sophia, who already has gone to jail for eleven-and-a-half of a twelve year term for the sake of white womanhood, is asked by her white mistress how much she loves her young white male charge. In the scene, Sophia dares to voice that the all-embracing arms of the black mammy is a concoction of white minds. She knows that being a mammy means one cannot mother her own; to have a mammy is to take someone else's mother. Therefore:

> "I love children," say Sofia. "But all the colored women that say they love yours is lying. They don't love Reynolds Stanley any more than I do. But if you so badly raise as to ast'em, what you expect them to say? Some colored people so scared of whitefolks they claim to love the cotton gin." (271)

Similarly, *Dessa Rose* problematizes the relationship between black and white women in the arenas of motherhood and childbirth. After Dessa escapes from her imprisonment, she finds herself in the bed of a white woman whose fortunes and power have declined because she is now without a husband. Dessa awakes to see this woman, Rufel, nursing her baby. However, this is not the beginning of a mutually satisfactory friendship, although Rufel certainly helps Dessa to stay out of the clenches of Adam Nehemiah. For Dessa, it will take more than the nursing of one black baby and more than Rufel's insistence that she liked her Mammy to make Dessa comfortable. The reductive label, mammy, shows no identity beyond the needs of white servitude. Dessa tells Rufel that Rufel never knew Mammy, and although Dessa comes to realize that Rufel, too, is at danger from rapists, Rufel is not raped. Obviously, Dessa sees black womanhood from a different perspective than Rufel does.

Williams tells us that she deliberately brings together two historical stories, that of a black woman who led a slave rebellion in Kentucky in 1829 and that of a white woman in 1830 who provided asylum to runaway slaves in North Carolina. Although she brings their stories together, it is clear by the work's end that Rufel must follow a different path from Dessa. When Rufel is contemplating echoing the sentiment of her biblical namesake, Ruth, who utters to another woman, "Whither thou goest, I will go; and where thou lodgest, I will lodge: thy people shall be my people, and thy God my God. . . ." (Ruth 1:16), Dessa stops her in her tracks. Rufel will not be going with her. When Rufel helps Dessa to get out of the situation with Adam Nehemiah who has found her and is trying to convince the sheriff that Dessa really is the devil woman and not Rufel's bondwoman as Rufel and Dessa are pretending, Dessa is grateful. She turns to Rufel and stumbles over the correct appellation—"Miz Lady, Mis'ess." To this Rufel responds, "'My name Ruth,' she say, 'Ruth. I ain't your mistress.' Like *I'd* been the one putting that on her" (255). Dessa had not "put mistress on her." Rufel had assumed an expected role of power, and it is this unconscious assumption of power that makes it impossible for her to become a Ruth to Dessa's Naomi.

Dessa will tell her story literally over the heads of black girls as she braids their hair, and they, their children's hair. If Rufel tells her story, it will be out West somewhere. Dessa's story, which began as the story of a black female trickster, ends with the story of a black female trickster, Aunt Chole. As a trick within the larger trick, Chole, "old auntie" who "might've been a granny and then some" (253), gives the authoritative reading of Dessa's body. Adam Nehemiah wants the sheriff to undress Dessa, so that her scars may prove her guilt. Such a disrobing should not be done in front of white womanhood, represented by Rufel, so the sheriff sends for Aunt Chole, who with milky, blind eyes and "heavy, calloused hands" takes the coin in her mouth that Dessa feels she needs to bribe her with, bites the coin, places it in her bosom and announces, "I ain't seed nothing on this gal's butt. She ain't got a scar on her back" (254). Furious and knowing he has been tricked, Adam Nehemiah accuses the sheriff of "taking the word of some nearsighted mammy" (254).

In black women's contemporary narratives, even mammies that appear nearsighted, rarely are. As with *Tar Baby*'s blind Marie-Therese, they still have enough insight to point the way to and through cultural myths, as Marie-Thérèse does for Son. She "sees" as well as any Tieresias. If she fails to do so, if she fails to perform the trick within the trick, if she buys too wholeheartedly into her role as mammy, nurturer, keeper of the homes of others, she becomes Morrison's Pauline Breedlove. Known as "Polly" to the little white girl that she takes care of, Pauline is Mrs. Breedlove to those in the black community. When her daughter,Pecola, who has no self-esteem, drops a blueberry pie in the home of Mrs. Breedlove's employer, Mrs. Breedlove slaps her, yanks her, humiliates her. Contrastingly, when the white girl starts to cry, Polly soothes her with "honey in her words" (87) and a promise that she will make another pie. The work criticizes her overly solicitous mammy-attitude toward the white child and abusive neglect of her own black child.

## MATERIAL CULTURE: REBELLIOUS MILKMAIDS AND
## DIASPORIC TRAVEL

> *And here comes the white man who says, 'Oh my god, not only are you poor and black and ignorant, you're still breast feeding. You're outdated.'*
> —Contemporary lay midwife, Shafia Mawushi Monroe, in "It Just Ain't Fair"

> *There was no nursing milk to call my own.*
> —Sethe in *Beloved*

Although few of the historical grannies speak of breastfeeding, an activity taken for granted by their clientele, some scholars and current black lay midwives such as Shafia Monroe link the issue over milk with the decline of lay midwifery: "The system did a very good job. They took away midwifery, home birth, and breast-feeding. In the 1950s, we were still breast-feeding and white America had stopped. . ." (qtd. in Dula 213). It is in this context that Monroe speaks of the doctors' assessment of black lay mid-wives as ignorant. Of course, medical opinions about breast-feeding now support what the grannies knew all along, but their only evidence was their "research" as black women on black women's bodies. Such evidence was discredited as poor women who could do no better. In "Mothers, Babies, and Breastfeeding in Late Capitalist America: The Shifting Contexts of Feminist Theory," Linda Blum notes: "If today, we may have learned to trust *some* women's bodies, it is only those of the proper race and class, not to mention marital status, age, and sexual orientation" (300).

In slave narratives there are accounts of female slaves bearing the pain of swollen breasts, not permitted to nurse their offspring due to laboring elsewhere on the plantation, most commonly, in the fields. There are also accounts of blood and milk flowing together as nursing mothers bore their share of whippings (Angela Davis 9). African American novelists make much of milk as a commodity and trope for black motherhood, although I would add that these are not totalizing constructions of motherhood. Tied to their agency as black women are their milk-producing breasts. Mbiti comments:

> African women, as a rule, suckle their children anywhere taking out their breasts openly and without any feeling of embarrassment or shame. Breasts are the symbols of life, and the bigger they are, the more people appreciate them: they are a sign that the woman has an ample supply of milk for her child. There is nothing "naked" or "sexy" about nursing mothers exposing their breasts to suckle their children in market places, church gatherings or buses; and those who judge such mothers as being indecent must revise their understanding of the African concept of what constitutes "nakedness." (120)

A look at selected works from Morrison's canon shows how milk becomes a racialized commodity in narratives that deal with women as healers and midwives. Members of the community in *Song of Solomon* call Macon Dead III, Milkman, a name that "bears witness"[13] to the sentiment of the younger generation in the work that Ruth, Milkman's mother, has nursed him too long. Upon witnessing Milkman nursing when he was old enough to have stopped, Freddie contributes to the work's psychoanalytic underpinnings. The sexual politics that connect Ruth to her father now manifests itself with Ruth and her son. Ruth is terrified when she sees

Freddie peeping in the window. She knows that although her feelings are complex, Freddie will tell the community a story that reduces her secret, self-indulgent act to "simple shame" (14). Ruth jumps up so quickly that she drops her son on the floor. Freddie's remarks capture the transition between a community that respected mother's milk and one that began to see breasts as sexual objects: "I don't even know the last time I seen that. I mean, ain't nothing wrong with it. I mean, old folks swear by it" (14). Although Freddie notes that there "used to be a lot of womenfolk nurse they kids a long time down South" (14), he recounts a story of excess: a mother he knows who "wasn't too quick" nursed her child until the boy was thirteen. Then, in an act of rhetorical signification, he remarks, "But that's a bit much, *ain't it?*" (14, emphasis mine). From henceforth baby Macon is a natural milkman and, according to Freddie, "Look out womens. Here he come. Huh!" (15). Although not knowing the circumstances whereby his son, Milkman, received his name, Macon suspects that it was not due to the association of milk with clean milk cans "standing on the back porch, glittering like captains on guard. It sounded dirty, intimate, and hot" (15). Macon connects his wife's milk to her sexuality; both are sour.

Marie-Thérèse, the nurturer and community seer in Morrison's next work, *Tar Baby*, is adamantly against the substitution of formula for mother's milk: "'Enfamil!' said Therese, banging her fist on the table. 'How can you feed a baby a thing calling itself Enfamil. Sounds like murder and a bad reputation'" (154). She de-authenticates man-made milk. Of course, we must note that baby formula is a threat to Marie-Therese's job as a wet nurse. "Thérèse is not only characterized as a visionary, she is also the archetypal earth mother by virtue of her 'magic breasts',", notes Sandra Pouchet Paquet (508). Claiming to still have milk in her breasts that are over eighty years old, Marie-Thérèse is the agent who sends Son on a counter, nationalistic journey, thereby mothering him in a way that is antithetical to Ruth's self-indulgent breast feeding of Milkman.

If ever there is a work that connects black women's milk with resistance, it is Morrison's next work, *Beloved*. Sethe explains that Nan, the plantation's midwife, "had to nurse whitebabies and me too because Ma'am was in the rice. The little whitebabies got it first and I got what was left" (200). Herein is a narrative of racial economy, the racial division of reproductive labor. Prior to her mammary rape by Schoolteacher's sadistic nephews, Sethe already has had her milk twice stolen. Forced to work in the rice field, her mother could not nurse her, and forced to nurse white babies first, Nan had little milk for her. As Jean Wyatt points out, *Beloved* is a text where getting milk to one's baby becomes high adventure (475), where rebellion gets inscribed on women's bodies by burning a circle and a cross under the breast, as with Sethe's mother. Sethe ascribes value to her milk and is determined that "nobody will ever get my milk no more except my own children. . . . I know what it is to be without the milk that belongs to you" (200). Denver, Sethe's daughter, speaks of drinking her mother's milk alongside her sister's blood (152). Metaphorically, the writers connect milk and a sisterhood nurtured by pain.

In *From Trickster to Badman*, John Roberts relates African tales showing that the journey to procure food is one of the primary quests in some African traditions:

> The material conditions created by existence in the African environment and the African trickster's constant quest for food cannot be accepted as accidental or unimportant to an understanding of the meaning that African people derived from trickster tale narration. For example, the African conception of the trickster as a figure particularly adept at securing the material means of survival, especially food, under famine-like conditions and through deception and false friendship is aptly captured in [tales of Ture, the sacred spider trickster]. (25)

Following African trickster traditions, Marie-Thérèse, Sethe, and other slave women in *Beloved* are interested in the material means of survival, safeguarding milk, as well as the more ethereal rites of riding with blind horsemen or exorcising evil babies.

When looking at how the writers make use of traveling vehicles and their women healers, I would argue that, as with the midwifery bags, they shape the historical, material object into a trope. The fictional characters travel, but their trips follow diasporic itineraries. As developed in Chapter Three, these are the characters who are interested in ancestry, Pan Africanism, and trips to a mythical home. In *Praisesong for the Widow*, Great Aunt Cuney's stories of how the Ibos walked on water to return to Africa prepare Avey for her trip back into the bowels of Caribbean culture. As with those who are prophetic midwives,[14] Great Aunt Cuney knew before Avey's birth she would be the one destined to travel her own version of the Middle Passage (42). Bambara's Minnie Ransom heals Velma by taking her on a spiritual journey, revisiting the past and integrating politics and history. Yet another example is Nana Pezant in the film *Daughters of the Dust*. Although members of her family may be moving mainland, Nana is most interested in a type of cultural travel that bekons one to "call on your ancestors. . . . Let them guide you. You need their strength."

In *Mama Day*, Miranda does not bemoan the use of cars in the island's annual CandleWalk ritual. Rather than focusing on cars as material objects that mar traditional landscapes, she, unsentimentally, recognizes folkways are dynamic.[15] Methods of travel change and those changes are beneficial as long as the community's long-term trip is the same—a road to the future built upon the past.

Any discussion of literary grannies and their emphasis upon travel should not neglect *Song of Solomon's* Pilate. Akin to Western African market women who walk many miles (Gay Wilentz 65), Pilate travels with map and geography book in hand. The work politicizes geography with Guitar declaring, ". . . I do believe my whole life's geography" (114) and speaks of Christ's Messianic mission as a lesson in geography (115). Throughout *Song*, Pilate travels, looking for family. While twelve years old, she walked for seven days until she was taken in by a preacher's family who required that she attend the one-room school. Of course, the teacher is delighted to have a student interested in geography. When Pilate must leave the preacher's home due to the preacher's sexual abuse of her, she walks out with her geography book: "I figured I ought to make tracks" (142). Pilate roams for some twenty years, traveling from the rural South to the urban North and back again to the rural South, her final trip an attempt to deliver her spiritual child, Milkman Dead. As important as her literal traveling, however, Pilate as midwife and rootworker traveled the routes of her historical past: "her mind traveled crooked streets and aimless goat paths, arriving sometimes at profundity, other times at the revelations of a three-year-old" (149). By the work's end, Pilate has traveled to mythical Shalimar with a message that is both profound and simplistic: ". . . If I'd a knowed more, I would a loved more" (336). Unlike most of the historical grannies who traveled by any means, except by airplanes, Morrison's Pilate flies.

# THREE

# God and the Grannies
## Testifying Theory

*The first thing I did was get down on my knees and pray to God,
. . . then I got up off my knees and got me a smart lawyer.*
—Midwife Gladys Milton, "Gladys Delivers"

THE TRAJECTORY OF THIS CHAPTER'S ARGUMENT IS THAT THE historical grannies were women who, without a formal pulpit, preached a gospel of womanist ethics and theology, and that black women writers build upon this tradition by imbuing their fictional grannies and women healers with a spirituality, a sense of mission rooted in the tenets of black feminist criticism. By looking at the ways the historical grannies grounded their beliefs and activities in traditional black religion and the ways the literature reformulates the spiritual sensibility, we end up with a different and indigenous way of theorizing—testifying theory.

To testify theory is to acknowledge that African American testimonial discourse has been a site for "insurgent black intellectual life."[1] It is to affirm that one of multiple locations for theory production is the oral tradition and that testifying as a speech act within black church services has always been preceded by the open invitation, "Can I get a witness?" It is not simply the learned who may answer this call, but anyone who is lucid, the granny as well as the scholar. Alongside all the physical healing that the grannies have done, by currently telling their stories, they can rightly say: "We heal our tongues. . . . We give testimony. Our noise is dangerous" (Mirikitani 202).

Propelled by their sense of a divine mandate, both the historical and the fictional grannies voice an ethic of caring and activism that is anchored in their self-defined theology, a spirituality that draws from Mae Henderson's trope of speaking in tongues, Audre Lorde's definition of the erotic, and Cornel West and bell hooks's "politics of conversion" and a "breaking of bread." That so many of the tropes and conceptual frameworks within black feminist criticism are spiritual in origin is not surprising, given the historical role of the African American church in emancipatory politics and identity formation. I make the same case for the rootedness of the grannies' lives that bell hooks makes for Sojourner Truth:

> When feminists, particularly White feminists, appropriated the words of
> Sojourner Truth, they conveniently ignored the fact that her emancipatory
> politics emerged from her religious faith. People need to remember that the
> name Isabel Humphrey took, Sojourner Truth, was rooted in her religious
> faith, that the truth she saw herself seeking was the truth of Oneness with God
> and her sense that, by choosing God, she was choosing to serve in the
> emancipation struggle of Black people. (*Breaking Bread* 51–52)

The grannies were spiritual women. When asked how did the grannies know of all future deliveries in the community, midwife Sadie Nickpeay quickly answered, "At church. You know, years ago, we'd be in church all days" (McFadden Video). The grannies saw themselves as doing the Lord's work, and they trace their history back to a biblical emancipation story—Moses.

Whereas preachers and politicians in the communities envisioned themselves as a type of Black Moses leading their people from bondage to freedom, the grannies rested securely in the knowledge that Moses would not have lived had it not been for subversive Hebrew midwives and a mother who refused to follow the laws of the land when those laws conflicted with their spiritual beliefs. Because the Israelites were rapidly multiplying, Pharoah instructed senior midwives Shiphrah and Puah: "When ye do the office of a midwife to the Hebrew women, and see them upon the stools;[2] if it be a son, then ye shall kill him: but if it be a daughter, then she shall live"(Exodus 1:16). The Egyptians needed the daughters as house servants, whereas the sons were potential soldiers, fighting from within enemy territory.

As threatening as a command from Pharoah was, Shiphrah and Puah showed remarkable courage by defying the order. Fearing God more than they feared Pharoah, the midwives did not kill the newborns, claiming that pregnant Hebrew women, unlike Egyptian women, delivered quickly, so quickly that the midwives, walking very slowly, undoubtedly, could not get there on time. God blessed the midwives, and stories of their courage helped many women, including the mother of Moses, to resist when Pharoah issued a second command—that all boy babies be thrown in the river (Exodus 11:17–22).

The bible is full of stories of midwives doing their jobs.[3] The grannies saw themselves as participants in this rich history. In *Motherwit*, Onnie Lee Logan attributes the white patients who came to her in her later years of practice to their renewed interest in following Scripture (Logan 128). When going to a delivery, many grannies carried their bibles. The bibles were both a symbol of their licensure from God and the document used to record the birth for the household. Those, who like their enslaved ancestors, were unable to read Scripture memorized passages and knew what "the Good Book said." Whereas all of the grannies in my study claimed to have carried a bible with them, some grannies have gone on record protesting the use of the bible in the birthing room, unless specifically requested by the pregnant mother. In Susie's interview of midwife Augusta Wilson, Wilson expresses a different angle to the midwife's relationship with her bible. Wilson, who delivered approximately five hundred babies throughout northern Florida, said that she did not carry a Bible to the patient's home because she felt it changed the room's ethos:

> . . . You have to keep their minds off the baby. So I always joked, cut the fool with 'em. Reading the Bible—it's always making 'em think about they gonna die or something like that. . . . (75)

Wilson goes on to explain that if you can get the mother relaxing and laughing, ". . . first thing, here the baby, and then some don't think about the pains or what they was going through" (Susie 76). In Susie's introductory remarks for the Augusta Wilson interview, she points out the painful experience that Wilson had with one publically pious family whose baby died. According to Wilson, when called to attend the birth of a family with membership in a local Holiness Church, there was so much "spiritual fervor" or religious commotion, depending on one's point of view, that "the young woman in labor became frightened and her contractions stopped." Although Wilson told the family to take the young woman to the hospital, they delayed. The authorities took away Wilson's license without a hearing (Susie 73). Wilson felt that too much showcasing of religion in the birthing room had hampered her effectiveness.

Despite Wilson's experience with one religious family, most of the midwives in Susie's field study were "ordinarily religious women" (13) who were themselves a part of the room's religious fervor. In interview after interview, the grannies speak of their religious background, although most can remember at least one midwife who was not, in the terminology of midwife Mary Lee Jones, "a church woman": "But *most* of us Christians. *Church* people—I don't know about the Christian" (Susie 192). More often than not, the grannies conceive of themselves as praying women, praying that God will show them how to cut the cord properly, praying that God will show them who their successor should be, praying that God will bless their hands (Susie 13–15). In "African American Midwives in the South," Holmes notes that

> although not a formal prerequisite for midwifery practice, the ability to
> summon the Holy Ghost for support, guidance, and "miracle working," as the
> case might require became apparent in many of the midwives' practices. Even
> before leaving their homes, these midwives frequently assumed the meditative
> state of prayer in preparation for attending a birth. (277)

Indeed, as part of the midwives' manual, *Lesson for Midwives*, was the Midwives' Prayer. The standard prayer asked that parents would be more loving toward their children and that God would guide their meetings so they could "render service more pleasing to [Him] and more acceptable to [their] fellow man" (vii). The emphasis upon prayer can best be summarized by one of Holmes's informants who said, "I prayed; I pray yet; I pray" (278).

The revocation of their licenses, especially for still-born births, was devastating for the grannies. Most sought solace in a God who could know the mortality rates for high risk pregnancies were not entirely the faults of midwives. The case of midwife, Gladys Milton, shows the tight intricacy between prayer and realism, the spiritual and the secular. In 1989 at sixty-four years old, Milton delivered a still born child, a situation the Florida Department of Health and Rehabilitative Services attributed to Milton's unsafe procedures. The pregnant woman had come to Milton during the last trimester of her pregnancy. Because she had delivered some three thousand babies, it was against Milton's better judgment to take the young woman as a patient, but the woman's mother prevailed on Milton to help her daughter. During delivery the baby's shoulders became lodged in the birth canal, and after trying everything in her manual, Milton performed the only episiotomy of her career, delivering a ten lbs. ten oz. baby (see Griffin, "Gladys Delivers"). It took Milton three years to clear herself legally of the charges, a total of fourteen infractions. The two most serious infractions were that Milton should have detected the mother's old scar tissue and that Milton should have been able to tell that the baby was going to be one pound larger than the weight permissible for lay midwives to deliver. How did Gladys Milton and those grannies for whom legal battles became increasingly more prevalent as times changed manage to withstand such ordeals? As quoted in the epigraph, Gladys did what any spiritual woman with one foot in heaven and the other on earth would do: she got down on her knees and prayed to God; then she rose up and got herself a smart lawyer (Griffin 60).

## A HIGH AND HOLY CALLING

Unlike European midwives and white American midwives who were for the most part self-selected or selected through some type of apprenticeship relationship, however informal, grannies speak of receiving a "calling" from the Lord.[4] By using the same terminology that their preachers used, the grannies were claiming for themselves holy authority. To be "called" by God was to receive via dreams, visions, intense prayer, or the workings of the Holy Spirit on one's heart (or in some cases the heart of one's mentor) some sort of signal that God had selected the person for his ministry. One granny speaks of having received her calling while picking cotton (Dougherty 151–52). As with preachers who tell of having a Saul-on-the-road-to-Damascus experience,[5] the grannies remember and speak of the circumstances when and where they first received their calling.

One of the reasons why so many of the husbands of grannies did not oppose their profession was that they shared the belief of a calling from God. Few felt qualified to dispute what God had ordained. With such a heavy reliance upon the spiritual dimensions of their practice, it is no wonder that when the State and County Boards began selecting their candidates for lay midwifery friction resulted. For the grannies, a legitimate practice was one generated by divine mandate. For health officials, legitimate practices were conducted by lay midwives who sat in classes and kept themselves credentialed. Dougherty goes as far as to assert that "the midwives recruited through the health department were held in disdain by midwives with established practices" (117).

In the case of the grannies, their most ardent claim was that God had taught them how to catch babies. Catching babies was a gift of the Spirit, the physical manifestation of their spiritual calling. When the ministers are ordained, upon having been called by the Lord, all the other ordained ministers and elders in the congregation would "lay hands on them." The literal laying on of their hands upon the head of the soon-to-be ordained minister symbolized God's blessing on the person's life. Similarly, some grannies enacted laying on of hands ceremonies, ceremonies that were especially meaningful given the role of the grannies' hands in the delivery process.

## PAYMENT FOR A SPIRITUAL GIFT

*When you add it all up, the real cost of my love is no charge.*
—Singer Shirley Ceasar, Queen of Gospel

*Before the baby was born God stepped in and the boyfriend paid me for delivering the baby.*
—Midwife Claudine Curry Smith, *Memories of a Black Lay Midwife from Northern Neck Virginia*

By conceiving of their skills as spiritual gifts and their mandate to practice as God's calling for their lives, the grannies' attitudes toward payment were complicated. They deserved payment, but their clients often were poor and many could not pay in currency. "I had a Christian heart about that. If they didn't have nothing, I didn't worry 'em for nothing . . ." (Holmes 280) and "I got [paid in] promises. . . . It was more or less what you call charity" (McFadden Video) were typical attitudes toward not receiving a cash payment.

Another common response was that God would one day pay them. In the video interview *Granny Woman*, midwife Sarah Maddux discusses the disgust of doctors for midwives who were willing to deliver and attend to the mother for virtually nothing because of their strong belief in a future spiritual payment. Mrs. Maddux repeatedly tells her interviewers that charity pays the biggest dividends: "You better have a star in your crown than a dollar in your pocket. You see, this dollar gets gone but this star shines on."

As a further testament to heavenly rewards, midwife Claudine Smith relates the story of a sixteen-year-old unmarried girl who came to her because her mother would not give her any money, admonishing her to get some help from her boyfriend. The young girl was willing to work for Mrs. Smith after the baby was born. Smith's response was, "If I don't get paid for that baby and I delivered it for you, God will pay me. . . . I've already been paid 'cause I got two legs and two good hands" (Smith 30). In the end, midwife Smith did not have to exercise her Christian virtues as fully as planned, because "before the baby was born God stepped in and the boyfriend paid me for delivering the baby" (Smith 30).

As equally common as divine intervention was payment in forms other than money. The grannies received chickens, pigs, flour, potatoes, all sorts of material rewards for their work. The grannies were part of a community system based on an ethic of caring and honesty. Midwife Smith proudly explains,

> I didn't keep a billing system. I could remember who owed and who didn't owe. Most of them that did owe they would kind of stop by. In my 31 years, I can't recall not over four people not to finish paying the bill. Everyone paid something, or they would promise me if they didn't have it. By living in a little town like we have, you're going to eventually run into each other every once in a while. (Smith 24)

When times began to change and some poor clients began receiving federal and state funding, many health professionals felt that the grannies were being shortchanged. As late as 1970, one of the nursing consultants reviewing the status of lay midwifery for the Georgia State Department of Health, concluded: "Midwives are impelled by a need to serve, and they never refuse a poverty mother. They are serving mothers eligible for Title V care (MIC) and they should be on a payroll" (Bredesen 21). This consultant observed that the state and county health boards have monitored the grannies' lives without seeing that they received the pay to which they were entitled, pay that would help in the fight against rural poverty: "We lay down all sorts of duties and restrictions, but provide no pay" (Bredesen 21).

## THE GRANNIES AS WOMANIST THEOLOGIANS

*Theory is a powerful black figurative negotiation of a blackmothered past.*
—Houston Baker, *Workings of the Spirit*

*When patients saw the midwife coming, they thought they saw Heaven! They thought the midwife could ease their burdens for them.*
—Midwife Maggie (Miss Mary) Smalls, "Mary had a baby. Sing Hallelu," in Daise, *Reminiscences of Sea Island Heritage*

Health Boards required the grannies to attend several types of meetings. One meeting was with nurses who demonstrated to the grannies proper obstetrical techniques. Another meeting was the meeting of the midwives clubs. Ostensibly, midwives clubs were to re-enforce the rules and regulations the grannies were learning.[6] However, these club meetings ended up as supplementary church service sessions. In addition to the many prayers and testimonies, all the songs about midwifery were sung to the tunes of well known hymns.[7] To sing "We Midwives will Greet you as Your Dearest friends" to the tune of "Since Jesus Came into My Heart" and to sing "We Are Midwives Banding Together" to the tune of "We Are climbing Jacob's Ladder" was to emphasize the granny's relationship with Dr. Jesus: "You don't pay no 'ttention to no Doctor, he human just like us. The only Doctor I trust is in Dr. Jesus cause he ain't never failed me yet" (Midwife qtd. in Davis and Ingram 192).

The subterfuge use of midwives clubs gave the granny the pulpit that traditional religion denied her. The grannies held their state mandated meetings, but did so through a religious process they found empowering. Thus, the midwives clubs were politicized sites where the grannies spoke in many tongues—that of health care reform and that of religion.[8] Biblical glossalia speaks of known and unknown tongues. The grannies' tongues spoke both a discourse with which they were familiar and another discourse that was pleasing for officials to hear. Even as they were testifying to their spiritual experiences, they were testifying against what they saw as a birthing process that was becoming less intimate, less humane. Akin to the way the spirituals had complex messages, one meant for the master's ear and one for the slave community's own liberation struggle, the speaking, singing, and testifying during the Club meetings were, to use Henry Louis Gates's framework, an example of survival through figurative language. Gates asserts that it is the figurative that has allowed the survival of the Afro-American tradition:

> The Afro-American tradition has been figurative from its beginnings. How could it have survived otherwise? I need not here trace the elaborate modes of signification implicit in black mythic and religious traditions, in ritual rhetorical structures such as "signifying" and the "dozens." Black people have always been masters of the figurative: saying one thing to mean something quite other has been basic to black survival in oppressive Western cultures. (*Black Literature and Literary Theory* 6)

Gates proceeds to describe "metaphorical literacy"—the ability "to decipher complex codes" (6). When the authorities saw how religious the grannies were, noting that content and form of the club meetings as just another church gathering, they were as naive as those who heard slaves singing, "I'm on my Way to Canaan Land," not realizing Canaan was as close as Canada. Often, black religious experiences have been dismissed as other-worldly, whereas the community of believers see themselves speaking to all worlds.

Embedded within the hymns, prayers, and testimonies of the grannies was a dialogue resonant with many of the tenets of black feminist criticism as developed by Collins in *Black Feminist Thought*. In Collins's discussion of the contours of an afrocentric feminist epistemology, she argues that "Afrocentric feminist epistemology is rooted in the everyday experiences of African-American women" (207) and lists several characteristics of an Afrocentric feminist epistemology, many of which I see in the everyday experiences of the grannies. Certainly, the grannies used concrete experience as a criterion of meaning. They rooted their testimonies and stories of obstetrical care in their mother wit, in what they knew to be true based on hundreds to thousands of deliveries each. Even today, very few of them are willing to problematize experience, asserting as Onnie Lee Logan does: "That's all I knowed" (21).

Two other characteristics from Collins's discussion in the aforementioned chapter are the ethic of caring and the ethic of accountability. Collins lists the components of the ethic of caring as "the value placed on individual expressiveness, the appropriateness of emotions, and the capacity for empathy" (215–17). Accountability includes the person and the person's relationship to his/her ideology. As moral counselors and spiritual guides, the grannies certainly demonstrated the ethic of caring and accountability.

Elizabeth (Betty) McCauly Gurley is a good example of a granny who ministered to the physical and spiritual needs of whole families in Hunstville, Alabama, and its environs (Whitesburg Pike). Known as Big Mom to her grandchildren, she was born on December 25, 1876 and died in 1974. She was a heavy-set woman with intense, deeply set eyes. Although only five feet six inches, her granddaughter remembers her as standing "taller than God." Her funeral was very well attended because she had done so much for the community. Other than delivering babies and baking millet cakes for the engorged breasts of the mothers, Big Mom would find out if anyone in the household or neighborhood needed pot soot for hemorrhaging, unfried fat back for fevers, and a gel of cough vine and moss for ear aches. Additionally, she would preach her own brand of a sermon before leaving. Another major attitude toward life and knowledge that manifests itself in the grannies' collective stories is a resistance to binaries. Of utmost importance is Holmes's observation, based on years of studying black lay midwifery, that the "spiritual dimension of midwifery is in harmony with a traditional cosmological view that does not fragment the secular and the religious" ("African American Midwives in the South" 276). The grannies were not religious on one day of the week and secular the other six days. They conceived of their lives as one sacred mission. Such a mission affected their methods as well as their knowledge base. Rather than the dichotomous thinking of dividing the spiritual from the sacred, we have the kind of thinking reflected in the aforementioned quotes from grannies who called on God and a good lawyer all in the same breath, who saw the boyfriend's payment as godly intervention.

## THE LITERARY GRANNIES AND HEALERS AS SPIRITUAL WOMEN

> *I don't need [Reverend Pike to reacquaint me with the Lord]. I can make my own acquaintance. What I need him for is to reacquaint me with my children*
> —Baby Suggs in *Beloved*

### THE EROTIC

Black women writers, too, place their grannies and women healers, within a spiritual arena, albeit one with much larger dimensions than traditional black American church services. Historically, the early black women speakers and writers such as Sojourner Truth and Maria Stewart claimed their authority from God. After a dramatic spiritual awakening, Bambara's Minnie Ransom, "fabled healer of the district," receives her gift "known to calm fretful babies with a smile or a pinch of the thigh, known to cool out nervous wives who bled all the time and couldn't stand still, known to dissolve hard lumps in the body that the doctors at the county hospital called cancers" (113). Having left a Bible college to go to New York, Minnie is seen by others as "batty, fixed, possessed, crossed, in deep trouble." Worst, they felt that someone of Minnie's class and background should have shown more dignity when struck by the Spirit:

> Said they'd heard of people drawn to starch or chalk or bits of plaster. But the sight of full-grown, educated, well-groomed, well-raised Minnie Ransom down on her knees eating dirt, craving pebbles and gravel, all asprawl in the road with her clothes every which way—it was too much to bear. And so jumpy, like something devilish had got hold of her, leaping up from the porch, from the table, from morning prayers and racing off to the woods, the women calling at her back, her daddy dropping his harness and shading his eyes, which slid off her back like slippery saddle soap. (51–62)

The contemporary works that contain the granny figure have strong spiritual sensibilities, although this sensibility renames itself in several ways. Audre Lorde speaks of the sense of the erotic by returning the word to its roots:

> The very word *erotic* comes from the Greek word *eros*, the personification of love in all its aspects—born of Chaos, and personifying creative power and harmony. When I speak of the erotic, then, I speak of it as an assertion of the lifeforce of women; of that creative energy empowered. (Lorde 55)

The concept of healing in *The Salt Eaters* is spiritually erotic in that it is centered on a love ethic undergirding communal care and requiring accountability. This love ethic is present in and through everyday acts, woven into the very fabric of the community. For example, Minnie feeds the loa (the ancestors) every morning by placing food and water at the tree. Ransom performs her healing in front of "the gallery," an ever-watching presence (7). Velma's refusal to let the community in blocks her healing. At first, she tries to "steel herself against intrusion . . . to go smooth, be sealed and inviolate" (5). To be sealed like an egg timer (19) is to reject the laying on of hands that the community feels she needs. After all, any person who slits her wrists and sticks her head in an oven needs spiritual healing, and Minnie becomes Velma's physician and preacher.

Similarly, Pilate speaks a spiritually erotic gospel in *Song of Solomon*. Her quote is a testimony to the way "love in all its aspects" (Lorde 55) can permeate one's being: "I wish I'd a knowed more people. I would of loved 'em all. If I'd knowed more, I would a loved more" (340). Throughout Pilate's life, she demonstrates an all encompassing love by offering food to everyone. She gives a pregnant Ruth the corn starch she craves, Milkman a perfect soft-boiled egg, Reba and Hagar whatever she has around her or whatever they crave. Fruit and the smell of ginger feed Pilate's eroticism. The "moon falling from her mouth, roses between her legs and tiaras of Spanish moss" (3) feed Indigo's eroticism. Having made velvet pads for her dolls so they could share "marvelous menstruation moments" (19) with her, Indigo becomes a lay midwife in adulthood.

## THE WHOLISTIC

*Can you afford to be whole?*
—Minnie Ransom in *The Salt Eaters*

That the grannies were hesitant to divide their lives into categories of secular and sacred, traditional and orthodox, mind and body, modern and folk is no accident. They lived in communities that in various ways critiqued dualistic thinking. As discussed earlier in this chapter, the grannies' brand of religion, unlike accusations leveled against traditional Christianity, did not embody a dualistic worldview.[9]

Neither does black women's fiction promote dualistic thinking. In "Paradise Lost and Found: Dualism and Edenic Myth in Toni Morrison's *Tar Baby*," Lauren Lepow defines dualism as

> any system of thought that polarizes what we perceive—[it] is a narrowing world view, for it inevitably cuts the individual off from the "other," the not-I or the not-good or the not-ordered. Dualism creates warring antitheses: the "other" is an enemy to strive with and, ideally, to dominate. (362)

Lepow's well-taken argument is that "Morrison continually requires us to confront the . . . literally self-defeating and self-destructive qualities of dualistic thinking, demonstrating that half a reality is insufficient for anyone" (364). Morrison speaks of black women as both harbor and ship,[10] anything less is incomplete. Similarly, Trudier Harris notes that Morrison "allows no dichotomy between form and substance, theme and character. In her literary uses of folklore, she has solved the problem of warring genre that plagued her predecessors" (*Fiction and Folklore* 7–8).

Patricia Hill Collins's and Barbara Christian's contentions that we are both/and rather than neither/or is true of the ideology espoused in much of black women's writings.[11] In *The Salt Eaters* the structure of the Infirmary breaks down these binaries. A cross between Western medicine and other assorted types of medicine, the Infirmary employs Minnie precisely because she has a gift, her experience as a granny. Additionally, *The Salt Eaters* has many characters who break down binaries. Meadows, a traditional doctor, gets reattached to the community, and he too starts breaking down the barriers between traditional medicine and healing, which he has seen Minnie do. Another character, Campbell, has the "ability to discuss fission in terms of billiards, to couch principles of thermonuclear dynamics in the language of down-home Bible-quoting folks." Campbell was able to do this because he

> knew in a glowing moment that all the systems were the same at base —
> voodoo, thermodynamics, I Ching, astrology, numerology, alchemy,
> metaphysics, everybody's ancient myths — they were interchangeable, not at
> all separate much less conflicting. (210)

Campbell's philosophy is generally supported in Bambara's narrative. Velma's healing is an altar call for the community's healing; the sickness comes from the connections that they cannot see. Velma is the only character who can see the relationship between industrial pollution and racism; between the personal and the political; she is at home with "the political workers" as well as the "psychically adept" (147). As such, Velma's healing highlights the need for the black community to move beyond chasmic ideological fractures. As one of the Seven Sisters argues, "the material without the spiritual and psychic does not a dialectic make" (104). By materially and psychologically catering to all members of a family, the grannies demonstrated a worldview that merges the material, spiritual, and psychic. Medical folklorist David Hufford notes that

> In recent centuries Western academic medicine has undergone a more or less
> intentional process of separation from other facets of culture. This

separateness, though still more apparent than real, appears very unusual when compared with the situation in other cultures, where health systems are strongly related to such other aspects of culture as religion and artistic expression. ("Folk Healers" 308)

The emphasis in *The Salt Eaters*, as with so many works in African American literature that discuss healing, is one of wholeness and not what Bambara calls "wasteful and dangerous splits" (Hull 224). Michelle Wallace adds that the "undermining of facile dualisms in binary oppositions of class, race, and sex is a priority in fiction by black women" (63).

## THE ALTAR CALL

> My concern, then, is a passionate one, for the literature of a people who are not in power has always been in danger of extinction of co-optation, not because we do not theorize, but because what we can even imagine, far less who we can reach, is constantly limited by societal structure.

—Barbara Christian, "The Race for Theory"

> At the same time one must not concede all the theoretical positions of power to men and white women.

—Carol Boyce Davies, *Black Women, Writing and Identity*

It is traditional in black church experiences to end the service by metaphorically "opening the doors of the church" or giving an altar call. This is the moment when the tone changes. It is the time that emphasizes one's response to the message the preacher has just given. It is at this final point in the service that the preacher discusses the consequences of the message. This is the time when believers reaffirm their sacred calling or when new believers accept their calling. It is in this sense that I offer my own version of an altar call, a call arguing that however blessed other frameworks may be and are, the works by black women writers need also to be read in the traditions of black feminist criticisms.

In her well-known essay, "The Race for Theory," Barbara Christian speaks of how those who enjoy the primary tasks of thinking, reading, and writing about works by women of color may feel intimidated or devalued by the continual race for theory, a race that sometimes leaves the literature itself in the dust. Indeed, we see our colleagues teaching a wide range of critical approaches from cultural poetics to cultural materialism, from new historicism to poststructuralism, from the Tartu School to the Nitra School. This is during the very time when the works of many black women writers have become popular in and outside of the academy. Christian feels that

> the new emphasis on literary critical theory is as hegemonic as the world
> which it attacks. I see the language it creates as one which mystifies rather
> than clarifies our condition, making it possible for a few people who know
> that particular language to control the critical scene—that language surfaced,
> interestingly enough, just when the literature of peoples of color, of black
> women, of Latin Americans, of Africans began to move to "the center." (338)

Although I share Christian's concerns, concerns that are often misinterpreted, my emphases are different and two-fold: first, the scholar in me wants to know what happens to black women's studies, especially such literature as Toni Morrison's *Beloved,* Sherley Anne Williams's *Dessa Rose,* Gloria Naylor's *Mama Day,* Rita Dove's *Thomas and Beulah,* Audre Lorde's *Zami,* Jamaica Kincaid's *Annie John*—and a long list of very strong works—when they are subjected *exclusively* to critical approaches that, although useful and illuminating, do not give primacy to black women's experiences and intellectual traditions? What is the cumulative value of theoretical frameworks that have asked few or insufficient questions about black women's agency or that leave too much space between "high theory" and theoretical forms that are indigenous to the communities of black women? As Carol Boyce Davies points out, "theory, as it is reified in the academy, still turns on Western phallocentric (master) or feminist 'gynocentric' (mistress-master) philosophy" (39). Davies's work moves toward a "negotiat[ion of] a variety of identities, theoretical positions and textualities without falling prey to schisms and dualistic or binary thinking that dismisses one dynamic to privilege another (Davies 57). The scholar in me wants to know why theoretical frameworks that have historically been articulated and advocated by black women—frameworks that could help the academy think through issues with clarity and fewer binaries are the frameworks that are most often dismissed. Rose Brewer rightly points out that "alone, [gender, race, class] are rather sterile categories infused with meaning developed out of many decades of social thought on class and race. . . . It is the simultaneity of these forces which has been identified and theorized by Black feminist thinkers" (27).

Second, the professor in me wants to know what happens to students of color when they are in graduate programs that teach texts by women of color, given their popularity in the last several decades, but the programs steadfastly retain their theoretical frameworks so that although the texts have changed, the great thinkers remain Foucault, Derrida, Cixous, Lacan—anyone except someone from the very tradition that generated the literature. Those of us in the academy, who occupy what Chandra Mohanty calls "oppositional space within institutional space,"[12] need to offer courses such as "Black Feminist Criticism" or "Womanist Theories," not to add another theory course to an already fat menu, but because the integrity of our texts demand that we do so, and students of color need to hear a discourse that legitimizes them as citizens of an academic community.[13] Those who think, theorize. If black students are made to think their people have not generated theory, or have not been fluent in theoretical language, they become less sure of themselves and their people as thinking, acting subjects.

Very few graduate programs offer Black Feminist Criticism courses or womanist theory courses. Some fail to do so because of a mistaken belief that womanist theory is the new kid on the block and most new kids run home after their first major fight. There is a wait-and-see posture adopted toward Black Feminist Criticism, and womanist critiques are very much like the attitudes that were first adopted toward the literature itself before it began winning National Book Awards, Pulitzer Prizes, Nobel Prizes. This wait-and-see attitude is quite different from the attention devoted to Anglo-centered theories, many of which, although in retreat, continue to attract large numbers of devotees. There are scholars who can demonstrate the historical range of many theoretical schools, but who see womanist criticism as some sort of step-child of feminist criticism (the proverbial child who gives birth to a child). Or, they see womanism as a post-civil rights/black power phenomenon, wanting a long line of historical antecedents, antecedents that we know include the writings of Maria Stewart, Ida B. Wells, Anna Julia Cooper, Linda Brent, Mary Church Terrell, Frances Harper—all the people that Alice Walker calls "my momma's generation." Sometimes, womanism has gone by other names, from Alice Walker's discussion of "contrary instincts" to Darlene Clark Hine's "culture of dissemblance."[14] Afrocentric womanists boast a history of intellectual thought that goes back to the motherland. Certainly, womanist theories do encompass a breadth that allows for what Houston Baker, in *Blues, Ideology and Afro-American Literature* calls,"generational shifts."

Rather than accusing Black Feminist Criticism of having no history, some dismiss it on grounds that such a discourse would lack rigor. The erasure of black women from the history of intellectualism has been so effective as to make the term "black female intellectual" oxymoronic. According to bell hooks,

> It is the sexist/racist Western conception of who and what an intellectual is that rules out the possibility that Black women will come to mind as representatives of intellectual vocation. Indeed, within White supremacist capitalist patriarchy, the entire culture works to deny Black women the opportunity to pursue a life of the mind, makes the intellectual realm a place of "off limits." Like our 19th century female ancestors, it is only through active resistance that we claim our right to assert an intellectual presence. Sexism and racism working together perpetuate an iconography of Black female representation that impresses on the collective cultural consciousness the idea that Black women are on this planet primarily for the purpose of serving others. From slavery to the present day, the Black female body has been seen in Western eyes as the quintessential symbol of a "natural" female presence that is organic, closer to nature, animalistic, primitive. (*Breaking Bread* 153)

In such a scenario, Black women have no epistemological or methodological concerns to add to the construction of knowledge. Professors and scholars deliberately or naively engage in what Toni Morrison terms "willful critical blindness," an act, certainly, of playing in the dark (*Playing in the Dark* 18). Adding and infusing courses in black feminist criticism in the academy is not easy. As Morrison asserts, some literary critics have been so opposed to African-American literature that they also avoid racialized discourses in texts by white authors: "What is surprising is that their refusal to read black texts—a refusal that makes no disturbance in their intellectual life—repeats itself when they reread the traditional, established works of literature worthy of their attention" (*Playing in the Dark* 13). In a socio-political context where some American critics have relegated racialized works by white authors as "minor," black women writers have had to raise their voices even more loudly, if to disturb the aforementioned intellectual lives.

Before offering a course in Black Feminist Criticism, one has to be in an environment or generate an environment, that has been shaped by profound consideration of a number of questions: How neutral is theory? Will the master's tools dismantle the master's house?[15] Should history be interrogated or unproblematically celebrated? How are questions of representation also questions of power? Do experts hail only from French academies or can they be Paule Marshall's "Poets in the Kitchen" women in whom art is deeply embedded, and for whom workshops are always word-shops? (12). Patricia Hill Collins points out that

> reclaiming the Black women's intellectual tradition involves examining the everyday ideas of Black women not previously considered intellectuals. The ideas we share with one another as mothers in extended families, as othermothers in Black communities, as members of Black churches, and as teachers to the Black community's children have formed one pivotal area where African-American women have hammered out a Black women's standpoint. (15)

Other issues to be considered are the epistemologies of location, the social construction of oppression, and the general questioning of knowledge claims. We cannot assume that the writings of those who practice or advocate womanism will be subsumed in existing theoretical frameworks, especially if these scholars practice what Cornel West calls insurgent black intellectualism: a "model [that] privileges collective intellectual work that contributes to communal resistance and struggle"(*Breaking Bread* 144). Even feminist scholarship has the tendency to reduce Black feminist criticisms to a monolithic category.

It is for all of the aforementioned reasons that I routinely teach graduate black feminist criticism courses that service the Departments of English, Women's Studies, and Black Studies. Such courses need to be constructed so that there are multiple voicings. The views of theorists cover a wide spectrum, from those who see theory as colonizing discourse to those who see it as an instrument for contesting hegemonic assumptions. Hazel Carby cautions us that "black feminist criticism be regarded as a problem, not a solution, as a sign that should be interrogated, a locus of contradictions" (*Reconstructing Womanhood* 15).

In addition, unlike conventional theory courses that use primarily philosophical essays, womanist theorists often use forms that the academy sees as unconventional: allegories, slave and fictional narratives, testimonies, and a wide range of cultural products, including blues and jazz (con)texts. In my most recent theory course, I used one work that presents theory in distinctly Afrocentric forms: bell hooks and Cornel West's *Breaking Bread* uses a call-and-response dialectic that foregrounds "mutual witness and testimony" from both males and females, a testifying community that testifies theory. Critic Mae Henderson speaks of the way that "black women writers enter into testimonial discourse with black men as blacks, with white women as women, and with black women as black women" (20).

*Breaking Bread* is a work whose dialogue is rooted in the oral tradition, a work that meets what Henry Louis Gates, Jr., describes as the challenge of black literary criticism: ". . . deriv[ing] principles of literary criticism from the black tradition itself, as defined in the idiom of critical theory but also in the idiom which constitutes the 'language of blackness.'" Indeed, the term "womanist" itself comes from "the black folk expression of mothers to female children, 'You acting womanish,' i.e., like a woman. . . . Interchangeable with another black folk expression: 'You trying to be grown' (*In Search of Our Mothers' Gardens*, xi). Womanist theorists are "grown" and make judicious use of many types of verbal lore to signify and testify their stature as thinking women.

Another text that I use is Patricia Williams's *The Alchemy of Race and Rights: Diary of a Law Professor*. This text theorizes judicial decisions and the intersection of race, gender, and class through a mixture of personal memoir, allegory, parable. Using a fluid, shifting, yet tight prose, Williams gives a black woman's voice to what has been a silencing discourse—Law. At the beginning of this alchemical project, Williams states that "subject position is everything in my analysis of the law" (3). To deconstruct the forms in which one theorizes law is to open spaces wherein one can challenge its "neutrality."

Another important principle in designing a black feminist criticism course is to use a novel to show how our narratives theorize. How does a womanist text look, feel, move, perform? Because so many of the texts in African American literary studies follow Toni Morrison's mandate that a work be "unquestionably political and irrevocably beautiful," a number of fictions are useful for raising some of the current issues in criticism, one in particular being Sherley Anne Williams's *Dessa Rose*. Because *Dessa Rose* is a story about a white historian who is trying to write/exploit a black woman's story, the novel raises questions about the multiplicity of positions, speaking for others, the production of texts, the construction of desire, the privileging of voice, decolonizing language, and many other current debates. A fourth prerequisite is the use of some writings from black popular culture. Many critical schools maintain a sharp separation between high theory and low theory. Because womanist theory shuns these polarities and false dichotomies, a womanist theory course should not end up canonizing a few of our scholars as high theorists. The popular culture text that I have used is Michele Wallace's *Black Popular Culture* which has a wide range of critical essays on gender, sexuality, black images, the production of black culture, postnationalism, and essentialism. Several of these essays are by critical thinkers, such as Marlon Riggs, who was not entrenched in anyone's academy.

Finally, womanism needs to be presented as a theory rooted in practice. Alice Walker's trope, "everyday use," captures the spirit of womanism. In her short story, "Everyday Use," she raises issues about the role of art: Should the mother give the grandmother's quilt to her daughter Maggie who is, as her educated sister Dee says, "backward enough to make them everyday use"? (33) Or should Dee be given the quilt so that she, in her moment of embracing what is popular, can hang it on her college room's wall where it will certainly be attractive, but a long way from the community that stitched it?

It is also important to read a work that shows how theory gets applied to issues that are important to the community, for example *Race-ing Justice, En-gendering Power: Essays on Anita Hill, Clarence Thomas, and the Construction of Social Reality*, edited and with an introduction by Toni Morrison. Using a wide range of interdisciplinary thinkers, this text is an important historical and cultural statement on the intersection of race and gender in American culture, all seen through the lens of a contemporary debate that was analyzed in the streets as well as the classroom.

Connected to the critical acclaim of texts by black women writers ought to be a resurgence of womanist thought. As Henry Giroux points out, African American feminist criticism

> is woven out of forms of testifying, narrative, and theorizing that reconstruct the meaning of difference while simultaneously rewriting the meaning of history as a basis for sustaining community memories and developing viable forms of collective struggle. (235)

We can not leave such an important task solely in the hands of theoretical schools that decenter our contributions. As Frieda Tesfagiorgis points out, we need to be always in the process of "claimin' discourse," realizing that "the act of claiming a particular discourse, in and of itself, asserts a claim for visibility and registers a theoretical position" (236).

There is a home environment where black feminist criticism gets everyday use. In discussing Walker's "Everyday Use," Mary Helen Washington argues that "'Everyday Use' tells . . . of the difficulty of reconciling home and art, particularly when the distance from home has been enlarged by education, by life among the 'gentlefolk,' and by literary recognition" (in Christian, *Everyday Use* 103). In similar ways, bell hooks discusses the concept of 'homeplace':

> Throughout our history, African Americans have recognized the subversive value of homeplace, of having access to private space where we do not directly encounter white racist aggression. Whatever the shape and direction of black liberation struggle (civil rights reform or black power movement), domestic space has been a crucial site for organizing, for forming political solidarity. Homeplace has been a site of resistance. (*Yearning: Race, Gender, and Cultural Politics* 47)

No matter how many other places or literary landscapes the texts by black women writers visit—and their strengths will carry them far—there are communities, cultural landscapes that have generated and continue to nourish these texts. For African American women's texts, their contexts — womanist theory, is not just *any place* or *some place*, it is *homeplace*. And it is in this context that we need to bring our theory back home.

# FOUR

# Women Who Work Magic

## Literary and Cultural Icons — Song of Solomon

*Black people believe in magic. . . . It's part of our heritage.*
—Toni Morrison, interview with Mel Watkins

*These are the kinds of women that made good midwives: they
had magical qualities, and the community knew it.*
—Debra Susie, *In the Way of Our Grandmothers*

BEFORE I BEGAN MY OWN ETHNOGRAPHIC WORK, I THOUGHT
that African American women writers were romanticizing the historical
grannies and folk healers. After all, in African American women's narratives, the grannies and women healers have tremendous powers, from
Pilate's ability "to step out of her skin, set a bush afire from fifty yards, and
turn a man into a ripe rutabaga" (94) to Sapphira Wade's skill at using the
heat of lightning to kindle her medicine pot. The literary women seem
limited only by their authors' creative imaginations. Yet after listening to
the historical grannies tell their stories, I learned something that surprised
me: the historical grannies have been complicit in the shaping of themselves as larger than life, albeit unwittingly so.

That is, however fabulous we read the writers' fables, there are equally
extraordinary folk beliefs in the histories of the grannies. The granny's
beliefs and her community's beliefs helped shape her grandeur such that
activities and events in the literature, which some scholars read as magical

realism,[1] I read as occurrences rooted in a tradition that the granny's kin, clients, and friends viewed as natural, plausible, rational. As Barbara Rigney points out, "Morrison does not permit us to escape into magic realism; instead, we confront the fact that evil as it is manifested in history has cosmic reverberations" (Rigney 77). Thus, I concur that we do not have magical realism, a term still rooted in the way men have written the unusual,[2] as much as we have the everyday magic of women, a workable magic rooted in what has been tested and tried by the culture. If there is a magical realism, as Morrison critic Dorothy Lee points out, it is one "that disregards conventional verisimilitude in its blend of the fabulous with carefully delineated historical circumstances, . . . evok[ing] a specific past and present experience" (164). I see the history and lore of the granny are a part of what Lee calls "carefully delineated historical circumstances." However, even as I suggest a cultural basis for the magic, I will target some differences between the literary and the historical granny lore, differences that give them both an energy not to be subsumed by the other.

In this chapter I discuss *Song of Solomon* as the earliest representative example of the fusion and tension between the conjuring activities of the historical granny and the magic of the literary imagination. The way I read *Song of Solomon* has pedagogical implications, for I suggest that those who grow up in communities where the presences of grannies are still felt would not read the magic as otherworldly or unbelievable, but as occupational lore. What appears mythic to some readers might just be mother wit to others.

By selecting *Song of Solomon* as the primary focus of this chapter, I will proceed with a different type of movement from earlier chapters. Whereas the structure in the previous chapters was to show first the granny's history and the literary intervention in and recovery of that history, the movement in this chapter is in the opposite direction. I select a representative work from the literary tradition and then demonstrate the cultural underpinnings of what in the literature appears fantastic by demystifying some of the literary and folk magic through my analysis of the historical lives of the grannies and the African influences nurturing the magic. The viability of the literary icons exist in tandem with the cultural icons.

I see the granny lore and Morrison's lore as participating in the same tradition—each dynamic in its own right; each distinct in its own right. My interest is as much with the culture that produces a Pilate as it is with Morrison's production of that culture. Hence, I offer a double-dutched methodology, a turning of two ropes in the presence of a company of participants. Because jumping double-dutch requires at least three people, it depends more on a company or community of children than jumping solo does.

Good rope turners make good jumpers. The more persons who jump at one time, the more efficient the turners of the ropes need to be. I can do a double-dutched reading of the literature and its socio-cultural underpinnings because authors Morrison, Naylor, Bambara, Marshall *et al.* are expert rope turners. They know the historical traditions, the rope's long length, and as they turn their narrative ropes, they know how to maintain rhythm and balance with the legacy of their cultural inheritance. Children call persons who cannot do the counter rhythmical turning that double-dutch requires "double-handed." If both or even one of the turners is double-handed, no one can jump, for the sound of the ropes will be offbeat. All of the literary writers in this volume are grounded in the history and folkways of their respective communities. Although as conjurers they are double-headed and double-voiced, none is double-handed.

When first organizing my two sets of data (the grannies' and the writers'), I was like the person who, when first learning double-dutch, starts from a central space, the middle, and closely watches each time the turners' hands go down, then jumps. By the time I had finished all of my research, I could hear the ropes turning without consciously having to force an analogy. I could hear each text turning in the other.

Therefore, when I discuss Pilate, I do so with an ear that listens to hear when the sound of the other rope of my analysis, the historical granny, is turning. Sometimes the sound of the ropes' reverberations is an echo, other times a strong whir. Each participates in interactive ways in African American expressive culture, which is why the version of reading double-dutch that I use for my methodology is an African American one. Young black girls expressed to me that French double-dutch makes a concession by allowing the ropes to move toward the jumper in outward circles. Doing so makes it easier for those boys and/or girls who have not done as much jumping or who have jumped in other traditions. For me to jump French double-dutch would be the equivalent of my grounding my volume in discursive strategies that appeal only to the academic elite. To listen to the grannies as storytellers and to listen to Morrison as a storyteller is to read/hear *Song of Solomon* as a performance within the dynamics of African American cultural transmission and production.

## SELF-DELIVERY AND THE SENSE OF THE IMMORTAL

*I can cure big navels. Doesn't cost nary a thing.*
—Folk healer Jessie Mae Newsome

*Even if you weren't frightened of a woman who had no navel, you certainly had to take her very seriously.*
—Toni Morrison, *Song of Solomon*

Morrison's Pilate is born without a navel to a woman whose death immediately precedes her daughter's birth. Modern technology continues to make the latter occurrence possible; only Morrison and God have made the former occurrence possible, Morrison with Pilate, God with Eve. Pilate "had come struggling out of the womb without help from throbbing muscles or the pressure of swift womb water" (27). Her stomach was "at no place interrupted by a navel" (27). Connected more to Christ than to the biblical Pilate, her namesake, she "inched [her] way headfirst out of a still, silent, and indifferent cave of flesh, dragging her own cord and her own afterbirth behind her" (28). Self-resurrected and self-delivered, Pilate is no ordinary woman.

The lack of a navel is a source of mystery for those who know Pilate. They need to be careful how they question her on this anatomical difference. When Guitar says that he wants to ask her something and then backs down by using rhetorical signification instead of a direct question, ("Somebody said you ain't got no navel"), Pilate responds in a manner that fans of *Jeopardy* can appreciate: "Don't sound like a question. Sound like an answer. Gimme the question" (37). Pilate has reason to be particular about how she responds to a question on the anatomy that has isolated her, othered her from the community of women and anyone who is "born natural" (143).

Around Pilate, other women "felt pity along with their terror of having been in the company of something God never made" (144). Pilate never knew that she was supposed to have had a navel until she had her first sexual experience at age fifteen. As naive as Pilate, the boy with whom she is intimate tells the men that he did not know there existed people without navels. The men send for the community's root woman to investigate the situation. Pilate thought that "the little corkscrew thing right in the middle" of one's stomach was a part of the masculine body. She had seen one on Milkman, her brother, and she certainly saw the one on her lover's stomach.

That she as a female should have had a navel never dawned on her. Once the root woman enlightens her, Pilate realizes that she has to be careful with future lovers. Each time a man discovers her abdominal smoothness, Pilate has to keep travelling. And because marriage would mean keeping the secret forever, she avoids that commitment. Fortunately, when Pilate gives birth to Reba, the two midwives in attendance "were so preoccupied with what was going on between her legs they never even noticed her smooth balloon of a stomach" (147). Eventually, tiring of the secrecy, Pilate begins to face the issue head on:

> It occurred to her that although men fucked armless women, one-legged women, hunchbacks and blind women, drunken women, razor-toting women, midgets, small children, convicts, boys, sheep, dogs, goats, liver, each other, and even certain species of plants, they were terrified of fucking her—a woman with no navel. They froze at the sight of that belly that looked like a back; became limp even, or cold. (148)

As with Morrison's other marked woman, Sula, Pilate is the pariah, the transgressive other that the community nevertheless needs.

As I hear Morrison's discussion of Pilate's navel, I also hear the navel stories of the historical grannies, two ropes twirling. Situated between occupational lore and belief lore, stories of navels abound in the oral narratives of the grannies and black women healers. Smooth navels were a testament to their professionalism. Large navels were a challenge to their skills. One woman with regional fame for her natural and magical cures is Mrs. Jessie Mae Newsome of White Springs, Florida.[3] During the summer of 1992 while going through records at the Bureau of Florida Folklife Programs, I found out that I was within walking distance from Newsome's house. Delighted that I had identified myself as a feminist folklorist, Beth Higgs, the Bureau's cultural anthropologist who, very much interested in Women's Studies herself, gladly agreed to take me by Newsome's house. To be a black feminist folklorist was enough of an oddity to secure an interview. As I talked with Newsome ("Miss Jessie," to me), it was clear that our ease with one another had more to do with her relationship with Beth Higgs and my resemblance to one of her relatives than any label I carried. As James and our children drove off to visit an alligator farm where they paid to watch someone feed alligators, I listened to Miss Jessie give details of the many navels she had cured. Her cure was to have the child stand against a tree and make a mark called a "navel mark" on the tree[4] denoting where the child's head is. When the child is tall enough such that her navel is at the navel mark, her navel will no longer be protruding.

"You mean protruding navels naturally go away as we age?" I responded.

"No, I mean I have cured many big navels with my marks," Miss Jessie insisted.

Newsome's response must have left me looking bewildered, for she immediately called her granddaughter to the front porch where we were sitting: "Punkin, show her your navel." It was obvious that "Punkin" had cooperated in times past to dispel any disbelief. Not wanting Punkin, who at the time was in her early teens, to have to show me bodily evidence, I affirmed my belief. But even as I was speaking, Punkin was uncovering the neatest little corkscrew in those parts.

Navels, the results of umbilical cords connecting the child to its life-support system, have generated much lore. For smoothness, some grannies suggest taping a quarter on the navel. This is supposed to work as well as a belly band, a piece of cloth tied around the waist. In Morrison the lack of a navel becomes the trope for symbolic immortal delivery of the self. Questioned by some readers on why Pilate dies in the work, Morrison in an interview emphasizes "she was not born anyway—she gave birth to herself. So the question of her birth and death is irrelevant" (McKay 413–39). Quite literally, some grannies discovered their birthing skills upon delivering their own babies, cutting their own baby's umbilical cords. Although in ways different from Pilate, they, too, self-delivered.

Other than an emphasis on self-delivery, Pilate's navel provides the framework in which to view her as ageless. That there has been a literal interest by the grannies on navels is worth noting, as typified by Jessie Mae Newsome's story. Perhaps more interesting is that those who have actually made a living or gained a reputation from umbilical cords also construct themselves as ageless, although in ways quite different from the literature.

In Morrison's fiction, Pilate and Circe, Pilate and Macon's midwife, seem to transcend time—Pilate because she can fly and Circe because she has been living for generations, delivering several branches of the same family tree. As Dorothy Lee points out, "Milkman first sees [Pilate]

Author and Mrs. Jessie Mae Newsome. (Photo by Elizabeth Higgs)

posed like some ancient mother goddess one foot pointing east and one west . . . , suggesting in the directions her connection to both life and death (65). Of course, Circe too is an immortal goddess. Although she does not literally change men into swine as her Homeric namesake, Milkman lets us know that Circe's cooking specialty is hog maws (52). Both Pilate and Circe have seductive, transcendent powers. Pilate, along with Circe, is a "vessel of secrets from the past, a figure beyond white logos [logic]" (Powell 757). This touch of immortality is common to the depictions of the literary women. Naylor's Miranda has served her community for decades as a midwife, her life spanning three centuries. She is going to "peek" into the twenty-first century for "pure devilment and curiosity" (312).

Curiously, the emphasis in literature on immortality and transcendence is not at odds with the grannies' construction of themselves. How do the historical grannies, born with navels, have the transcendent qualities that Pilate's lack of a navel gives to her? How do they approximate such immortality? How have those who existed outside of fiction made similar claims, seizing for themselves a piece of immortality? How have their lives participated in a conversation that has constructed black women healers and midwives as ageless? Through fluid constructions, many of the historical grannies achieve that same status, the sense of having performed from time immemorial.

A study of the registration records of grannies dating from the first eras of required licensure reveals a tendency among them to be inexact about their age. Although those who are still living today are proud of their advanced years (most are at least eighty years old), they had reasons to be vague about their ages when health boards first began inspecting and registering them. Knowing that health officials were skeptical of their ability to adapt, the grannies had to balance the large numbers of babies they were claiming to have delivered, from several hundreds to thousands in some cases, with their ages and years of service. Within her community, age could not wither her, for the granny was part of social phenomena, rather than medical aberrancy. Their elusive numbers were not a mathematical problem for the people they served, people who equated age with experience and wisdom, and people for whom relationships[5] were more important than vital statistics. The numbers were a problem from the point of view of health boards which needed for the grannies to know new techniques and progressive methods based on the most recent research.

Interestingly, the grannies managed to go through annual interviews and still the data are elusive—elusive birth dates, elusive years of service, elusive numbers of babies delivered. Case examples can be seen among the hundreds of records that I examined from Georgia's Registration records. To test my sense that the information the grannies gave was fluid, I focused on a detailed study of the registration records of six grannies,[6] chosen at random from the many records I browsed through. It is difficult to determine the starting dates of service for many of the grannies. In 1929, E. M. gives her starting date as 1920, with nine years of service to her credit. Subsequent registration records gradually shift her starting date. The most marked changes are in 1936 when her number of years of practice make her starting date 1903 and one year later in 1937, her starting date tabulates to 1927, a difference of several decades. L. W.'s registration records also suggest legendary service. Her implied year of birth as listed on her earliest dated card is 1891 and her latest year of birth is 1903, a difference of a dozen years. Two two-year cycles show intriguing gaps: in 1948, her year of birth tabulates to 1893, but one year later it is set at 1900; in 1960, her year of birth is set at 1902, but in 1961 her birth year becomes 1896. E. J. initially registers her birth date as 1892. In 1955, 1956, and 1958, she gives her exact birthday as May 28, 1892. This type of exactness did not prevent her from giving information in other years, from 1934 to 1967, that would calculate her birth year as 1893, 1894, and 1901. B. B.'s year of birth would appear to be most accurately as 1897, which her earliest records imply. Eventually, 1903 becomes her "new" year of birth, a year she uses fairly consistently from the mid-1950s through the late 1960s. By 1970, much less specific guesses can be made as to her year of birth, projecting her into the legendary realm, as far as age is concerned. As with the others, her birthday is a floating signifier.

Among the many possibilities for the discrepancies are vague memories, inaccurate record keeping, and confusion between dates of certification and actual dates of initial practice. Another possibility is that as community icons, caught between their traditional society that revered them for their ancient wisdom and another society that wanted them younger, they chose a multiple, shifting, construction of black female subjectivity. And this, I suspect, is why so many of their histories begin by sounding like slave narratives, where the years are often sketchy, deliberately and non-deliberately so, but where the larger fact—the quest for human status—is firm.

Much of African American fiction and autobiography is rooted in the conventions of the slave tradition.[7] Many of the grannies stories, especially in terms of how they deal liberally with age, signify on the slave tradition. For the black person to not know with exactitude his or her birthday was common in the slave community, where few detailed records of birth dates of slaves were kept and where the economy dictated time in terms of harvest and seed-time. What was important to the slave was, "I was Born." James Olney, a leading authority on slave narratives, discusses the many slave narratives that start off with the affirmation, "I was born." Olney notes the importance of this existential claim at the beginning of slave narratives by Frederick Douglass, Moses Roper, Harriet Jacobs, and a long list of other writers. Olney translates the "I was born" prelude as meaning: "I subscribe myself . . . I underwrite my identity and my very being, as indeed I have done in and all through the foregoing narrative that has brought me to this place, this moment, this state of being" (Olney 157). Unlike eighteenth- and nineteenth-century Anglo autobiographers who not did not bear the burden of proving their humanity, writers of slave narratives had to claim their identity by affirming that they were born into the human family, regardless of omission of dates.

As with their slavery forbearers, many of the grannies know where they were born, but the selves that are constructed for health department records do not seem to know when they were born. When threatened, they negotiate between their personal selves and their fictive selves, speaking themselves into being in much the same way as slave narrators wrote themselves into being.[8] Slave narratives have conventions that infuse the way those who write and those who speak tell their journeys. This is a case where the literature is not a simple re-creation of the social text, but a case wherein the literature changes the social text.[9] Whether grannies actually read slave narratives, as the novelists have done, is immaterial. They certainly heard enough stories in their churches, beauty and funeral parlors, and homes that made use of the conventions. These were stories that stressed how, despite humble and uncertain beginnings, the person, relying on a faith in a God who is no respecter of persons, is mission driven to go on a journey where accusations of fugitive plottings dog their tracks and where literacy and freedom become intertwined.[10] Although both the authors of the slave narratives and the grannies offer authenticating evidence for the stories they share, there is a vagueness about their own births as they shape narratives of adventure that make them subjects and agents of their own story, giving to themselves multi-layered identities.

In the literature, women with birthing skills and healing powers are known especially for their multilayered identities, for their roles as shape shifters. There are times when Pilate appears large and there are times we are told when she shrinks herself through perfecting the age-old techniques of maskwearing, as she does when she goes to jail to retrieve Milkman and Guitar. In order for Pilate to save her surrogate son, Milkman, she assumes another self, reminiscent of the self created in similar scenes by so many African American writers.[11] With no historical sense of what Pilate is doing, Milkman gives Pilate's antics a dismissive laugh: "She came in there like Louise Beavers and Butterfly McQueen all rolled up in one. Yassuh, boss. Yassuh, boss . . . "(205). Milkman further marvels that Pilate was "prepared. She had it all together when she got there" (205). Neither he nor his father knows how Pilate knew how to perform in this scene. Pilate knows because she is from a long line of black foremothers who had to re-create themselves for purposes of their children's survival. Even when they appeared to be betrayers, they were undermining the establishment with their "yassuhs."[12] Unfortunately, Milkman cannot distinguish the subversive from the servile. His references to Louise Beavers and Butterfly McQueen are revealing.

Too often, Louise Beavers and Butterfly McQueen have been seen as the quintessential mammies, unaware of their own exploitation. Louise Beavers (1908–1962) spent her life playing those limited parts that were offered to her: mammies and maids in *Uncle Tom's Cabin*, *Imitation of Life*, and other pictures that needed a mammy to validate the main actress as a mistress. Forced to stay fat to maintain her mammy status, to be the representative Aunt Jemima for pancakes when she hated pancakes, and to use southern negro dialect with which she was uncomfortable, Beavers groomed herself for survival.[13] Butterfly McQueen (1911–1995), best known for her part as Prissy in *Gone with the Wind* (1939), was also viewed as a shuffling, sell-out of her community. In his autobiography, Malcolm X says he felt anger and shame when he saw her performing as Prissy, whose famous line was, "Lawdy, Miz Scarlett, I don't know nuthin' 'bout birthin' babies." Yet *Black Women in America* notes that McQueen elevated the convention of the hysterical domestic to an art form (777) and quotes McQueen as saying, "But after I did the same thing over and over I resented it. I didn't mind being funny, but I didn't like being stupid" (Stark quoted in *Black Women in America* 778). The real Butterfly McQueen was no Prissy. At sixty-four years old, she earned her B.A. degree in Spanish. This narrative of her life must be read alongside the mammy narrative. In discussing the Anita Hill/Clarence Thomas conflict, Wahneema Lubiano notes that "narratives [can be] so naturalized, so pushed by the momentum of their ubiquity, that they seem to be reality. That dynamic is the work of ideology" (329). Louise Beavers and Butterfly McQueen had selves that resisted their public mammy selves. Milkman decries the power of the mammy mask. He misunderstands the protean experiences of African American women, experiences Cheryl Wall labels as "unmistakably polyvalent" (10).

### PILATE AS AFRICAN HEALER AND MIDWIFE

*If you ever have a doubt we from Africa, look at Pilate.*
—Macon Dead in *Song of Solomon*

*We claim our inheritance of ritual and stories, and we survive.*
—Abena Busia, "Words Whispered Over Voids"

Self-delivery and immortality are not the only two qualities that give Pilate and the grannies their iconographic stature. Their connections to African practices, which they revive and revise, give them legendary status. Pilate's various connections to Africa are unmistakable. The context of this section's epigraph is Macon's derision of Pilate's African features. He tells Milkman that Pilate does not favor their light-skinned pretty mother who died giving birth to her, but her father, a regular Pennsylvania African (54). Pilate is as dark as Ruth is lemony, and for Pilate, darkness is not a handicap. She appreciates the texture of blackness: "You think dark is just one color, but it ain't. There're five or six kinds of black. Some silky, some wooly. Some just empty. Some like fingers. And it don't stay still" (40–41). Pilate continues by pointing out the shifting nature and rainbow breadth of blackness.

It is Pilate, folk healer and midwife, who in the text represents the African rootedness of many African American folk beliefs and rituals. It is Pilate who ignores Western family relationship labels, refusing to differentiate between a brother and a cousin: "I mean what's the difference in the way you act toward 'em? Don't you have to act the same way to both?" (44). Pilate is situating herself in African traditions where terms such as "sister" and "brother" are fluid. Kinship is larger than the confines of the nuclear family.

Pilate is connected with African influences in other ways. The very air around Pilate's house "could have come straight from a marketplace in Accra" (185). Critic Gay Wilentz is among a small group of those who have discussed Pilate within an Afrocentric cultural discourse and rightly so, for Pilate "looms large," despite Morrison's intentions (McKay 143). Wilentz discusses Pilate as a "West African market woman"(65), noting the chewing stick between her lips, her scent of African ginger, her house that could be relocated in an African village compound, and her various mystical powers. Wilentz reads the story as an African dilemma tale and argues that "[Morrison's] discourse is based in the values and traditions of an African heritage which informs the African-American community and its writers" (74).

I place Pilate's empirical beliefs and magical beliefs within African traditions. Pilate and the grannies are atavistic[14] storehouses of ethnobotanical, as well as ritual cures. It is not always easy to distinguish between empirical and magical beliefs, especially in traditions where meaning and magic are created in synergy. As folklorist Pat Mullen points out in his study of Texas Gulf Coast fishermen lore, empirical beliefs "together with magical beliefs . . . form a complex system of occupational belief which is unusual in modern times" (Mullen 61).

"A natural healer" (150), Pilate combines the medical and the magical, each to ensure the greater potency of the other. When she assumes the task of getting Ruth pregnant, she uses a combination of roots and conjuration. To impregnate Ruth would be no easy task, for Macon, Ruth's husband and Pilate's brother, had stopped fondling Ruth and was now fondling only his keys—symbols of his love for the materialistic. Each key represented another tenement from which he could exact rent. Earlier in their relationship, he thought he had won Ruth's hand in marriage because of "the magic . . . in the two keys" (23). The person with undisputed magic, however, is Pilate. At twenty years old, Ruth goes to see Pilate because Macon has stopped having sex with her. Ruth will never visit Pilate again until several decades later when she returns to see why

Hagar, Pilate's granddaughter wants to kill Milkman. Pilate, who has an enduring interest in family lines, takes it upon herself to be a fertility specialist for Macon and Ruth: "He ought to have a son. Otherwise this be the end of us" (125).

Fortunately, Pilate's fertility cure comes after Dr. Foster's death. Dr. Foster, the only black doctor with white patients, would not have approved of Pilate's role in his daughter's life. Rather than send for a "dirty" midwife (71), he delivers Ruth's children himself. He makes it clear to Macon that midwives are not good enough for his daughter. Dr. Foster internalizes all the stereotypes about black lay midwives, despite his first-hand encounters with racism in his profession: black women had to give birth on the steps of Mercy Hospital, not in its interior. Hence, they call Mercy Hospital "No Mercy Hospital." Indeed, the only person in the community who wants to go to a hospital is Reba, who with "her picture-show thinks of hospitals as nice hotels" (95). Dr. Foster thinks of the hospital as a place of reliable medicine. Yet when he is dying, doctors bring to him radiathor, what Macon calls science's brand of a magic potion. According to Macon, Dr. Foster ends up dying because "for the first time in his life the pompous donkey found out what it was like to have to be sick and pay another donkey to make you well" (72).

Pilate is not limited by the stereotypes of her profession, nor by lack of access to a hospital. She begins her treatment by giving Ruth some "greenish-gray grassy-looking stuff" (125). Pilate is closely tied to nature and the forest and thereby begins her cure with the ethnobotanical. She knows where to collect aphrodisiac roots and the best type of water to use to mix the roots—rain water. *Song of Solomon* is a work that draws upon knowledge from the animal and plant kingdoms to facilitate healing. According to Circe, cobwebs draw the pus out of wounds, stopping the bleeding (167); Pilate tells Ruth that eating cherries prevents you from having "to wear them little windows over your eyes" (134). As Ruth places the medicine/potion in Macon's food, she feels "like a doctor, like a chemist doing some big important scientific experiment" (125). Indeed many of the herbal potions of women healers have chemical properties that make them work. And work it does: "Macon came to me [Ruth] for four days. He even came home from his office in the middle of the day to be with me. He looked puzzled, but he came" (125).

Shortly after the reader accepts the possibility that there are roots that can induce what the work calls sexual hypnosis, Morrison complicates the cure. Upon learning that Ruth is pregnant, Macon is furious and forces Ruth to use all types of folk remedies to abort the baby, from castor oil and soapy enemas to knitting needles and stomach punches. To prevent an abortion, Pilate gives Ruth Argo cornstarch because "when you expectin, you have to eat what the baby craves, . . . 'less it come in the world hongry for what you denied it" (132). How babies come in the world and leave the world are central to Morrison's African influenced cosmology, a cosmology she further delineates in her later work, *Beloved*. Following the cornstarch, Pilate does another act that makes common sense, even medical sense. She wraps Ruth's crotch in a "home-made-on-the-spot girdle" to be worn for the first four months of her pregnancy (132).

However, just when everything is sounding plausible, we later learn that through a ritual cure, Pilate the conjurer finished the job that Pilate the midwife and healer had begun. To insure that Macon would never "ram another thing up in [Ruth's] womb," Pilate placed a male doll with a chicken bone between its legs and a circle on its belly in Macon's chair (132). When Macon saw the doll, he took no chances. Fearing that Pilate is the oxymoronic charming snake who bites its loving master because that is what snakes do, Macon will battle her on her own turf. If he did not understand what was going on with the sexual hypnosis, he certainly now understands that Pilate is working within a realm where the psychology of knowing what the ritualized scene means is sufficient to cause enough trauma to inadvertently bring about what one most fears. As with Greek tragedy, this type of black magic prompts an inexorable fate. Macon tries to burn the doll by dousing it with alcohol. In keeping with the pregnancy motif, it takes *nine* burnings to do so. Ruth's stomach is so reminiscent of the circle on the doll that Macon never dares bothering her again.

How does one make sense of a belief system that merges the plausible and the improbable without labeling either in an evaluative way? I turn to the granny, Pilate's historical counterpart. One of the early articles on the granny as folk practitioner argues that the granny "did not adopt the doctor's techniques because they were rational, nor did she abandon her own because they were irrational. She simply substituted his kind of magic for her own or practiced them both side by side. When the magic did not work, it wasn't the magic that was at fault; it was the Lord's will" (Mongeau 503). In this respect the grannies were very much like the healers in Native American communities who blended old and new techniques without ascribing superiority to either. In Leslie Silko's story, "The

Man to Send Rain Clouds" the indigenous healers, after using their own medicines, accept holy water, the priest's contribution to health and wellness, not because the holy water is better, but because it cannot hurt to have such a back-up. Similarly in Silko's *Ceremony*, Betonie's cure is eclectic. The bear cure paraphernalia, telephone directories, and other representations of modern life all fill Betonie's room.

Much as Native American healers revisit their ancient healing rituals through modern changes, black midwives carried African healing practices into the New World. Alongside natural remedies with probable chemical properties, the roots, the berries, the oils, and the teas, the women brought to their trades a knowledge of curing and a concept of health that had African influences. Their parents and grandparents were enslaved Africans—not Americans awaiting a belief system, but Africans with a system already in place that gets transformed in the New World. The grannies and their grannies before them were diasporic Africans. As Linda Holmes points out, the apprentice system of the granny midwives "provided formalized mechanisms for passing on various cultural expressions and knowledge." Holmes interviewed women who "recalled the specifics of how they maintained a culturally appropriate rubric for the labor, delivery, and postpartum process" ("Medical History: Alabama Granny Midwife" 390).

Although some of the pharmacopeia changed given the change in landscape, other types of beliefs remained virtually intact. Take, for example, the fact that Morrison's Pilate chews everything:

> She chewed things. As a baby, as a very young girl, she kept things in her mouth—straw from brooms, gristle, buttons, seeds, leaves, string, and her favorite, when he [Macon] could find some for her, rubber bands and India rubber erasers. (30)

The passage continues to describe how Pilate's "lips were alive with small movements" (30). She is a woman who "hummed and chewed things all the time" (135). Pilate's oral behavior from childhood paves the way for oral behavior that is both psychological and literal as she matures into adulthood. Pilate is giving, open, and generous with her love and her possessions. Her moving mouth transmits an oral tradition.

This emphasis on the oral behavior of Pilate is very appropriate for a work so heavily embedded in the oral tradition as *Song of Solomon* is. Full of a mixture of Greek myths and African American folk myths, *Song of Solomon* is very much a speakerly text—a text that Henry Louis Gates, Jr., describes as "a text which aspires to the status of oral narration" (*The Signifying Monkey* xxvi). Pilate's oral behavior reverberates with African lay midwifery's emphasis on the role the mouth plays in childbirth. Bambaras cut the umbilical cord with their teeth. Given all the emphasis on cleanliness in the birthing room in Western societies, such an act would be regarded as unclean and unsafe. Mbiti reports that the Bambaras, among others, make charms from the cords that they cut with their teeth. The Akamba eat a certain type of dirt thought to have certain minerals (Mbiti 111).

One of the items that Pilate likes to chew on is a fresh twig (48). Described as a "tall black tree" (50), Pilate identifies with twigs and bark. Fresh barks and twigs have always been a part of the folk medicine of the grannies. The experience of midwife Betty Gurley was typical. She usually carried a twig from a particular tree named "cough vine" for the pregnant woman to bite down on during the throes of labor. The vine had a minty flavor and a hollow center (Crawford Interview). Additionally, the grannies used barks, leaves, and twigs for their medicinal teas. Midwife Gurley used to make a tea from the leaves of the mullen tree for the mother to take immediately before and after the birth. Other teas from trees mentioned by the grannies include peach and sassafras.

Many other beliefs seem grounded in modified African philosophical views, blurring the distinction between medicinal and ritual cures. One prominent example is the belief that the literal splitting or cutting power of axes can be transformed figuratively to other activities. According to her granddaughter, Midwife Betty Gurley kept an axe in her back yard during storms in order to "split the tornado" so that it would bypass her house (Crawford Interview). Even more prominent was the belief that an axe could cut labor pains. American society's disdain and ridicule for such a nonsensical belief showed itself when this belief became the hallmark of black women's stupidity in *Gone With the Wind*. Scarlett is exasperated with Prissy when Prissy claims that the only thing she knows about cutting the pain is to place an axe under the bed. The grannies I talked to had all heard of the axe under the bed, but were hesitant to discuss it. To assert belief, or even to begin to explain belief, gets misunderstood. In his story of "The 'Granny-Woman' in the Ozarks," Otto Ernest Rayburn notes that "the custom of placing an ax under the bed during confinement is widely known in the Ozarks, but not many people will admit that they practice it" (146).

I contend that when the grannies spoke of the axe under the bed, the coin under the mattress, the hen's feather under the bed, the husband's hat in the room, the tied-up thigh to keep the pain from slipping from the abdomen to the legs, and a host of other beliefs, they were doing something other than technical curing; they were reformulating myths, myths that were a part of their ancestral heritage and general women's lore. Mbiti points out that among some African groups, all weapons, especially of iron, are removed from the homes of pregnant women (110). Although I do not wish to speculate on why some African societies have this prohibition, I do wish to suggest one way in which the axe under the bed becomes functional. There are stories that men tell of how they were scared to death when they saw grannies coming with a five pound axe.[15] Perhaps, the axe under the bed has roots in the woman's need to relieve pain by taking action against the man who has placed her in her situation. This is not too far removed from pregnant women who in the larger American culture find yelling at the men who placed them in their situation therapeutic, threatening them if ever they place them in such a situation again. To see a midwife coming with an axe could certainly serve as a sign that the woman is empowered with a weapon should the man not respond sympathetically to her pain.

As with their medical counterparts, some grannies maintained beliefs that were clearly questionable. An example of an unfounded but pervasive belief among many doctors and men of science during the nineteenth century was that the development of a woman's brains affected the usefulness of her uterus. The more a woman used her brain, expending energy from the nervous system, the more likely her sexual organs would remain undeveloped: "Physicians argued that those women who dared to engage in serious intellectual pursuits, such as the study of medicine, faced the grave risk of being unable to produce normal, healthy children" (Litoff, *American Midwives* 13). The grannies,too, maintained unfounded beliefs, but such beliefs seem rooted in less sinister motives.

Some of the grannies' questionable beliefs include the many omens that are supposed to jinx the birth of babies. One finds evidence of these omens in the fictions, in African birth lore, and in the actual practices of the grannies. In *Song of Solomon*, one of Milkman's friends, Freddie, tells the story of his birth. As his mother was walking down the street with a neighbor, another woman appeared before them and when the neighbor greeted the woman with a "howdy," the woman changed into a white bull right before their eyes. Such an event immediately sends Freddie's mother into labor. When his mother looks at the baby to whom she has just given birth, she screams, passes out, and dies. Freddie is left an orphan because ". . . they couldn't get none of [his] people and nobody else to take a baby brought here by a white bull" (110).[16]

Other omens and jinxing activities can be found among many groups. Among the Yoruba, pregnant women need to be careful of what they see at night. All types of *abiku* or spirits of dead children can try to hurt or replace the child in the womb. It is also believed that should the pregnant woman walk over someone's crossed legs, she will miscarry. Among the Hausa, many ascribe a wide range of birth defects as well as neurological and epidemic diseases and illnesses to the presence of spirits, especially those that affect the pregnant mother (Wall 198–99).

Grannies perpetuated this type of lore. In his story of the Ozark Granny, Rayburn notes that whatever the malady—two faces, one ear, hooflike feet, or pop-eyes, the granny has an explanation. For example, if the child "don't have good sense," some Ozark grannies believed it is due to the mother having "stepped on a toad-frog about three months, 'fore the youngen was born" (Rayburn 145–46). Often, grannies attributed a baby's peculiar looks to an event during the mother's pregnancy. Pregnant mothers who attended circuses ran the risk of having children who looked like animals. In a similar vein, mothers who looked at too many ugly people jeopardized their children's physical appearance. Another folk belief is that the number of knots on the umbilical cord signal the number of children the mother will have.

A large number of beliefs, however, resist classification. Natural healer, Jessie Mae Newsome, claims to have cured many cases of chicken pox by having the child lay on the ground in front of the chicken coop and letting the chickens fly overhead, scaring the pox. Another such folk belief is rubbing a wart with a copper penny will remove it. In "Parallels Between Magico-Religious Healing and Clinical Hypnosis Therapy, "physician Robert Sammons tells the story of his father, who is also a physician. A nonbeliever, his father tried the copper penny cure and the wart was removed as promised (53). Cures that "can't hurt but just may help" are among those that resist classification. Gynecological examples of beliefs that blur the distinction between the probable and improbable abound. There are many beliefs that purport to predict the gender of the child based on the way the mother carries the fetus, the mother's cravings, or her complexion. Many of the activities purported to induce labor, such as riding over a bumpy road and using a laxative have worked for some people. The emphasis upon walking to induce labor has received more and more medical credibility. Wolof women walk up and down before delivery (Mbiti 112); grannies often speak of walking counterclockwise (Dougherty 161).

Some beliefs resist classification because their utility is not measured in terms of effectiveness, but in terms of how the community chooses to respond to its own traditions. Lore concerning placentas is in such a category. Midwives in both the Old World and the New World invest the placenta with meaning and power. Today, scientists are still researching the various properties of placentas. The Banyoro of Uganda bury the placenta on the right side of the doorway if the child is a boy and on the left if the child is a girl (Roscoe in Imperato 117). Burying the placenta is common cross-cultural lore. In some Caribbean islands, the placenta, usually referred to as the "navel string" is often buried in the backyard. It is believed that doing so will keep the child always connected to home.[17] Similarly, in a dream sequence Rudolfo Anaya's midwife, Ultima explains the midwive's role in burying the placenta: "*I will bury the afterbirth and the cord that once linked him [Tonio] to eternity. Only I will know his destiny*" (6).

As equally prevalent as burying the placenta is burning the placenta. Elderly Spanish-American midwives speak of burning the placenta. Then they give the mother three pinto beans and some herbal tea. The three pinto beans represent the trinity, ever watching over the mother and child (Marquis qtd. in Bredesen 33). Some of the American grannies also believed in burning the afterbirth: "You couldn't take no fire out of the fireplace when they burned the afterbirth" (midwife in Holmes, "The Insurance Crisis" 81).

The lore concerning cauls is another intriguing example of African influenced lore that survived the Middle Passage. The slave community had many folk beliefs about babies born with cauls or veils, and these beliefs were still prevalent during the heyday of the grannies. Babies born covered with amniotic fluid, commonly known as a caul or veil, are thought to be special or to have special powers. This belief was also wide-spread among European lay midwives, although among the European lay midwives the medicinal value of cauls and its protective powers, especially against drowning, was tempered by the view that cauls were used in witch-craft (Forbes 99–105). Although there is a long history of European fasci-nation with cauls, a history that some scholars trace to the Romans via the Orient, those who have studied the veil at length argue that the beliefs are most persistent among blacks in the Deep South (Rich 328).

Early in the century, Newbell Niles Puckett did work on black children who were born with veils. These children were supposed to hear and speak to ghosts. According to Puckett's informants, those born with cauls had to keep them throughout their lives. Anyone losing his/her caul would still hear ghosts but would not be able to speak to them. Puckett's informants also said that even deaf persons born with a veil could hear ghosts. Puckett reports that some grannies believed enough in the power of cauls or veils to steal them (Puckett qtd. in Rich). As a follow-up to Puckett's work, folklorist Carroll Rich collected stories of the veils from black informants throughout Louisiana. One of his informants, upon being asked exactly how a veil looks, replied, "You ever see a hog killing? Well, you ever seen that fat on the chitlings with all them little holes in it? That's just the way it is over a child when it's born" (Rich 329). Those of Rich's informants who themselves were born with veils testify of many types of power: the power to tell when someone will soon die; the power to know when others talk about you; and the power to cure thrush, a child-hood disease that affects the tongue. In his early work on Gullah folk beliefs, folklorist William Bascom collected caul lore, noting that "like their African ancestors, the Negroes of the Sea Islands regard abnormali-ties of birth as prognostic of the future" (29). In addition to the powers that Rich's informants named, Bascom's informants speak of the caul's ability to foretell if "whiskey has been doused" (Bascom 29).

African American novelists have been experimenting with characters born with a caul/veil. Milkman, the first black baby allowed to be born at Mercy Hospital, appears to be "deep" to the women who come to visit Ruth. They inquire if he was born with a caul and tell Ruth that she "should have dried [the caul] and made him some tea from it to drink. If you don't he'll see ghosts" (10), they warn. When Ruth asks them if they believe in these types of notions, they deny believing so, "but that's what the old people say" (10). By the narrative's end, Milkman must indeed come to terms with the ghost of his father(s). Morrison affirms the caul lore.

A more recent literary work from the tradition of African American women's literature that makes creative use of the lore of the veil is Tina McElroy Ansa's *Baby of the Family* (1989). As with Milkman, Lena, the baby of the family, is born with a caul in Mulberry, Georgia in 1949. Whereas Milkman's birth was the first black birth permitted at the all white hospital, Lena's mother, Nellie, chooses to give birth to Lena in an all black hospital, St. Luke's Hospital. She prefers the kindness and attention that the town's one black doctor and founder of the black hospital gives his patients rather than the lack of respect received from the large white county hospital, where she must enter by the back door.

Dr. Williams, the black doctor who founded and owns St. Luke's, delivers Lena. Ordinarily, Dr. Williams is very much a man of science and technology. Very disturbed that his hospital did not have the up-to-date equipment that the white county hospital had, Dr. Williams took it upon himself to secure such items as incubators. And although Nurse Bloom, a former country midwife, seems to be the nurse he most trusts, Dr. Williams routinely hires nurses from the top of their Tuskegee Institute class. As a professional, he keeps abreast of his field. Yet when he delivers Lena, a baby with a caul, a baby who "brought with her a touch of the supernatural into a place that owed so much to the scientific" (3), he cannot shake off all the mythology and rituals that are a part of such a birth. Folk culture erupts; there is always seepage: "Seeming to forget his usual delivery-room procedure, formed over nearly a quarter century of practice, he turned the next two minutes into a ritualized dance that had nothing to do with modern medicine" (5). Both the cleaning woman and the cook come to gaze upon baby Lena. Most delighted is Nurse Bloom who becomes once again Mother Bloom, enacting the necessary rituals.

Carefully, she removes the gossamer veil, the thin membrane that looks as if it were "draped there by a band of angels" (3). Mother Bloom preserves the caul through a chanting, cleansing, and drying process. Interestingly, Nurse Bloom admits that the modern technology available at the hospital is the most efficient way she has ever found of preserving the caul. Once again, the notion that folk practitioners resist the new is proven wrong by their eclecticism. By using the hospital dryer, Nurse Bloom can perform the ritual in forty-five minutes, a ritual that would have taken her all day in the country over a red-hot brick. She then gives the new mother a baby bottle full of tea made from the water in which she soaked the caul. She tells Nellie that her child is a special child, and that drinking caul tea will protect the child from evil.

Because Nellie is a "modern woman," she eventually burns the caul and never gives Lena the caul tea. In fact, to her the caul in water reminds her of chitterlings soaking in a sink, reminiscent of Puckett's informant who linked cauls and chitterlings, an interesting linkage of cultural rituals and ethnic food. Contrastingly, Nurse Bloom sees the dried caul as "an ancient map of some unexplored territory" (21). Nurse Bloom makes all kinds of claims for the caul: Lena will see ghosts, she will be wise, she will be able to foretell things. All these predictions and more come to pass because "God . . . touched her in the womb"(17). As Lena struggles to ascertain why she is so unlike everyone else, she thinks she is crazy. She does not come to understand her veiled existence and its role as a blessing and not a curse in her life until after her grandmother dies. The dead grandmother returns to apologize to Lena for not preparing her for understanding the properties of the caul. *Baby in the Family* is a book about understanding what happens when the community forgets its lore. When Lena's mother does not give her the tea, she is denying Lena the community's ritual. Lena is a young girl of middle-class background whose life remains forever changed by age-old lore.

Lore involving placentas and cauls keeps an element of mystery about the activities that take place within lay midwifery communities. Through the burial rites associated with placentas and the care given to cauls, along with all their ethnobotanical expertise, the women healers and grannies become ritual specialists, as well as functional practitioners, not that they feel a need to discern between the two. Whether the need is physical or emotional, Pilate, in the tradition of the grannies, asserts, "What difference do it make if the thing you scared of is real or not?" When the husband of one of the women for whom Pilate worked stands in his kitchen and tells her that he is about to fall off a cliff, she does not tell him that there is no cliff in his kitchen. Rather, she holds onto him so that he does not fall. The husband would still be living had not his wife walked in and failed to believe Pilate's falling off the cliff explanation. Pilate lets go and the husband drops dead (42–43). Emotional realities are as consequential as physical ones. If the grannies want to mix the ethnobotanical with the ritual, they do so in the spirit of wellness for the whole body.

Ntozake Shange begins *sassafrass,cypress, & indigo* with the inevitability of magic: "Where there is woman there is magic" (3). Although African American women writers give readers a range of activities performed by the healers and midwives, their construction of the magical is what makes these characters stand tall and their tales memorable. To think that the literary or historical lives of grannies would be divested of magic and myth is to misunderstand a society that has survived by believing the unbelievable and speaking the unspoken. Indeed, W. E. B. Du Bois's definition of the Negro as the seventh son born with a veil (*The Souls of Black Folks*) is predicated upon survival magic. This definition extends qualities that make individuals larger than life to broader, cultural qualities that speak to the group's need to be seers, to be larger than their circumstances, because they have been destined to be so. As Gina Dent points out, blackness itself "is still a mythic construction" (18). If blackness is a mythic construction, the grannies' lives then become myths within a larger myth of blackness.

## PILATE AS FOLK PERFORMER

> The only cure
> I know
> is a good ceremony . . .
> Leslie Silko, *Ceremony*

Throughout *Song of Solomon* Pilate is a performer. During the opening scene when Robert Smith is about to commit suicide, Pilate, wrapped in an archetypal folk quilt, puts on a musical performance that competes with Robert Smith's flapping wings (8). Her music provides the backdrop for Smith's fatal leap. As Pilate sings a song of flight, "O Sugarman done fly," Smith jumps. Her singing contextualizes his flight within a tradition of soaring slaves, some because they have found themselves, others because they have gone mad. Always singing, Pilate attracts an audience. When Milkman is passing by her house one day, he stands outside the window listening to Pilate lead a melody with Reba and Hagar (29). The scene is replete with images that conflate folk women and goddesses. Reba, Hagar, and Pilate appear as an African American version of the three Greek fates. Reba is cutting toenails, Hagar is braiding hair, Pilate is stirring her pot. Because of the rhythm of the music, Pilate "swayed like a willow over her stirring" (30). Singing and stirring, Pilate captures Milkman's interest by her dual performance.

Pilate stirs her mixtures in several large "crocks," as she calls them. Crocks were to the grannies what test tubes are to scientists. They were the depositories for their mixtures, potions, and experiments. Grannies speak of their Franklin stoves and their large black crocks. But before one places Pilate too squarely in the same centuries-old picture of midwives and healers working tirelessly over the hearth, look again. Pilate's crock is just as likely to be brewing illegal spirits as it is to be brewing stews. The illegal activity causes Macon to refer to his sister as a "raggedy bootlegger" and all three women, Pilate, Reba, and Hagar as "a collection of lunatics who made wine and sang in the streets like common street women! Just like common street women!" (20).

Pilate's performance as a poor street woman comes across as genteel poverty when compared to the material deprivations of the grannies. As a maker of wine, she appears more as a female Dionysus. The historical grannies had to make ends meet through more mundane jobs. Without complaining because it was "the work of God," Onnie Lee Logan explains that "all at the same time when I was deliverin babies at night I was workin full-time for the Mearses, livin on the place. Their maid full-time" (Logan 104). Logan goes on to explain that she never wasted a minute, for she had so much to do. Claudine Smith was a bus driver, oyster shucker, domestic, and a nursing-home aide. When she had to deliver a baby, her family picked up her other chores (Smith 12–13). After thirty-one years of midwifery and thirty-seven years of school-bus driving, she did not receive a pension from either. Other grannies supplemented their income by providing food services, working in beauty parlors, weaving, raising chickens or whatever form of moonlighting that was necessary to fulfill their calling.

Few hearing their stories would envy the material starkness of their lives and the lives of their clientele. The grannies went to homes without the basic utilities and sometimes had to carry with them everything from basins to bed linen. So impoverished were some of their clients that Arkansas grannies complained that husbands from poor families should stop making babies (Freedman 5). According to state training manuals, grannies were supposed to see that their patients ate lean meat and drank fresh milk. However, poverty dictated that their substance be grits, greens, and fatback (Bredesen 7).

Contrastingly, Pilate's poverty is as narcotic as the smell of pine and wine in her house and as inviting as sweet spicy ginger (40). She lives in a two-room house with no back door, no bathroom, no telephone, no house number, no electricity, and no gas. Rather than pay for utilities, she uses candles and kerosene lamps. Yet the narrator calls this house with its smell of pine and wine an inn, a haven, a safe harbor (135), echoing Morrison's earlier usage of "safe harbor" in *Sula*. Like its owner who soon will be airborne, the house's basement "seemed to be rising from rather than settling into the ground" (27). Pilate's poverty has its roots in an indifference to money rather than a traditional sacred calling (139). Unlike Macon, a "propertied Negro" whose motto is "own things. And let the things you own own other things" (55), Pilate lives by a different gospel: "I wish I'd a knowed more people. I would of loved 'em all. If I'd a knowed more, I would a loved more" (336). Echoing the biblical command, "Love they neighbor as thyself," Pilate becomes the soothing, spiritual presence in Milkman's life. For others, Pilate remains outside the norm. Even someone as outside the norm as Guitar sees Pilate as a step beyond the norm. To him she is nappy headed and crazy (182). Harsher than Guitar's criticism is Macon's. To Macon Pilate is a "raggedy bootlegging bitch" (204).

For readers, Pilate is the one woman in the text who is a grown-up woman when the other females are still doll babies (196). In a restricted society, to be a grown-up woman is to be a male. Morrison's Pilate refuses to live a gendered life . When her illiterate father, Macon Sr., randomly chooses from the Bible the name "Pilate," the midwife in attendance does not want to accept the name. To Macon Sr. the group of letters appeared strong and handsome. To the midwife, the name is first of all a man's name, and secondly a Christ-killing name. Macon Sr. refuses to relinquish the name, even when the midwife asks him, "You don't want to give this motherless child the name of the man that killed Jesus, do you?" (19). Given the death of his wife, Macon Sr. feels that naming the child "Pilate" might be a fitting affront to a God to whom he had prayed all night long, but who did not spare his wife. Horrified by this type of theology, the midwife wants the piece of paper with the name on it thrown "right in the Devil's flames" (19). Macon Sr. places the name in the Bible and that is where it stays until Pilate, at the age of twelve, retrieves it. Pilate never changes the maleness of her name, although her life does challenge the theology behind the name. More of a Christ figure than a Pilate figure, she is comfortable with her identity. However, Pilate's brother, Macon Dead, is embarrassed to have a sister who defies gender constructions. Pilate has cut her hair and does not dress the part of a woman. Macon looks at her sailor's cap, her lack of stockings, her unlaced men's shoes and inquires, "Why can't you dress like a woman?"(21). Pilate's only reply is, "I been worried sick about you too, Macon" (20). For Pilate, "tack[ling] the problem of trying to decide how she wanted to live and what was valuable to her" (149) was a personal quest. Her choices "kept her just barely within the boundaries of the elaborately socialized world of black people" (149).

Pilate hums her tunes, poses her riddles, sings her songs, and tells her stories. As singer of riddles and teller of tales, she is both black sphinx and ageless griotte, concealing and revealing information. *Song of Solomon* is a story about the telling and re-telling of stories. Like the grannies, who because they have witnessed the cycles of life, have many stories to tell, Morrison makes *Song of Solomon* a repository of stories. There is a story behind everything: how one gets one's name; how one arrives at a particular place, how one flies. Each time someone tells a story, the narrative shifts. An accomplished storyteller, Pilate "savors" a good story (18) and the stories contained in her green sack, brass ear box, and folk songs unravel and tighten the work's puzzle: how Pilate's song becomes Milkman's prophecy.

Skerrett refers to Pilate's storytelling as "an art of love and nurture, closely associated with food—an egg, a peach—and structured to meet the needs of others, not self (197–98). She does not tell Macon's vindictive stories, Guitar's horror stories, or Ruth's defensive stories. A protean healer and mythic performer, Pilate draws her story from the same wellspring the granny draws hers—a growing body of culture rooted in the dynamism of the oral tradition.

# FIVE

# Conjure Discourse in Conjuring Communities

## Mama Day *and Fieldwork in Paradise*

*You had not prepared me for Paradise.*
—George in *Mama Day*

WHEREAS MORRISON'S *Song of Solomon* (1977) IS THE FIRST fully developed portrait of the type of midwife with extraordinary powers in whom I am interested, Naylor's *Mama Day*, written a decade later, is the strongest example of a whole community of conjurers and healers. Naylor centers women who have midwifery, rootworking, and healing skills and who perform these activities in communities where healing rituals are ancient, but fluid. Because of Naylor's comprehensive approach to indigenous medical and belief systems, *Mama Day* is a work where I see a total fusion of what I have been describing in earlier chapters. With *Mama Day* we have an elderly black midwife, several conjuring women, sacred places and ethnobotanical groves, and a plea for counter-discursive practices when interpreting history or creating icons.

As with the previous chapter, in this chapter I read double-dutch. In jumping double-dutch, there is always a search for the most appropriate rope. Regular ropes are too thin and light; ropes borrowed from clotheslines are often too heavy. The better the rope, the easier the jumping. I end with *Mama Day*, not because the story is artistically better than other works I might have chosen, but because for my purposes, it is a better rope. Comprehensive in scope, *Mama Day* brings together character, landscape, cultural rituals, and an African-based epistemology. Therefore one rope that this chapter will be turning is Naylor's narrative with its emphasis on conjure women, conjure narratology, and conjure communities. The way Naylor turns her rope makes it easier for me to turn the other rope of my analysis, the historical tradition. This chapter knots the historical tradition to the granny's community, making them inseparable. To discuss granny midwives without discussing the politics of entering and living in these communities is insufficient. After discussing how Naylor invites readers to enter the Willow Springs community, I try to follow her instructions. Accordingly, I end this chapter with my own narrative on entering and leaving communities based on ethnographic encounters in Mississippi, one of the sites of my fieldwork. I move from Naylor's problematized paradise to an informant's self-constructed paradise. In the final analysis, the grannies, the literary writers, and I all perform as *sistah* conjurers, each using the power of storytelling to heal our communities, ourselves.

## CONJURE WOMEN

> *The island got spit out from the mouth of God, and when it fell to the earth it brought along an army of stars. He tried to reach down and scoop them back up, and found Himself shaking hands with the greatest conjure woman on earth.*
> —Gloria Naylor, *Mama Day*

*Mama Day* begins with the power of an African born conjure woman, Sapphira Wade, a "true conjure woman"(3). As a primordial mud mother[1] who produces "earth men" (48), Sapphira is not fixed by time—producing seven sons in one thousand days, nor color—appearing to be everything from "satin black" to "biscuit cream" (3). She is the "ancient mother of pure black that one day spits out" her great granddaughter's golden colors. Legend has it that she heats her medicine pots not with household fire, but with an element more cosmic—the heat from lightning. She is able to work with any natural force and allegedly "turned the moon into salve, the stars into a swaddling cloth, and healed the wounds of every creature walking up on two or down on four" (3). She is the slave woman "who *took* her freedom in 1823" (111), repositioning who was master and who was slave. Bascombe "fell under the spell of a woman he owned" (206). Sapphira ends up poisoning him and taking the deed to the land.

If Sapphira's African birth, fiery medicine pots, and liberatory actions are not enough to claim conjure woman status, her giving birth to seven sons is definitely the material of legends. Within folklore and various religions,

> there is a widespread belief that the seventh sibling of the same sex, Seventh Sister or Seventh Son (especially a Seventh Son of a Seventh Son), has unusual abilities. This idea seems to have appeared in Europe in the sixteenth century and is now found worldwide. The most powerful West African gods were seven in number as well, and appear in the New World as the Seven African Powers, or Spirits. (Snow 52)

Building upon these beliefs, black women's literature presents conjure women who, like Sapphira and Ajax's mother in *Sula*, give birth to seven children of the same sex,[2] affirming their God-given powers. The children help their mother with her rootworking activities and the mother passes on to them "the weight of her hoary knowledge" (*Sula* 108–9).

Mama Day is the daughter of the seventh son of one of Sapphira's seven sons, thereby increasing her powers threefold. Evidence shows that some of the historical grannies believed that the seventh son of a seventh son could "remove warts, take out fire from a burn, stop blood, and do other miraculous things" (Rayburn 147). For Mama Day to be the daughter of the seventh son of a seventh son is to acknowledge the specialty of her family genealogy. Early on in the narrative readers suspect that Mama Day will serve a special function for George, who has no genealogy. Although not one of the official "earth men"(48) in Sapphira's lineage, his name's root,"geo," associates him with the earth. George has the possibility of becoming an "earth man" because of his surrogate son relationship to a power source—Mama Day. Yet in an act of gender subversion, Naylor allows Sapphira's sons to be on the family chart that precedes the novel, but does not place husbands there. As Morrison's Baby Suggs would say, "A man ain't nothing but a man, . . . [b]ut a son? Well now, that's *somebody*" (*Beloved* 23). The final tree limbs have neither sons nor husbands. The tree's trunk are all women. Power that started with a woman ends with a woman. It takes the seventh son of a seventh son to produce a Mama Day.

For all of her extraordinary powers, however, we first see Mama Day (Miranda) as a delightful elderly woman who has spent her life doing midwifery, rootworking, and healing. Through the decades, she and her sister, Abigail, check on each other with their common question, "You there, Sister?" When the weather is damp, Miranda's arthritis acts up and she jokes that Old Arthur is the "only man I been able to roll out of bed with since I passed my seventies" (36). Sometimes the night liniment that she rubs on her legs makes them feel "spry enough to join in the front line of them kicking girls at Radio City" (202). To keep her stockpile of nature's remedies full, she is always looking for "a little useful bit of something in the bush" (78). In return for all of her nurturing of the Willow Springs community, Mama Day receives such foods as vegetables, jellies, meat, and ginger cakes. One former patient gives her an old Ford.

Very early in the narration, Cocoa tells us that Mama Day has second sight (14). Well grounded in human psychology, Mama Day understands the part that the mind plays in healing, "'cause the mind is everything" (90). Her knowledge of humankind allows her to "disguise a little dose of nothing but mother-wit with a lot of hocus-pocus" (97). Her mother wit, "the collective wisdom acquired by the experience of living. . ." (Dundes xiv), stands her in good stead: "they don't make enough wool—even up in New York—to pull anything over her eyes" (133).

At the beginning of the novel, Mama Day's power, like that in "The Revenge of Hannah Kemhuff," is more the threat of power than the execution of it. All speak of the power Mama Day supposedly has and that she herself intimates she has. Most of the time, all she needs to do is to threaten. She warns the pedophile school principal that she "could fix it so the only thing he'd be able to whip out of his pants for the rest of his life would be pocket change" (68). She reminds the receptionist in Dr. Smithfield's office: "You been knowing me a long time, ain't you, sugar? So if you don't [call Dr. Smithfield tonight], you know I ain't phoning back to find out why" (77). She prophetically tells the white deputy who disrespects Parris,"You'll address him proper before the night is over" (80).

Naylor contrasts Mama Day's effectiveness with Dr. Buzzard's lack of power. The family tree at the beginning of the work makes clear who Mama Day's ancestors are. Descended from the African, Sapphira, and fourteen men with biblical names covering the Old and New Testaments,

Mama Day's stock is solid. Although the virtues, Peace, Grace, and Hope have all died, Cocoa will bring the family into the twenty-first century. Contrastingly, those who have studied hoodoo medicine know that Dr. Buzzard has a dubious family tree. Although Naylor does not contextualize Buzzard historically, it is no accident that she selects Dr. Buzzard as Mama's Day's likeable, professional rival. Dr. Buzzard is not just a character in Naylor's novel, but he was a historical person and a legendary one. When Naylor presents Dr. Buzzard in her text, he carries the name of actual men who called themselves "Dr. Buzzard." Within folk medicine, tales of Dr. Buzzard abound. Some sources say he was a white hoodoo doctor in South Carolina who was so good with roots, herbs, and spells that he gained the respect of black clients, who in turn named their children who were born with special gifts after him. Another version popularized around Beaufort County,[3] South Carolina, claims that Sheriff J. E. McTeer, Jr., a white root doctor who has been interviewed by television talk shows and medical schools, wanted to clear the county of those black root doctors who were making what he considered to be outrageous claims, such as a cure for cancer. In this version of the story, the powers of Sheriff McTeer awe Dr. Buzzard, who in turn helps to make McTeer a world famous root doctor:

> Early in his tenure as sheriff, McTeer had to admonish Dr. Buzzard and the other Beaufort Root doctors—Dr. Bug, Dr. Eagle and Dr. Hawk, all now deceased—for claiming to their clients that they could cure such physical illnesses as cancer. Dr. Buzzard challenged him to make him stop. Two weeks later, Dr. Buzzard's son drove off a causeway and drowned. Buzzard, believing this to be a sign of McTeer's power, brought him a gift of two white chickens, promised to stick to psychic medicine and taught Sheriff McTeer all he knew about Root, witchcraft and Voodoo. Dr. Buzzard's father had been a witch doctor in Africa, and Sheriff McTeer considers Buzzard to have been the most powerful and authentic of all Beaufort's witch doctors. (Moussatos 31)

In yet another variation of the story, Loudell Snow and Jack Santino in separate articles describe a Dr. Buzzard, Jr., practicing in the Washington, D.C./Alexandria, Virginia, area. Dr. Buzzard, Jr., argues that he has the "gift" because his father, Dr. Buzzard, was the seventh son of a seventh son and born with a caul over his face (Santino 156). Dr. Buzzard, Sr. received his name because he flew out of a jail by transforming himself into a buzzard. Snow argues that Dr. Buzzard, Jr., belongs to the younger generation of American born "con men and conjure men" whose views have been Anglicized:

> In American Black folk belief today, such wondrous feats in the American-born are likely to be intermingled with a European contribution, a pact with the Devil. Successful con men/conjure men have a readily available pool of folklore to underwrite their putative abilities. (Snow 58)

What most separates Buzzard's history from Mama Day's is its very different interplay of race and gender. Despite a family tree where the seventh son fathers a seventh son, Sapphira and Mama Day form the trunk of their family tree. Validating a womanist epistemology, they, as women, are the ones who wield power and as blacks, they pride themselves on African ancestry. In their Kwanzaa-like Candlelight ritual, they face east toward Africa and acknowledge the "Great Mother," the conjure woman who shook hands with God (110–11). Buzzard's family line is more male-centered and his powers have more Euro-centric elements, for he crosses the line between shaman and shyster.

Interestingly, Naylor depicts an affable, comic Buzzard. Clearly not in Mama Day's league, he is as watered down as his moonshine (51). More con man than conjure man, Dr. Buzzard does not serve the community in the same way Mama Day does. Buzzard has all the trappings of power, but none of the substance. He calls himself doctor, wears a necktie of bones, and has "mojo hands" (92). Yet, we come to see him as Mama Day calls him with her string of epithets: addle-brained, shiftless, no good, twisted-mouthed, slimy-backed slew-footed son-of-a-crow, to name a few (46,191). She calls his moonshine "devil's brew" and is always punning on his name: "he don't do crow's squat for a living" (196). And although Buzzard claims to rope and tie up haints, he is so scared of others' hexes that he never leaves strands of hair anywhere. It is with one's hair that evil forces work their spells.

Mama Day's strength is grounded in an ancient African mother. Buzzard is a root doctor without being well rooted. In the narrative, he has no antecedents, no genealogy. Naylor gives his historical genealogy of being the seventh son of a seventh son to Mama Day. Because the community is all embracing, there is room for everyone. That Buzzard wins the poker games because he cheats is expected and respected. Neither potent or harmful, he knows the real power in the work resides with Mama Day and Ruby. Ruby is said to have "stuff that can dance rings around Dr. Buzzard's mess; some say she's even as powerful as Mama Day" (112). Thus, Naylor sets up Ruby as another foil to Mama Day. In Willow Springs there is a range of conjure possibilities.

Mama Day's life valorizes wisdom, kinship, and community. Through Reema's boy's experiences in academia, Naylor subordinates knowledge from institutions of "higher" learning to wisdom practiced in Mama Day and Abigail's homeplace. Their "other place" is an alternative location for understanding the world. As bell hooks notes:

> Black women and men must create a revolutionary vision of black liberation that has a feminist dimension, one which is formed in consideration of our specific needs and concerns. Drawing on past legacies, contemporary black women can begin to reconceptualize ideas of homeplace, once again considering the primacy of domesticity as a site for subversion and resistance. (*Yearning* 48)

Through the wisdom gained in Mama Day's homeplace, she is able to fight political battles. As one engaged in resistance, Mama Day is a social agent who protects Willow Springs from real estate developers. She knows that their rhetoric of "community uplift" obfuscates the fact that when the other sea islands became "vacation paradises" blacks who heretofore performed a range of activities were reduced to servants, needed only to clean the vacationer's toilets and cut their grass (6). In Mama Day's culturally mediated perspective, the welfare of the self and the welfare of her kin and community are inseparable. Her quilt making is a material demonstration of an Afrocentric belief, for she sews together clothing from the lives of various family members in order to give Cocoa personal, familial, and communal histories.

Mama Day is also distinctive because she serves the community in multiple ways. As an indigenous healer, she prescribes lard and baking soda to bring down fevers, warm castor oil and jimson for childhood worms, star grass and red raspberry tea for strengthening wombs, ague-weed to clean out the system, choke-cherry bark to chew on to stop labor pains, and so many effective remedies that Dr. Smithfield accuses her of trying to steal his patients. As a midwife, Mama Day performed a c-section so well when delivering one of Reema's boys that Dr. Smithfield had to acknowledge her expertise, and what fertility pills could not do for Bernice, Mama Day did. Although she has no children of her own, as midwife she is "everybody's mama" (89).

"Mama" is what many children of the community called the historical grannies. No matter how old they became or far away they traveled, the children delivered by grannies saw them as "mamas." The grannies were proud of their many children: "I don't care how old they is, they still my children and they give me big kisses" ("Delivered With Love" Video). The historical grannies often delivered several generations of the same family, many having delivered most of the community. Midwifery allowed them to *know* their communities. As othermothers, they used commonly heard folk threats to warn their "children" when they stepped out of line: "I brought you into the world and I can take you out"; "I knew you before you knew yourself."

As a community midwife living among those she serves, Mama Day retains some of the historical grannies' spirit and attitude. She tells Ambush that she knows him because she brought him in the world, his wife, and his mama too. How could any of them surprise her? "I knew you before you knew yourself," she says with authority (43). With equal authority, she muses over how she will combat Ruby's powers: "'Don't make me tangle with you, Ruby,' she thinks deep into the smoke: 'I brought you into this world'" (157). Those readers who know the lore know to add the implicit remainder of this sentence, "and I can take you out."

Mama Day is a granny who knows the ages of those in her community, not because she kept all the forms, but because she remembers everyone's birth in relationship to another's. She knows Ruby's age because she remembers that Ruby could talk when she delivered Ruby's baby brother, Woody. Named after Woodrow Wilson who was the current President, Woody died during World War II. For Mama Day, all these details corroborate Ruby's age: "So what that make Ruby?" (69).

Mama Day is a midwife well versed in human anatomy as well as folk psychiatry. She cleans her fingernails, splashes a little alcohol and performs her own version of a pap smear. She knows how warm wombs should be, how much moisture uterine walls should have, and how to diagnose ovarian cysts (72–77). Although Pearl calls Mama Day's work "bush medicine," Dr. Smithfield knows a good doctor when he sees one (149).

CONJURE NARRATOLOGY

*Mixing it all together and keeping everything that done shifted down through the holes of time. . . .*

—Gloria Naylor, *Mama Day*

On the very first page of *Mama Day*, Naylor begins her conjuring work, using the above epigraph to warn us of her intentions. The mixing and shifting of which she speaks resembles oral storytelling. As with other black writers who place orality in the foreground, Naylor writes a novel that one has to hear. Repeatedly, the communal narrator and Cocoa ask readers to listen and to do so in a distinctive way—by placing moss in their shoes: "As soon as I put the moss in my shoes, I could hear them. . . ." (223), Cocoa explains. The story remains out of reach for both characters and readers who do not put moss in their shoes. The characters who wish to hear must literally place moss in their shoes. Figuratively, moss as a trope suggests that readers too must have a way to move from outside their own worlds to inside other worlds. Without moss in their shoes, readers can neither hear the voices from the past nor use an appropriate interpretive framework. And in *Mama Day* hearing is the preferred way of knowing:

> You done heard it the way we know it, sitting on our porches and shelling
> June peas, quieting the midnight cough of a baby, taking apart the engine of a
> car—you done heard it without a single living soul really saying a word. (10)

Reema's boy substitutes scholarly ways of knowing for the folk practice of listening via moss and thereby hears only his own nonsense reverberating. Unlike Reema's boy, George had not been exposed to listening to a polyrhythmic discourse prior to coming to Willow Springs. Before entering the Day's family graveyard, he asks Cocoa to give him the history and meaning of placing the moss in one's shoes. Cocoa lets him know that it is not history and meaning which he needs, but respect (217)—respect for how one enters and exits a community. Similarly, Naylor does not tell readers why moss and not some other plant. What she does say is that without the moss, readers will not know where George is in 1999 nor how John-Paul and Grace come to voice. Without the moss, readers remain in their own places, unable to travel with the Day family to the "other place." Moss is as much Naylor's conjuring tool as jumping double-dutch is mine, and without reading double-dutch, readers end up separating the literature from its underpinnings.

There are several other ways that demonstrate Naylor's narrative alchemy in her role as *sistah* conjurer. Although published in 1988, *Mama Day* takes place in 1999, not to give readers Orwellian predictions, but to demonstrate how a character such as Miranda Day can "tie up" one century and "peek" into the next. Poised on the millennium, the text argues for the continuation of rituals and beliefs that have existed from time immemorial.[4] They exist because they are dynamic and not static. That during Candlewalk gadgets have replaced gifts from the earth and car light has replaced candle light is of no worry to Miranda who respects the changes of each generation. All of the Candlewalk stories stem from some version of the Great Mother etiological tale (111) and as such are survival strategies for whatever century.

Another feature of the way Naylor writes her story is to withhold secrets from public consumption.[5] When we as readers arrive at "the other place" for the fertility ritual Mama Day will perform on Bernice, we know we are in a real house with a real rocking chair, but are unprepared for the mystery of birth that takes place. Something inexplicable is happening to Bernice, in this re-writing of Yeats's "Leda and the Swan." Feathered throats and egg shells and "a rhythm older than woman" take over in a way we are not meant to understand or explain. Abstractions begin to perform: Fear trembles, Hope voices, Confusion waits and "Knowing takes the egg while the shell's still pulsing and wet, breaks it, and eats" (139). The fertility scene, as with the scene when George is in the northwest corner of the chicken coop, plays loose with pronouns as well as nouns, leaving readers without boundaries, just ancient conjurations, ending in Bernice's impregnation and George's death.

Equally unbounded is the way the Willow Springs community uses 1823. Whatever happened between Bascombe and Sapphira Wade in 1823 is but an historical springboard for an 18 & 23 epistemology. "18 & 23" is many things: the history of Willow Springs; the way blacks manipulate the system; a type of deep black skin color; a rite of passage, anything the community wants it to be and to mean . . . "the God-honest truth: it was just our way of saying something" (7). This floating, unstable, and changeable trope certainly qualifies as a type of hieroglyph, a term nuanced by Barbara Christian's observation:

My folk, in other words, have always been in [sic] a race for theory—though more in the form of the hieroglyph, a written figure which is both sensual and abstract, both beautiful and communicative. (336)

By using an hieroglyph, as commonly done by womanist critics,[6]Naylor emphasizes multiplicity and complexity over stable, unified meanings. As an expression, "18 & 23" begins in a master/slave relationship and widens its meanings through centuries of redefinitions by Miranda Day's black community. Its changing usage is a critique of the patriarchal and racist institution that generated the events between the slave woman and her master in 1823. The residents of Willow Springs can add their own meanings, which is also the way much folk language evolves. Hieroglyphs allow readers also to participate in the creation of meaning. "18 & 23" is an event or activity, as well as a rhetorical strategy understood in the tradition of the hieroglyph. The way Naylor tells her story and the way we as readers come to know it relies on intuition and inference. Naylor the artist is as much a conjure woman as Miranda the character. Each stews her potions from her own pot.

CONJURE COMMUNITIES

> *It's hard to know what to expect from a place when you can't find it on the map.*
> —George in *Mama Day*

Neither in Georgia or South Carolina, Willow Springs is stateless. It is a place where people chew mint sprigs, drink star grass tea, sprinkle salt on doorsteps and await "a stone city boy" (9). Its air, thick as water was "more than pure, it was primal" (175;185). In Willow Springs dreams are portentous, weather signs predictive, and nature profligate. In Willow Springs, one does not need clocks and calendars, "crude attempts to order our reality" (158). Therefore, "it's sorta easy to forget about time" (160). Willow Springs is the type of place where one expects to preface all appointments with the folk expression, "if the good Lord willin' and the creek don't rise." Rather than digital watches, crops and seasons control behavior (281). It is a place where so much is cyclical that even the live oaks in the graveyard stand in a circle (150). It is a place that clings to life, where we still hear George and where a dead Little Caesar travels to his own funeral in a seat belt and raincoat. "Places like this island were ripe for myths," muses George (218).

Yet Naylor is a conjure woman. As such, she deconstructs the very spell she casts, deromanticizing and deessentializing our expectations. Willow Springs is not utopia, and the best of intentions does not save souls. Mama Day plays God by effecting Little Caesar's birth and then cannot resurrect his dead body. The Days seek peace, but all the virtues, Peace, Grace, and Hope die. The chicken coop is full of "bloody straw, . . . smashed eggs, and scattered bodies"(302). It is always difficult for outsiders to know a community. Cocoa warns George: "You really don't know this place. But just go on and roll around in those woods with your clothes off, and the first red ant that bites your behind will tell you all about paradise" (222). George, who has only seen chicken "all wrapped up neat under cellophane," has a hard time watching Mama Day wring their necks (196). To live in Willow Springs and not be able to balance the real and the mythic is fatal. George dies. Fierce red ants and broken-neck chickens mar paradise.

*Mama Day* forces its readers to respect yet deromanticize conjuring communities. Although a work of fiction, it is arguably one of the best resource guides for doing fieldwork. The challenge for the fieldworker who is well versed in the literature and immersed in the actual communities is to do as Naylor has done. She creatively blends the texts of both the historical and literary grannies, decreasing the distance between imagination and reality, allowing practice and praxis to move closer together. Her challenge to fieldworkers is to do the same. Thus, I end this volume by accepting her challenge. I offer a corollary narrative from taped transcripts of my field work in Mississippi. As I replay the tapes over and over again, I am amazed at all the echoings of *Mama Day* and other works in the tradition that I hear. In my narrative, I deliberately avoid pointing out all these reverberations because I want to give readers their opportunity to read double-dutch. Naylor has certainly turned her rope well, and if I have turned mine well, readers will hear in this final narrative echoes of much of what has been said.

READING MISSISSIPPI

*Difference invades the text; it can no longer be represented; it must be enacted.*
—James Clifford, "On Ethnographic Allegory"

Although I, like Reema's boy, have never picked a boll of cotton in my life, I lay claim to extensive *field* work in Mississippi. Zora Neale Hurston had a knack for making fieldwork seem effortless. I can see her, like Reema's boy, "hauling [herself] back from one of those fancy colleges mainside, dragging [her] notebooks and tape recorder" (*Mama Day* 7). Yet, unlike Reema's boy, Hurston knew how to decrease the distance between academy and community. Naylor's open-ended narrative made me confident that I did not have to end up as misdirected as Reema's boy nor as dead as George. Yet for good measure, I thought I would equip myself with a supplementary manual to Naylor's fiction: Hurston's *Mules and Men*. Now, I thought myself prepared for fieldwork. Yet, I was equally armed with all types of caveats: Laura Mulvey[7] has taught me to worry about the gaze—is it penetrating? Fetishizing? Pornographic? Linda Alcoff[8] has cautioned me about the voice—Am I speaking for the other, alongside the other, to the other, with the other? Because of Maria Lugones[9] I am ever mindful of "playful traveling" and of Edward Bruner's assertion that, "No ethnographer is truly innocent."[10] Yet, I still desired to participate in the story I was writing, and although the literary texts are participatory narratives leaving many spaces for reader interaction, the ethnographer in me wanted to dialogue with "informants," a label so formal, it smells of betrayal. The folklorist in me wanted to sit through storytelling sessions, hearing from raconteurs whose stories were priceless long before African American women writers started to win National Book Awards and Pulitzer Prizes. The womanist impulse within me wanted to be surrounded with as many othermothers as possible. So, I decided to go searching for grannies, believing that the path of experience would cross the roads of a cultural text, perhaps hoping to hear what Janie Crawford's granny tells her, "I saved de text for you" (32).

I traveled throughout the South, talking with grannies and those who in their "rememoryings" tried to convince me they were grannies: "If I delivered my sister's baby while momma was at the store, does that count?" "If the only baby I delivered was my own, does that count?" I traveled throughout Florida, Georgia, North Carolina, Louisiana, Tennessee,

South Carolina, the Sea Islands, Alabama, and also a few places North and West, tracking down any rumor of a practicing, lucid granny. All the time I was running around, however, I heard a voice telling me, "You haven't been anywhere until you have gone to Mississippi." I would love to report that the urge to go to Mississippi was scholarly, for data support that there were more grannies in Mississippi than anywhere else in this country. However, the data became the excuse I needed to make what I had always heard was a necessary pilgrimage for any African American: "Until you go to Mississippi, you haven't been home."

Mississippi became mythic in my literary-fed imagination, much as Africa had been. Prior to teaching hundreds of Xhosas, Zulus, and Sothos, I had situated Africa somewhere between Joseph Conrad's *Heart of Darkness* and Graham Greene's *The Heart of the Matter*. Prior to my granny fieldwork, Mississippi was Faulkner's Yoknapatawpha; it was Anne Moody's *Coming of Age in Mississippi*, John O. Killens's *'Sippi*, and Mildred Taylor's *Let the Circle Be Unbroken*. It was hearing Margaret Walker say that only someone who understood racism in Mississippi could write a credible biography of Richard Wright, who was born in the Mississippi Woods, "a veritable hell" (Walker 13). Mississippi was Emmett Till's grand uncle, Mose Wright, standing in a courtroom in Money, Mississippi, pointing to the white men who killed his nephew for what Ishmael Reed calls, "reckless eyeballing." Mississippi was Medgar Evers trying to enroll in "Ole Miss" and James Meredith trying to register voters and dying for doing so. But just when I was beginning to think that Mississippi was the textbook case of oppression, I listened to a forum wherein Margaret Walker and Eudora Welty shared with each other personal reminiscences in a way as delightful and spirited as Naylor's Miranda and Abigail or the elderly southern ladies in *Having Our Say*. Mississippi was where I had to go, for it was also Delta cotton, the Delta Queen, and Delta Blues. Mississippi was Meridian, magnolias, and mockingbirds. Even a folk rhyme, a jump rope rhyme from childhood, beckoned me to come: "M-i-crooked letter, crooked letter-i-crooked letter, crooked letter-i-hump-back, hump-back-i. . . ."[11] Who could have predicted that one of the longest spelled states would roll so easily off the tongues of children, clapping to its rhythm?

RELIVING MISSISSIPPI

*It is not only the story itself which has meaning, but the circumstances of its*
*telling . . .*
—Abena Busia, "What Is Your Nation?. . ."

"You aren't going to Mississippi without knowing anyone there, are you?"
When Linda Stingily, a friend from California whose parents are from
Mississippi, asked me this, I was taken aback.

"I didn't *know* people in all those other places and did fine, thank you."

"But entering Mississippi is like entering Willow Springs. You need an
introduction to get the real story." Knowing all about Willow Springs and
Mama Day, Linda was working on a dissertation on representations of
educators in black literature.

Initially, I assumed that Linda's comment was her way of saying that I
was not southern enough to enter Mississippi. That I may not be southern
enough had not occurred to me. After all, when I first went away to college, it was my southerness, the sixty miles south of the Mason-Dixon line
background that I had tried to hide. When arriving at college in New
England from my southern Maryland home town, I was made to feel I was
very southern. I'll never forget sitting in the office of an esteemed professor of philosophy and religion who was teaching my honors course and
asked me where I was from.

"Merlyn," I said without a moment's thought.

"Merlyn?"

"Yes, Merlyn."

"Where's Merlyn?"

I was trying to decide whether he had a problem with hearing or geography when he asked: "What's the capital of Merlyn?" This I thought must
be a trick question to see if I was deserving of the honors program.

"Annapolis, of course."

"Oh, Maryland!" He snickered the three syllables and said something
about my southern accent.

Learning that around Bostonians I sounded southern, I set out picking
up bits and pieces of accents from roommates from Harlem, Bermuda,
Madagascar, Zambia, anywhere to make me less southern. Yet years of
teaching African American studies has made me want to be more southern. I tell myself that there are southern tenets that I never disobeyed,
southern rules that I never compromised. I never, to this day, wear white

shoes before Easter or after Labor Day; I've been heard to say "Yes, ma'am, I'll drink soda for supper"—much more mannerly and alliterative than saying, "Yes, I'll drink pop for dinner." I have memories of sitting on the front porch eating fried fish in a tin pie-pan for breakfast. So, when I had thought Linda was critiquing my southerness, I had taken offense. However, what she was really doing was offering me a means to decrease the distance from the academy to the community and to make sure I would not be perceived as a version of Reema's boy. I was ready to listen. She agreed to introduce me to some of her family members. Linda hails from a family full of elderly wise women whose names grow more exotic the closer they live to the Gulf coast—Doshea of Pulaski[12] and Balzoria of Moss Point, certainly a place for putting moss in one's shoes.

After Linda did her initial work on my behalf, I was ready to go to Mississippi and decided to drive for two reasons. I wanted to see cotton fields since I knew that grannies were sometimes called "cotton dollies." Also, it must cost more to fly to Jackson, Mississippi than any southern city I know. And so many people gave me conflicting flight informa- tion: "You have to fly to New Orleans." "No, you should fly to Houston." "I never go, except if I fly to Memphis." Already, my romance with Mississippi was beginning to suffer.

Before dawn one Sunday morning, I set out for Mississippi. I could have gone during the winter months, but I thought Mississippi would be more "authentic" when it was fiery furnace hot. With me was my research assistant, Antonia, from St. Lucia and our driver, M.C., originally from Mississippi, but who had settled in Ohio after college. He had agreed to take us around the backroads. We drove all night long. It was on this long trip there that I learned the most about double-voicedness and disrupting hegemonic discourse. Antonia claimed that the farther South we traveled, the more southern M.C.'s accent was becoming and the more patriarchal his views. M.C. countercharged that he could never understand "island people," that "feminism was a white thing that had messed up our minds," and that "research assistants are an unnecessary luxury." Working in a very hierarchal organization, M.C. had trouble understanding the familiarity between a graduate assistant and a bona fide Doctor of Philosophy. He questioned why she ate her meals with me, why she could take breaks from typing on the laptop computer, and why she was so vocal, given that she was "under" me. Antonia was constructing a false picture of M.C. as a totalitarian husband, a leader of patriarchy when in fact, I assured her that he was just teasing her. I had known his family for many years.

For all these spirited discussions, I served as translator, fearing that a ruptured relationship between the two might just jeopardize my project. My plea with both of them was a Polyanna-ish, "Can't we all just get along?" As I think back on this trip and the force of both Antonia's and M.C.'s convictions, I am just glad that we took the trip before Antonia had fully dreaded her hair and before M.C. had attended the Million Man March. Neither one needed any more empowerment. Although by the return trip, each of us had shifted some of our views. Twenty-eight hours of driving will do that.

Upon arriving in Mississippi, Antonia and I thought it best first to acculturate ourselves through archival work, which is far more benign than developing human relationships. Searching for information in traditional scholarly sources was easier than encountering live subjects. I had saved visiting Mississippi's archives for last because my earlier research on Mississippi had indicated that it was a state where midwifery had been more widely practiced than the other southern states I visited. During the year 1921 public health nurses helped the United States Public Health Service to conduct a survey of the number of lay midwives in the state. Five thousand practicing midwives were documented (Roberts *et al.* 59).

By 1947 midwives in Mississippi still numbered 2,192, thirty-five of whom were white. They attended 23,815 or 36 percent of the births (Ferguson 85). Although considerably reduced in numbers from the heyday of the 1920s, Mississippi was still very much reliant on lay midwifery. By 1980, however, Mississippi, with only twenty certified lay midwives, had taken its place beside other states, and by 1985 there was only one documented practicing lay midwife (Roberts *et al.* 61). Given the number of grannies in Mississippi, I spent hours going through public health records. I wanted to be knowledgeable about the area's health care system before talking to members of Linda's family. Linda had given me the name of her great-great-grandmother, midwife Easter Parker. Antonia and I found reconstructing the family line through census records intriguing. Figuring out the name and age variations made us feel like detectives. We began noting all kinds of family business: the 1910 Census lists a different timespan for the number of years Easter was married before having children; one son, who should have been listed, does not appear on the 1920

Census; although most family members were listed as "mulatto," a few were later reclassified as "black"—probably the effects of the Mississippi sun. By the time we had mastered the complex code for locating families on the 1880, 1900, 1910, and 1920 Census, we felt we knew the family.

By the next day, I was ready to talk to Mr. Fred "Carver" Parker, Linda's maternal uncle. From generation to generation, the Parker family, has passed down stories of midwife Easter Parker (1852–circa 1956). Every Parker family member whom I called when I arrived in Jackson instructed me to talk with Carver. Having just turned fifty-three years old the previous week, Carver was ready to speak as one of the family's griots—and he looks the part: a burly, white, full beard and a twinkle in his eyes. For the past twenty-six years he has driven a school bus in New Orleans during the week. His weekends, however, he spends at the family's homestead, Parker's Paradise in Lake, Mississippi. Driving a school bus is part of his commitment to the education of children. In a family of many educators, Carver is thinking about one day finishing the few remaining hours of his degree to get his teaching certificate and then teach elementary school. "I might do it for free," Carver reflects. A colorful character, Carver diminished my praising of his personality by adding, "I can be a son of a gun." Linda already had asked him if he would talk to a researcher from a university, a *sistah* with her own research assistant, another *sistah*.

Although Carver and I hit it off well, he did remind me of his earlier bittersweet experience with a journalist. This story would be a forewarning to me to not misrepresent him. This researcher/photographer had come to town interviewing men who had played Santa Claus for stores, events, or any activity. For years, Carver had been a Santa Claus because of his love for children:

> Kids think I'm Santa Claus. They flock over to my place and boast to other children, "I live next door to Santa Claus." When I go to Parker's Paradise, they think I've gone to the Pole. *Ain't nobody* can pay me a job that can make me feel better. (Carver Interview, June 1995)

Carver was one of the Santas whom the journalist wanted to profile. He agreed to an interview and photograph, thinking that this would be another opportunity to build dreams in someone's child. The journalist had stressed that he wanted all kinds of Santas—a diversity of people and experiences. He was interested in Carver because Carver was a black Santa Claus. Excited, Carver told all his friends and relatives to look for his picture when the article was due to come out. The Santa story made first page of the newspaper, but the end product shamed Carver. It turned out to be a story satirizing Santas inasmuch as there were pictures of a Santa stripper and other Santas in dubious activities. Carver felt that the article demeaned the vocation and he was embarrassed that his picture was with a group of pictures of Santas who did not take their role as seriously as he. According to Carver, "the journalist threw away the whole thing in order to make a dollar. What about all those children who saw the Santa stripper? What will they think of Santa Claus?" After telling me this story, Carver gave me some of the best advice I have ever received about collecting and cataloguing data:

> As Jed Clampitt[13] would say, you have to be careful because "you have a lot of stuff to decipher and get in a straight line." All the information you receive is like pouring out a box of Alpha Bits. You still have to do your own spelling.

Carver reflected for a while. Although he always wears a beard, he says that he has left instructions to shave it when he dies, so he won't look like Santa Claus in the casket: "Let the children have their memories. A dead Santa Claus would disillusion them. I don't want to be a part of any child's disillusionment." With this story fresh in my mind, I promised Carver that when he poured out *his* box of Alpha Bits, I would try to spell *his* words. I knew he would hold me accountable for the way I spelled it out. My role as translator was becoming more complex.

Easter Parker was Carver's great grandmother. He estimates that she was around twelve or thirteen years old when Emancipation occurred. Delivering both white and black babies, she worked well into her seventies. Antonia and I knew that the census records list her as unemployed before her husband's death and as a farmer when she became head of household. Although Easter worked as midwife in a particular section of Smith County, midwife is not listed as her occupation, probably because she never registered as one.

As with many older black families, it is hard to share family history without sharing how skin complexion affected their opportunities. According to Carver, Easter was caught up in the politics of color within her race, sometimes called "colorism." Carver asserts that Easter

> had just enough black blood to be classified as black. She was 1/32 black and that was just enough. Her father was a white dentist, but she couldn't carry his

name. So, she took her step daddy's name, Riley, Pappy Jack Riley [He was terrible with his fists]. Easter wanted to be white. She wasn't allowed to marry the white boy she liked, though. That would have made for trouble. Instead she married my great grandfather, John Parker, who was very light.

The oldest child born to the union of John Parker and Easter Riley Parker was Hunter Parker who married Hattie Flowers, who gave birth to Artis, Carver's father. Artis married Mary Dixon, a woman Easter considered to be dark-skinned and therefore unattractive, but whom others saw as a pretty woman with long wavy hair and cinnamon skin tones, a mixture of black and Choctaw. Carver remembers visiting Easter and Easter asking him, "Well, how's your old black mother doing, boy?" Artis had not married well when marrying well meant to keep the color in the family and if possible lighten the generations rather than darken them. As Carver was talking, I could hear Zora Neale Hurston's Mrs. Turner resounding in my ears: "We oughta lighten up de race" (*Eyes* 209).

After Mary Dixon Parker had six children, her husband Artis decided that he should let Easter deliver the rest of his children. Although very much against his dark-skinned wife, Easter had wanted to be the dutiful midwife to her. Therefore she was permitted to deliver the seventh and eight child. Baby number 7 lived only an hour; baby number 8 was stillborn. Not knowing what was going on, but knowing that Easter did not like dark-skinned Mary, Artis and Mary thought it best to change midwives. Therefore, the earlier midwife, Sylvia (Aunt Sylvie) Anderson, delivered Carver, baby number 9, and baby number 10, Odessa, called Dessa.

That many of the family members were mulattos who could "pass" is evident by another childhood story of Carver's. Carver tells of a trip he took with his father to the lumber mill. His father was "off hand, taken as white." Upon arriving at the lumber mill with his "very light and good grade of hair" father, Carver was startled to hear a white man approach his father, and assuming that Artis was white too, ask him: "That's a good looking nigger you have with you there. Is he off of your farm?" This question and the racist attitude undergirding it placed Artis in a difficult position. If he said Carver was his son, he would lose his right to be at the lumber mill. If he denied his relationship to Carver, he would risk losing a son. Carver is proud of the quick, cagey answer his father gave. By asking if the boy Carver was "*off of* your farm," the white man assumed a sharecropping relationship between a-white-appearing Artis and a darker Carver. Astutely, Artis replied, "He's *of* my place," an ambiguous response that affirmed both what the lumber mill workers expected to hear and what Carver needed to hear.

An earlier memory of Carver's goes back to the birth of his younger sister, Odessa. He remembers the night the granny midwife, Aunt Sylvie came to deliver Odessa. He has told this story over and over to family members. It was in 1944 and he was two years old. His family had no electricity, but the birthing room was very bright because of an Aladdin Lamp. In the main room was an open fireplace, making this room dimly lit. Although quite young, Carver recounts all the details. Because of bad roads, his father went to pick up Aunt Sylvie in the mule wagon. The roads were especially impassable after heavy rains. After Aunt Sylvie delivered his baby sister, Carver was permitted to come in the room. He saw the baby, "a little, scratty thing." Wearing glasses, a long dress, and her hair all wrapped up, Aunt Sylvie made an impression on Carver. However, the scene became traumatizing when Aunt Sylvie, after cleaning the baby, announced, "I have to take these extra fingers off. All of them don't belong there." She reached for the scissors and cut off the baby's extra fingers. Horrified, Carver grabbed the scissors: "I was going to stab her with the scissors to keep her from hurting my baby sister again," Carver chuckled. Aunt Sylvie explained why she had to cut off the extra fingers: there were too many fingers and they would grow back, even if she cut them off. To this day, Carver says his sister gets them surgically cut ever so often. Expressing some disbelief because my own sixth finger has never grown back, I had to be reassured that it is possible for an extra finger to grow. Carver ended this part of the conversation with, "She's my sister and I should know."[14]

Full of stories of midwives and their relationship to his family, Carver began naming other family members who had a story or two. He spoke of jars of grape wine and live chickens given to midwives for their services in some sort of bartering system: "Our neighborhood had lots of swapped things." A big day in the neighborhood was when the white doctor, driving an old Model A Ford that could go anywhere a mule could go, made two trips in one day to see Carver's ill brother, Joe Nathan, who had rheumatic fever and who would one day grow up to be a professor of agriculture. The doctor crossed a valley where the road was under water. He had to use a stick to feel for the road and then cross a bridge to get to them. Everyone in the family was glad the doctor came, for although Easter and Sylvia and other midwives in the community knew roots and herbs for headaches and fevers, they knew that rheumatic fever needed the doctor's special medicine.

It is easy to see that Carver enjoys all the old stories. He warns me that if his speech patterns aren't correct to blame it on Easter, who was full of linguistic idiosyncracies, "the remnants of which remain in my family." It seems that Easter "talked backwards." She would ask others to tell her the answer before she asked them the question. According to Carver, "The Parker family had been talking backwards long before Jeopardy made millions off of talking backwards." Easter would create language patterns that others would at first laugh at and then imitate. When Carver came to visit her, she would say, "It's a fur place to go," meaning "it's a long way off and you should start making tracks to get back home." Also, she would deliberately mix up her tenses. Instead of saying, "speak to me," she would say, "'spoke to me.' She did all of this for the heck of it," Carver explained.

Before I left, Carver made me promise that I would stop by and see Parker's Paradise: "You can't get a feel for the family without walking on our land. Linda says that Parker's Paradise is a good place for her to write her dissertation because she feels centered here. It's a private, natural place. You need to go there." After telling him that I was off to see his "Cousin Sis," he gave me some last words of advice: "Education is what you learn, not what they teach you. You writing this down, girl?" I assured him that I had everything in my field notes.

To visit Mrs. Maggie Moore, affectionately known to her family members as "Cousin Sis," I enlisted the aid of Linda's first cousin on her father's side, Mary Stingley Wesley.[15] Linda had called Mary in advance and assured her that she would like Antonia and me. As a social worker, Mary understood the significance of what we were trying to do and seemed like she had always been within our circle of friends. She felt it appropriate that we stop at a small locally owned soul food eatery before beginning our trip to see Cousin Sis. Both of us were particularly interested in Antonia's response to the foods, the flavor, all the folkways. She admitted that much reminded her of back home. After eating, we all jumped back in the car to take a forty minute trip to a rural area outside of Jackson to see Mrs. Maggie Moore.

Mrs. Maggie Moore is a granddaughter of Easter Parker. Born in 1920 to Albert and Nannie Parker, she was their second child and was delivered by Easter. Easter would later deliver Mrs. Moore's first three children. Mrs. Moore's house sits at the crossroads of two country roads and her hospitality was as warm as the Mississippi sun. It was from the record in the family bible, along with census records, that we were able to reconstruct the family tree. Carver had correctly warned me that "the family tree is diversified and scattered; you can't trace all the limbs back to the trunk."

Reportedly, John Wesley Parker who was born in 1904 was born with a handicap because of an incident involving Easter and her brother-in-law. A posse of white men were hunting down the brother-in-law for allegedly killing a white man. When the posse came looking for him at Easter's house where her husband was hiding him, Easter's husband said he was not there. The white men did not search the house because of the high stature that Easter and her husband had in the community. They later smuggled the brother-in-law out of the country, and never heard from him again. It is said that the experience so traumatized Easter that the baby she was carrying at the time was born deformed. Curiously, another woman pregnant at the same time also had a deformed baby, an empathetic response to the general fear that all in the community were feeling when the brother-in-law was accused of the crime.

Mrs. Moore's memories and the records I collected worked together to build a family genealogy. Each of us began sharing with the other. Due to the camaraderie with both of us reconstructing the family tree, Mrs. Moore was fast becoming "Cousin Sis" to me. Most of the time when reconstructing the family's history, Cousin Sis filled in details. However, sometimes my archival work was what she needed to spur her memories. Such was the case with Hunter Parker. Cousin Sis, a good listener as well as raconteur, smiled slyly when we mentioned that Hunter's name was not on the Census record. Because Hunter was Easter's first child, Antonia and I had speculated that maybe by the time of the 1910 records which we were studying, Hunter was not living at home. As if solving a family mystery, Cousin Sis remarked that there was talk that Hunter was Easter's child by someone other than her husband. Census records reveal many tales and obscure others. I learned from Cousin Sis that Easter became not just a small-time farmer when her husband died, but she managed a sharecropping business.

Cousin Sis remembers being intensely curious about her grandmother's midwifery bag because whenever she took her bag with her, a baby would appear. Thinking that perhaps the baby was in the bag, Cousin Sis remembers the first time she looked in it—no babies were in the bag. When Easter's house burned down, the bag was destroyed in the fire.

After having listened to Carver and Cousin Sis, I could see Easter with her angular nose and small lips, directing her son, Albert, to go and get the family Bible to record another birth. She had to trust that he was writing the information correctly and certainly must have felt that her records were safer than the health department's. Easter never bothered to register or become certified as midwife. No matter how much experience she had, she was not able to fill out birth certificates or other forms. According to Carver and Cousin Sis, Easter could neither read or write.

We left the kitchen and moved to Cousin Sis's front porch, easily carrying on the conversation there, Antonia and I adding details we had learned from our own investigative work, Cousin Sis adding from her distilled memories. Hearing the story of how Easter's name should have been "Esther" but her midwife misspelled it brought back to me all the tales of slaves and their descendants ending up with all kinds of peculiar names because the verification was not in the speaking, but in the spelling—the alphabet.

By the time I interviewed Cousin Sis, I had become a professional at developing rapport. I had used all my interviews in other states as practice sessions. I knew that there were several things I could tell the grannies or their elderly kin about me that would take me out of the world of the Academy and place me right on their porches beside them. As a black woman researcher primarily interviewing black women subjects, I thought I had a head-start. Each interview seemed like I was interviewing my own grandmother all over again. I knew that if I spoke of my faith, my twin sons and two daughters, and my six fingers, I could develop a certain ethos with my informants, if "ethos" and "informant" are not oxymoronic. Choosing from among the three aforementioned topics for building ethos, I thought I would first try the six-finger strategy. I had used it early in my career to bond with Lucille Clifton, who has all those six-finger poems. So, I showed Cousin Sis my six fingers and asked my routine question: "What did Easter do when a baby was born with six fingers?"

"She used to use horsehair to tie around the finger; if tied tight enough the extra finger would wither away."

Somehow Cousin Sis's memory of horsehair appealed to my imagination in ways that scissors and surgery do not. As we were getting ready to leave, Cousin Sis stood at the crossroads in front of her home. One road led to her church, Galilee, the other to Parker's Paradise. She reiterated that Carver would not forgive us if we did not stop there. Upon leaving, I remembered that we had not asked Cousin Sis about her children. We quickly exchanged photographs of children and then I asked, "Is your husband dead?" "He wasn't dead this morning" Cousin Sis smiled. We had assumed that since her husband was not at home all day then he was no longer living, only to find out that her eighty-year-old husband was still working full time. In Mississippi you learn something about what good, honest labor, and disciplined living does for the body and soul.

After our conversation with Cousin Sis, Antonia and I were eager to visit Parker's Paradise. Coming from the Caribbean, Antonia knew more about paradises than I did, so I did not know what to expect, except Mary seemed to be driving out in the middle of nowhere, all the time pointing out sites as if we were on Fifth Avenue. We were about fifty-five miles outside of Jackson. Finally, we turned on a dirt road and up ahead blowing in the breeze was a banner secured by two poles. The banner read, "Parker's Paradise." Not expecting such a royal entranceway, Antonia and I jumped out of the car and walked the rest of the way. Near the farm house were fields of corn and sweet potatoes. There were chickens, an old barn, restored wagons, and a tractor. Carver had also built an open air pavilion for family reunions. It had one of the largest barbecue grills I had seen and was full of chairs waiting for family members to come together. Carver had stocked the man-made fishing pond with fish.[16]

Created by Artis and Mary Dixon Parker, Parker's Paradise is where all their babies were born. This is the place where Sylvia Anderson and Easter Parker delivered Mary's babies and where even today their children's children return for summer refreshment. Parker's Paradise is a place where family members swap stories. As such, like Willow Springs, it is "ripe with myth." At the same time, it is a place of healing where stories of healers become as restorative as the healing itself. As Carver encouraged Linda, "If you think you can write good work here, then come home." His notion of going home to write echoed my own thoughts about homeplace as a site for theorizing and storytelling for black women writers. Parker's Paradise left me wanting to meet more people in Mississippi. Everything was happening according to the script that I had in my head of grannies, family, and community.

Mr. Fred "Carver" Parker at "Parker's Paradise." (Photos by Linda Stingily)

The entranceway to "Parker's Paradise."

The open-air shelter at "Parker's Paradise." (Photos by Valerie Lee)

Mrs. Maggie Moore, "Cousin Sis." (Photo by Valerie Lee)

When I returned from Parker's Paradise, M.C. had some good news for us. With great excitement, he gave me a call, informing me that his mother thought that work on the grannies was long overdue. In fact, M.C. was surprised to hear his mother say, "Boy, don't you know you were delivered by Mrs. Parker, the granny who is still living up by Tougaloo College?"

This was the defining moment for my research. As a man in his late thirties and the oldest of nine children, M.C. had no idea that he was the one child in his family delivered by a local granny. All the old-fashioned stuff with which I was working had in that moment touched his life. We could not leave Jackson without him meeting the woman whose hands brought him in the world. An awed M.C. developed a plan whereby we could get to visit Mrs. Parker. It turned out that M.C.'s eighty-year-old uncle was still from time to time visiting a relative of Mrs. Parker. The plan was to get Uncle George to introduce M.C. to his othermother and then M.C. would in turn explain our presence. The plan was a good one, except for one detail. M.C. was sure Uncle George would not believe that as a threesome, we were on a research mission.

"Who did you say these women were?" Uncle George got in the front seat and glanced in the back at Antonia and me.

"This is a professor and her research assistant, Uncle George, and put away that snuff. You're not going to embarrass me, are you? These powerful, important ladies are from the university; you can't be using your spit cup."

"But, boy, I thought you said they were grannies looking to visit their friends?"

"No, man, I didn't tell you that."

It was too late. Antonia and I now understood why we were not introduced earlier. We were thirty to forty some years younger than we had been described. Nevertheless, my joy at interviewing one of the last grannies (and by her account and the records at the archives, the very last granny) in Mississippi was enough to compensate for any breech of etiquette or misrepresentation of fact.

Uncle George delivered as promised. Luckily for us, Mrs. Bertha Parker was next door at her sister's home when we arrived. Uncle George walked right in and before we knew it, out walked Mrs. Parker. Mrs. Parker headed homeward with a gait much like Mrs. Wilcox in *Howard's End*: "Trail, trail, went her long dress over the sopping grass" (Forster 4).

She had the energy and vibrancy of someone much younger than her years. At seventy-nine years of age, she was not stooped in stature, but stood several inches taller than any of us. With extended arms, she embraced each of us as if we were all her babies.

"All my babies come back to see me," she announced. I was in high heaven that she so quickly and graciously invited us in her home. Her spriteliness, agelessness, and all-embracing attitude were already beginning to make me think that she was going to be one of those mythic grannies. The joke would be on me. No amount of moss in my shoes could have prepared me for an interview that would begin according to the rules, my rules, and end with Mrs. Parker taking full charge of the interpretation of her life.

Expecting the predictable, I was ready for the storytelling session to begin. Humbled to hear the details of his own birth, M.C. sat in one corner and Uncle George, suspicious of all the attention Bertha Parker was receiving, sat in another corner. Mrs. Parker's elderly husband made himself busy in the kitchen. Antonia, Mrs. Parker, and I sat at the dining room table. On the walls of the room was what must be the most common portrait found in the homes of elderly blacks—that of the two Kennedys and Martin Luther King. There were also several pictures of Jesus, community service plaques, and news clippings by journalists who had managed to reach Mrs. Parker before I did. I immediately noticed that she had none of the reticence or surprise of other grannies when told they were important to my research. Not living in Jackson and not an actual midwife herself, Cousin Sis had not had many interviewers to stop by. No one thinks to talk to family members, forgetting that grannies were community women, each with her own distinctive way of responding to her community. Contrastingly, Mrs. Parker, a very self-aware informant, had already received word from the academic community that grannies were in vogue again, not for delivery of babies, but for their stories.

She began by addressing M.C. and giving her testimony: "Yeah, the Lord is so wonderful. This has been a dream come true for me."

"This is really an experience for me too. I just always assumed I was born in a hospital," M.C. added.

"Yeah, the Lord's been so wonderful. The last person who came by here to interview me wrote this here article about me." She jumps up to fetch the article.

I looked at the paper; it turned out to be a high school theme, wherein

Mrs. Bertha Parker.

Mr. M.C. Adams in a reunion visit with his midwife, Mrs. Bertha Parker.
(Photos by Valerie Lee)

the last several pages praised Mrs. Parker for her years of midwifery. As a high school paper, it was very well done, and my eyes quickly read its contents. I proceeded, however, to impress upon Mrs. Parker that my work would likely have a larger audience.

"I have a larger project in mind and would like to interview you for my book."

"But a *white* girl wrote this paper on me and she did me all these thousands of dollars worth of good. She was looking for a midwife and this is her history of me. The Lord is very good. Here is my history." She passes to me the paper to look at again, but will not let me have one of her copies. In my head circulates Lyotard's "As narrator she is narrated as well. And in a way she is already told, and what she herself is telling will not undo that somewhere else she is told."[17] While I am musing, Mrs. Parker turns again to M.C.: "How old did you say you was, baby?"

"Thirty-seven."

"I once had one of my babies return to me when he was fifty-one years old. Of course, I don't know nothing about you, you been away so long."

"My mother said, 'Do you know who delivered you?' I said no. And she said, 'Boy, you don't know your history, do you?'" (Everyone laughed.)

"Yes, I carry a lot of history with me. I was a Madison County Certified Midwife. I was trained by a white man, Dr. Lawrence Jacobs and had no difficulty passing the exam. I was God's helper all throughout Madison/ Ridgeland communities. When the county health board said to get certified, I got certified. I was a cotton dolly who got certified. That's what they were called when they delivered the slave population."

M.C. snickered and repeated, "Cotton dollies. Well, well."

Undaunted, Mrs. Parker jumped up again and showed me written proof that, unlike those grannies who were overwhelmed by the new rules, she was able to keep up with her profession. I turned the tape recorder toward me and began to enter factual data about the particulars of the occasion.

"I had been working fifteen years before the Health Department kept records."

Her husband who rarely spoke, added, "Fifteen long years." "I am seventy-six years old now," continued Mrs. Parker. "That's the picture of my wedding anniversary over there." She points to one of the many pictures on her walls.

"What's the story you told the high school girl about how you became interested in midwifery?" I was trying to keep everything germane. I was feeling she had saved the text for me, but she would not let me copy it.[18]

"I was walking through the woods of Madison County and met my grandmother, who was a midwife. She knew all about roots and stuff in her time, but I used medicine in my time. Anyway, my grandmother was walking through the woods and carrying her bag. I thought grandma had a baby in the bag. She told me she found the babies in the woods, you know. So, I used to go to the woods looking for bags with babies. I was around eleven years old then. When I became twelve I knew better because I finally looked into the bag." (Mrs. Parker laughed). "Afterwards, I started to go with my grandmother to help her deliver babies."

"Were you following in the footsteps of your grandmother when you decided to become a midwife?" Just when I thought this was a redundant question, Mrs. Parker interrupted:

"No, God called me. I was baptized in 1926, stumbled across the bag in 1927. God helped me to deliver all my babies. I seen it all. Babies born with teeth. Some with one ear. See, I started with a white man. The doctor told me how to cut off babies born with an extra finger."

At this point, to keep myself in Mrs. Parker's good graces, I showed her my physical evidence of having had an extra finger cut off.

"Yes, yours is a smooth job, but I was so good that the doctor used to say, 'If Bertha can't do it, I can't either.'"

At this point she proceeded to tell me her areas of medical expertise. I was so impressed that I backtracked and asked a question whose answer I had assumed; I signified even: "Now were you a granny midwife or a nurse midwife?"

Rising in her chair, Mrs. Parker responded, "I was a granny. But I got a license from the white doctor when I was fourteen.[19] The health department was giving classes and I didn't have to do anything but get my license because if you could answer all the questions, you didn't have to take the class and I could answer all the questions."

I wrote on my note pad that there are two main types of granny midwives. Easter Parker represents those grannies who, although experienced, were not "malleable," from the health department's point of view. Mrs. Parker did go through the retraining process and became certified, representing those grannies who practiced through the transitional years. Other than the grannies, there were some black nurse-midwives, most notably Maude Callen of South Carolina.[20]

"Yeah I had worked with my grandmother and this white man. Boy, I used to ride with that man many places; he used to come by and get me."

"Did you ever put the axe under the bed?"

"Oh, no, dear. I know 'bout that of course, but I never did it. The older ones used to do it, but I was certified. I'm not superstitious like that." Her laugh was hearty. All the grannies I talked to knew about the axe and someone who used it, but each claimed not to use it herself—"traditions of *dis*belief" as Hufford would say ("Folk Healers. . ." 306).

"Were there other midwives besides your grandmother in your family?"

"My grandmother had a sister who was a midwife too."

"How many babies do you think you delivered?"

"God is so good. He helped me to deliver 1,000 babies. See what this says." She showed me a newspaper article written in 1981, "Ridgeland Midwife Delivered 1,000 Babies: Was God's Helper."

"Did you get paid for your work?"

"When you do something for God, you really get paid for it and you don't get paid in just 'thank you' either. Lots of times when I worked on babies I 'd get a peck of 'tatoes, corn, whatever they had. Sometimes I got two dollars. I used to keep this long sheet of paper that said so and so owed me this much and one day something told me to tear it up. And then someone would come up to me and give me something and say, 'I owe you this,' and I wouldn't even know it. I had torn up the paper. But that's really true. I asked God for salary and the Lord continually gives to me. I was praying to him like I had just got religion. I was stretching out to him. All this is in my history. Check the history."

"So, you have felt God's presence?"

"Nobody but God. I have seen babies born with six fingers and no toes, . . ."

"Six fingers. Now that keeps coming up around in this area. How common is that?"

"Well, I delivered 'bout four or five with extra fingers, and I've delivered four or five born with teeth. There were some with one ear. One delivery I had the doctor said the baby was already dead for two weeks. You talk about somebody praying. When that baby came the skin was peeled off, and when I came to catch him, it was like pulling the skin off a sweet potato. The mother was going through the change. She was fifty years old then. The baby was eleven pounds. It was snowing on the day I delivered the baby."

"You've seen everything, including snow in Mississippi," I was thinking. I thought I would press the six-finger issue again. Everything was going rather well and I wanted to use the six finger reference to test her skills, for I fancied I knew all about its removal. "If a baby was born with six fingers, did you have to cut off the extra finger?"

"No, not during the early years. I did afterwards, after working with the doctor. I learned how to cut. Yours looks real good, real good."

"A surgical answer," I mused, "No horsehair, no ball of string, no shoelace, just a medical cutting." As I was trying to sort out my own images, Mrs. Parker was not at a loss for words. Rising and walking, she continued to give me details.

"There's not no way a baby been born that I don't think I have already saw. If it had to be taken, the doctor had to do it at the hospital. And it ain't too many babies that I had to have a doctor. Doctor said, 'If she can't do it, I can't either.' And that's in my history too. And this lady, this girl who was going to college was asked if she could find a midwife and that's when she got in touch with me. She got a scholarship and she gave me $2,000 and a chance to go to Washington to be part of a show, but I was too old to go. They say whatever I need, just call and I've called them to get so many things."

The material angle of the conversation was beginning to make me nervous. Perhaps the politics of having a research assistant and a driver was backfiring. Rather than their presence authenticating me as a scholar, their accompaniment must have made Mrs. Parker think I had money. Knowing no pay would be forthcoming from this interview, I tried to steer the conversation in another direction. "What form of transportation did you use to travel all the backroads?"

"Oh, don't name that. Don't name that. Sometimes it be on a sled, on a mule's back, sometimes on a buggy, sometimes on a tractor. You name it; all that's in the history too. Sometimes I would get to a place where people didn't have no wood. I started bringing them to my house. I had home delivery then. I had home delivery for thirteen years."

"Do you still have your midwife's bag?"

"That picture on the wall shows the last one I had. I don't have one now. Some things, like castor oil, I couldn't keep in my bag. I gave my bag to my grandson in Chicago and he packed his tennis shoes in it!"

Mrs. Parker laughed at the conversion of her midwife bag to a gym bag. Somehow, I had wanted to imagine the bag encased in a dining room curio or at least consumed by fire, as Easter's was. No matter how many times I had taught Alice Walker's "Everyday Use," it was hard for me to accept that these bags, as valuable artifacts, would one day carry great-grandchildren's and grandchildren's shoes, bowling balls, and roller blades. But before I could ponder for long, Mrs. Parker had jumped up again—no numbness in her limbs.

"I think I have some midwife stuff in my bedroom. I'll go and see." Before I knew it, Mrs. Parker was up from the table again. She certainly must have been a double-dutch jumper when young.

"These are some of my things; this is for the baby's navel; see here I still have some towels, and here is my uniform."

"Oh, can I take a picture with your uniform on? Stand by your community service award plaque." Even as the words left my mouth, I remembered Toni Cade Bambara's story, "Blues Ain't No Mocking Bird" where white photographers visit an elderly couple and want to catch their "real" images. I am also very aware that my research assistant is quite critical of touristic gazes. After all, her dissertation speaks to the ways in which the Caribbean is represented in travel discourse.

"See, this how you dressed when you delivered; but you had to have your mask on too. These were health department rules. God has blessed me. He gives me everything I need. I just have to be patient."

Mrs. Parker was up again, this time patting down her hot-combed hair. "You know what happens with pressed hair?" She glances at Antonia, who has been unusually quiet, decreasing my need for translating Caribbean intonations. Antonia had removed her turban like scarf, unveiling her natural braids. I could read Mrs. Parker's thoughts: "To be so intelligent, I don't know why she doesn't do something with all that hair."

"I had to keep everything sterilized, fingernails had to be clean. Let me see if I can find my old cap before you take your picture. I did have a cap, just a tie cap to put on my head to keep all my hair out of the way. I did have some then." On her feet again, she left to find the cap with no success.

"When did you stop delivering babies?"

"Well I was in a car wreck in 1965 and I didn't deliver more than twenty-five after that because I was down for twelve months. I was lucky I could still walk. Before I healed, I was walking like an old granny."

I glanced over at the questions a silent Antonia had been scribbling. "Do you have children?"

"I got two daughters. My baby boy got drowned at twelve. Both of my daughters are nurses. I got nine grandchildren; I got twenty-six great-grand children; I got two great-great grandchildren. I was delivering babies before I had any babies and nobody see me when I was delivering my own."

"What do you mean by that statement? You mean, you didn't call in a midwife?"

"I called in one after the baby was born."

"Oh, because you already knew what to do? That must be hard delivering your own."

"I did my own. By this time my grandmother was dead."

We were talking and moving around the room taking pictures. I commented on Mrs. Parker's graceful stride. She walked as well as a fifty year old, but reminded me that she is in her late seventies.

"Now, how many babies do you think you delivered? This article says 1,000."

"That was during that time. That was in '81, and that was just 1,000 and some during that time. But in other papers, I'm listed as 2,000 to 2,100. That's what was written, but I delivered some before there were forms to fill out. I had to send the forms to the health department. I delivered white and black babies. I could have delivered more white babies, but then I wouldn't have had a chance to deliver my own. I delivered about sixteen white people, but they required me to do a lot more around their houses, and I didn't have the time. I delivered eight of my sister's twelve children; I delivered my brother's son; my cousin's children. Everyone. I weighed them in some of those bags you see over there. (I glance and see something that looks like a potato bag.) I had a scale."

"Have you ever delivered twins? I have twins." I thought this image of fertile motherhood would make the rest of the interview effortless.

"I don't know how many sets. I even have twins in my family; my cousin has twins. One of the boys in a set of twins came to see me around a month ago; he was overseas, and he stopped by to see me. He was forty-seven. Both his parents are dead now and he came to see me. I would say I delivered twenty-seven sets of twins." As she finishes her comment, she glances at Antonia, who must not have been looking maternal enough.

"Do you have children?," Mrs. Parker asked Antonia. We both showed her our children's pictures; Mrs. Parker commented on how much the pictures reminded her of her grandchildren.

"God told us to have babies. It's right there in Genesis. Go through pain. I knew how to do abortions but I was working for God. I taken his word. I didn't kill mine and I didn't want to kill anybody else's. I had my first baby three years before I got married. I was in college and they wouldn't let me return."

"You went to college?"

"Yes, I did a year at Tougaloo." Most of the grannies had minimal formal educations, and I had incorrectly assumed this of Mrs. Parker. I was hoping that she had not seen the surprised look on my face when she answered my question. To cover my discomfiture, I immediately wanted to ask another question, but Mrs. Parker began to control the conversation with her own set of test questions.

"I wouldn't take anything for God. Sometimes people come to me and think I can help them get pregnant. I can't do that, but God can. Remember Sarah was ninety years old. The Book of James has five chapters in it. Y'all start to read it. You need to be in God and God in you. The Lord is my Shepherd . . ."

"I shall not want," I completed this text and all the rest that she began reciting in order to prove I was worthy to record the memories of a God-fearing woman.

"Inasmuch as ye have done it unto the least of these my brethren. . . ."

"Ye have done it unto me," I added.

"I will look unto the hills. . . ."

"From whence cometh my help," I finished this text too. Mrs. Parker was smiling at me. We were speaking the same conversation. Quite surprised by my knowledge of Scriptures, she mumbled something about being glad I had not "educated myself past God." She walked into her bedroom and brought back the picture that would be our undoing.

"You must tell me what this is." Mrs. Parker showed Antonia, M.C., and me one of those three dimensional pictures, popularized in "magic eye" books, although her photograph was a xeroxed copy.

"Oh, I'm not good at looking at these pictures and trying to discern the picture underneath which is supposed to stand out if you hold it just right. I've never been able to see the hidden picture. My children can do it. It's probably a picture of Jesus, right? I think I see Jesus." I wanted us to quickly move on to something else.

"You have to be able to tell me what this picture says," reiterated Mrs. Parker. She passed the picture to me, and not knowing how to focus my eyes for 3D viewing, I passed it to M.C., hoping that this is a ritual a fellow Mississippian would be able to demystify.

M.C. laughed and whispered to me,"It probably says 'to whom much is given, much is expected' or 'a man is worthy of his hire,' meaning she wants you to grease her paw."

I then passed the photo to Antonia, who refused to look at it, saying she occasionally went to church, but she wasn't *that* religious. I decided to guess at what it said because it seemed to be important to Mrs. Parker who, in a turn of events, was testing our credentials, translating us. Were we "called" to interview her? I thought I should try once again.

"It says Jesus died for our sins." M.C. picked up on my notion that we may hit the right answer through guessing and added, "It says I am the Way, The Truth, and the Life."

"I am very disappointed. I thought you were Christian peoples, and you can't see what the picture says?"

Trying to salvage the earlier, lighter tone I began explaining my inadequacy. All of my protestations that I did not know how to hold 3D pictures for best viewing and that I had no stereoscopic depth perception were to no avail. I could not see the picture.

"But this picture is my history," continued Mrs. Parker.

"Oh, I see a baby being born." This was a good try on M.C.'s part, but he was as wrong as I had been.

"No. You see, you asked me to tell you what I know, but you won't do what that paper says to do. You were innocent in finding out what midwives do, but you can't be innocent in finding out about this picture."

At this point we were all confused. Was this not the same woman who told me earlier that she was not superstitious, who never believed in the axe under the bed? Whatever she saw in the picture, we did not see, could not see, would not see. It was almost as if no longer able to deliver babies, she was channeling her creativity into a new form. Babies were no longer the product; the photograph was. I was now reminded of James Clifford's caution that sometimes the informant looks over the ethnographer's shoulders. I thought too of Alice Walker's musing: What happens to our grandmothers and mother who had "springs of creativity in them for which there was no release" (*In Search of Our Mothers' Gardens* 233). No longer delivering babies, Mrs. Parker had lost her art form and "like any artist with no art form, she became dangerous" (*Sula* 121).

"Can you give us a hint?"

I was beginning to grow tired, but Mrs. Parker was warming up. This was no longer going according to script. Before coming to Mississippi, Antonia and I had viewed several videos where interviewers kept talking, but the grannies were tired. In one video the granny tells the interviewing team in at least six or seven ways that she is tired. Antonia and I listened to ninety-two and a half year-old granny Sarah Maddux say, "Well, now children. I really told you enough. You never will have enough. Any final questions you have to ask?" ("Granny Woman" video). We vowed we would never tax the granny's stamina. There were no videos on not taxing the stamina of researchers. Mrs. Parker did not let rest the 3D picture issue.

"This picture is just like your bible. You need to read the Book of James. What does it say at the top of the picture?"

By this time, I was glad that I could at least read. Slowly, I responded, "It says, "Look at directions for this miracle."

"Now, does it say to ask questions or to look?

"It says to look." But, again I reaffirmed that I must have a "lazy eye," "crossed eyes," everything except a "magic eye."

Wanting my research to go well, M.C. turned to his Uncle George, who mumbled something about he knew Bertha before she got so much religion: "I'm not looking. She ain't ever been that religious."

"Don't ask me any more questions. Do what the paper says. I got a three-year-old grandchild who knows what the paper says. You'se American and you should know what it says." Mrs. Parker's last comment made me think I was drawing all of my responses from the wrong categories. As interdisciplinary as I am, I couldn't pull together America, miracles, money, and Jesus all in the same picture. Now thinking it might be a postcolonial, diasporic issue, I turned to Antonia for help.

"Antonia, why don't you just take a look at it?"

"I don't want to look at it. I'm not able to see these pictures either."

Turning to Mrs. Parker in an attempt to distract her, Antonia asked, "Did you ever let others in the birthing room?"

"Occasionally, a husband would want to come in. I delivered one girl who wanted her daddy to come in. I told her that when she made that baby daddy wasn't there. I told her that if her daddy had been with her then, she wouldn't have had that baby. Look at the picture."

"But, we don't want to take up anymore of your time," Antonia responded.

"Well, I just hope you all could have got that picture. Let's have prayer."

We had prayer, and the politics of praying must have changed the mood. When we all walked outside Mrs. Parker named the different medicinal plants around her house. She graciously embraced us again and told us to be sure to study the Bible while we're at the university. Her last words were, "I'm just sorry you didn't get the picture."

Anthropologist Ruth Behar in *Translated Woman: Crossing the Border with Esperanza's Story* comments that Esperanza, "without putting down a word on paper, . . . has been writing the story of her life since she was five years old" (xii). Similarly, Mrs. Parker, without putting down a word on paper herself had been writing the story of her life ever since her encounter in the woods with her grandmother. I liked Mrs. Parker—gracious, assertive, conjuring us with her own agenda, jumping double-dutch faster than we ever could. She questioned my eyesight in ways in which I had expected only the old masters would do. From Mark Twain, I had learned: "You cannot depend on your eyes when your imagination is out of focus" and from Michel Foucault, I remembered:

> There are times in life when the question of knowing if one can think differently than one thinks, and perceive differently than one sees, is absolutely necessary if one is to go on looking and reflecting at all.[21]

Yet it was from my serendipitous encounter with Mrs. Parker that I realized I still had much to learn. In the presence of an ordinary woman with extraordinary presence, I was not the professor of literature. I was simply someone trying to see. All of my essentialist bonding with her, my manipulation of myself as a Southern black six-fingered woman, was not enough. In the presence of a *sistah* conjurer, one needs a magic eye.

# NOTES

INTRODUCTION

1  In her chapter "Toward an Afrocentric Feminist Epistemology" in *Black Feminist Thought*, Patricia Hill Collins names an ethic of caring and an ethic of accountability as two of several dimensions of an alternative epistemology. She defines the ethic of caring as "the value placed on individual expressiveness, the appropriateness of emotions, and the capacity for empathy" and the ethic of caring as the relationship between one's knowledge claims and values and ethics (216–18).

2  Morrison's concept of "culture bearers" emphasizes the storehouse of information, creativity, and instruction which black women ancestors have provided their literary daughters, who in following them, also become culture bearers through the stories they tell. See Nellie Mckay, "An Interview With Toni Morrison."

3  When I use "granny" in the singular, I do not want to erase the specificity of each woman's experience by essentializing or totalizing them. Indeed, throughout this volume, I record the voices of numerous grannies, in order to show the range of experiences. "Granny" is a convenient term that refers to the shared positioning that black lay midwives experienced in literature and life. As such, "Granny" is the constructed category and "grannies" are the historical women.

4  Gates uses "speakerly" to refer to a text that "seems to be aspiring to the status of oral narration." His foremost example of such a text is Zora Neale Hurston's *Their Eyes Were Watching God*, a "double-voiced," "signifyin(g)" text within the black tradition.

5  In searching for "cultural guides" to center black women's experiences, Elsa Barkley Brown in "African-American Women's Quilting" uses quilting as a trope for "the way in which they saw and constructed their own lives to provide the analytical framework by which we attempt to understand their experiences and their world and to provide the structural framework by which we attempt to teach this to others" (929).

6  hooks and West speak of a "community of faith," historically anchored in the black church, but broadened to include a range of dialogues, "a sense of communion and breaking bread, of sharing fundamentally that which is most one's own. Sharing the word" (*Breaking Bread* 2).

7  In "Beloved: A Spiritual," Holloway speaks of Beloved's role as a "cultural mooring place" inasmuch as she represents all mothers and children from slavery's history. For Holloway, "a cultural mooring place" is "a moment for reclamation and for naming" (522). Also, see Holloway's *Moorings and*

*Metaphors: Figures of Culture and Gender in Black Women's Literature.*

8  For a collection of ring and rope songs that have been traced to black children's experiences, see *Shake It To the One That You Love the Best: Play Songs and Lullabies from Black Musical Traditions,* Cheryl Mattox ed. Illustrated by Varnette P. Honeywood and Brenda Joysmith, this collection is a compilation of art, music, and historical vignettes.

9  Most folklorists agree that scholars need to do more than point out that a literary work contains folklore, a simplistic approach that fails to engage the complexity of how both the literature and the lore interact. See Roger Abrahams's critique of the "lore-in-lit" approach, "Folklore and Literature as Performance" where he argues that "commonly the study of folklore and literature has been studied as folklore *in* literature. This is because the study of folklore has been one of discovering survivals, and therefore strongly evolutionary and progressivist in bias. . . . The objective of the 'lore-in-lit' approach is essentially one of glossing—using one's folkloric knowledge to illuminate content or formal features of a work of art" (82).

10  There are double-dutch teams that compete at regional and national levels. As a sports activity, teams do all types of gymnastic feats while jumping double-dutch.

11  Roberts argues that the origin of the term is from the community itself and not from white authorities. I see "granny" as a term that, like "black," went from disfavor as an externally imposed term to its favorable reclamation by the community itself. Parts of this phenomenon are similar to Foucault's notion of "reverse discourse"—a marginalized community resists hegemony by valorizing the terms that have previously served to marginalize them. See *History of Sexuality, Vol.1.*

12  I have in mind the Sheppard-Towner Act, which I discuss in Chapter One.

13  See Molly Dougherty's "Southern Lay Midwives as Ritual Specialists" for a discussion of how midwifery requires "special ritual, economic, and social behavior" (151).

14  In her interview with Nellie McKay, Morrison comments: "Sometimes a writer imagines characters who threaten, who are able to take the book over. To prevent that, the writer has to exercise some kind of control. Pilate in *Song of Solomon* was that kind of character. She was a very large character and loomed very large in the book. So I wouldn't let her say too much" (418).

15  The current National Black Women's Health Project founded by Byllye Avery has been instrumental in bringing forth a wide range of black women's health issues. See *The Black Women's Health Book: Speaking for Ourselves,* edited by Evelyn C. White. The term "new dignity" is used in a government publication of the 1970s, "The Granny Midwife: Her Training, Licensure, and Practice. . . " So much had been taken away from the grannies that the publi-

cation argues for the return of a "new dignity." My position is that the black women's health movement and African American fiction writers are the ones restoring the dignity.

16 According to the National Center for Health Services Research publication, "The Granny Midwife: Her Training, Licensure, and Practice. . ." some grannies had problems communicating what was written in their manuals because of the small print and unfamiliar terms (7).

17 *Trials, Tribulations, and Celebrations,* edited by Marian Gray Secundy, with the literary collaboration of Lois LaCivita Nixon, is a collection of short stories and poems by African American writers who are interested in a socio-literary approach to health. Organized around the themes of "Illness And Health-Seeking Behavior," "Aging," and "Loss and Grief," this collection gives a sense of the relationship between ethnicity and healing.

18 *Plumes* won first prize in the literary contest sponsored by *Opportunity* magazine in 1927.

19 See Emily Martin's *The Woman in the Body: A Cultural Analysis of Reproduction* where she shows how cultural assumptions have infused the science of reproduction.

20 Here I echo W.E.B. Du Bois's theory of double consciousness as explained in *The Souls of Black Folks.*

21 In *The Book of Psalms* David has many poems that ask God to rebuke his enemies. Usually, these are general pleas for God to avenge the injustices done to the Israelites by their enemies. In contrast, Hurston is very detailed when chronicling the calamities and retribution of one's enemies. Her curse-prayers specify what vengeful acts will occur on which body parts.

22 I am indebted to folklorist Rosemary Hathaway for this turn of phrase.

23 David Brown speaks of conjure as a "black discourse" in "Conjure/Doctors: An Exploration of a Black Discourse in America, Antebellum to 1940."

24 I use "womanist" and "womanism" in this volume to specify the particular slant that feminism takes in communities of color. Coined by Alice Walker in *In Search of Our Mothers' Gardens,* "womanist," given its association with black oral traditions and speech patterns, does not carry the same negative baggage in communities of color that "feminist" carries. The term has gained widespread usage and is sometimes used interchangeably with black feminist criticism, although a case can be made for different nuances of meanings.

25 Henderson uses testimonial discourse to develop her trope of "speaking in tongues." Speaking in tongues includes both glossolalia (private, privileged communication) and heteroglossia (the ability to speak in diverse known languages). Suggesting that black women writers speak in tongues, Henderson ends her essay by charging black feminist critics with the "hermeneutical task of interpreting tongues" (37).

26  Clifford observes in "On Ethnographic Allegory" that "the theme of the vanishing primitive, of the end of traditional society (the very act of naming it 'traditional' implies a rupture), is pervasive in ethnographic writing" (112). He goes on to say that such a method "assume[s] that the other society is weak and 'needs' to be represented by an outsider (and that what matters in its life is its past, not present or future). The recorder and interpreter of fragile custom is custodian of an essence, unimpeachable witness to an authenticity" (113).

CHAPTER ONE

1  The Mammy figure is the stereotypically large, black woman who nurtures all the members of the white household where she is employed. Unlike the mammy stereotype, which has its origins in plantation life, the Sapphire stereotype has its origins in radio and television. Sapphire is the aggressive black woman who nags her man. In contrast to the asexuality of the first two, the Jezebel figure is the black seductress. See Donald Bogle, *Toms, Coons, Mulattoes, Mammies & Bucks* for the distinctive differences among the various stereotypes.

2  In 1522, German physician Wertt, who had camouflaged himself as a woman so he could study childbirth in the lying-in chamber, was burned to death for such a transgression. Some of the American colonies enacted laws against male presence in birth chambers. See Litoff, *The American Midwife Debate*,4 and Donegan, *Women and Men Midwives*, 18.

3  All of the Ehrenreich and English quotes are from *Witches, Midwives, and Nurses* except for the quotes which specifically mention *For Her Own Good*.

4  Useful histories include any of Litoff's works; Ehrenreich and English, *Witches, Midwives, and Nurses: A History of Women Healers*; Wertz and Wertz, *Lying in: A History of Childbirth in America*.

5  Although Wollstonecraft had wanted only female attendants during her daughter's Mary's birth, her delivery became complicated when she could not expel the placenta. Therefore, a male attendant, assumed to be more knowledgeable, was sent for. Tragically, he retrieved the placenta by using his own hands, causing Wollstonecraft to hemorrhage to death (see Wertz and Wertz, *Lying-In: A History of Childbirth in America* 43–44).

6  Ehrenreich and English in *For Her Own Good* report that "in the late fifteenth and early sixteenth centuries there were thousands upon thousands of executions—usually live burnings at the stake—in Germany, Italy, and other countries. In the mid-sixteenth century the terror spread to France, and finally to England. One writer has estimated the number of executions at an average of six hundred a year for certain German cities—or two a day, 'leaving out Sundays'" (35). Similarly, Achterberg in *Woman as Healer* reports that "fires

burned throughout Europe." In about 1600, a contemporary observer noted that "Germany is almost entirely occupied with building fires for the witches. Switzerland has been compelled to wipe out many of her villages on their account. Travelers in Lorraine may see thousands and thousands of the stakes to which witches are bound" (Robbins, 551, quoted in Achterberg). The Inquisition acknowledged burning 30,000 witches in 150 years (Achterberg 85).

7 For information on this early lay midwifery center near Summertown, Tennessee, see *Spiritual Midwifery* by Ina May Gaskin, one of the founding members of the original group of three hundred people who settled there. They adverstise themselves as "a group of midwives who deliver babies and provide primary health care for our spiritual community of eleven hundred long-haired vegetarians" (14).

8 Although the initials "TCB" stand for Traditional Childbirth, the acronym plays upon a common folk phrase in African American communities, "take care of business." Discussions of the group's co-founder, Shafia Monroe, can be found in the works edited by Bair and Cayleff and in Dula and Goering.

9 Those authors who have concentrated on the history of the grannies include Linda Holmes, Holly Mathews, and Beatrice Mongeau.

10 In *Hausa Medicine: Illness and Well-Being in a West African Culture*, Wall details the nuances of meanings of *lafiya*, which is translated broadly into English as "health" instead of the connotations of "harmony" and "balance." In *Body and Mind in Zulu Medicine*, Harriet Ngubane makes the same case for the meaning of good health among the Zulu: "good health means the harmonious working and coordination of his [sic] universe" (27). The emphasis on harmony and balance has not always assured protection for midwives in Africa. Contrary to Shafia Monroe's quote in this chapter's epigraph, Mbiti acknowledges that some women were burned as witches in Africa (see *Concepts of God in Africa*, Southampton, Great Britain: The Camelot Press, 1970). Nevertheless, an emphasis on health as harmony and balance helped quickly restore the stature of midwives.

11 Judith Walzer Leavitt describes how women came to view forceps as "hands of iron," although for men forceps "constituted the favorite instrument of physician intervention"("Science Enters the Birthing Room: Obstetrics in America since the Eighteenth Century, 287).

12 To conceive of delivery as catching babies is quite different from conceiving it as grabbing or pulling babies. Also note that most cases wherein the midwife would have been tempted to place her hands within the mother are the very cases that, because of their complications, were given over to doctors. The most well known case of a midwife killing a patient due to unclean hands

invading the mother was the earlier case I spoke of—the case of Mary Wollstonecraft and the male midwife whose hand caused her to hemorrhage to death.

13 I randomly selected six granny midwives and followed their careers for a period of approximately 30 to 40 years each by reviewing their "Application for Certificate to Practice Midwifery," a certificate given by the Georgia Department of Public Health. In total, I examined over 400 records from the mid 1930s to the late 1960s. Each certificate has such information as: Years Practiced, Intelligence, Literary, Courses of Instruction, Relationship with Doctors, Condition of Midwifery Bag, and statistics about number and condition of deliveries. Some of the information in Chapter Four draws from these certificates, which are presently housed at the Georgia Department of Archives and History.

14 Biblical commentators have long presented a portrait of Pilate as someone who, despite his attempts at washing his hands to symbolize his innocence in the crucifixion of Jesus, is never clean from the act. Legend has it that after the crucifixion, he kept washing his hands over and over. The desire to make himself clean drove him mad.

15 With the exception of Morrison's Pilate who carries her rocks in a bag, rarely do the women healers in black women's literature carry bags. Thus, the writers miss an opportunity to integrate material culture with the lives of their woman healers. Yet, the literature does explore the type of syncretism represented by the bags. Bambara's Minnie Ramson and Morrison's Miranda Day benefit from traditional knowledge, as well as specialized knowledge. As with their Latina counterparts, the *curandera*, their approach is eclectic. They are not static healers bemoaning whatever is modern. The expectation is that the rituals and cures will change.

16 As a tribute to Mrs. Maggie Smalls's standing in her community, the Penn Center, a historical site built in 1862 by Northern missionaries for the education of freedmen, has Smalls's uniform and certificates on the wall. The Penn Center served as an institute for the training of the grannies. Although Mrs. Smalls died in 1987, her children, grand children, and the many people she delivered (over 2,000) on St. Helena's Island keep her stories alive.

17 For this pun on grannies who travelled both geographical backroads and medical ones, I am indebted to Alex S. Freedman, "The Passing of the Arkansas Granny Midwife."

18 As with Eudora Welty's story, "A Worn Path," the point of the story is not whether the child is dead or alive, but the journey of the caretaker.

CHAPTER TWO

1 Although I proceed to discuss how black women fiction writers reclaim hands, I would note that black women poets also do so. Nikki Giovanni has a

prose poem, "Hands," which is a tribute to the many activities that the hands of black women perform.

2 Morrison uses the term "disremembered and unaccounted for" to describe Beloved at the end of *Beloved* (274). It is an apt term to describe a host of stories "not to pass on" by and about black women.

3 Morrison uses the phrase "erupt the funk" in *The Bluest Eye*. Susan Willis's article, "Eruptions of Funk: Historicizing Toni Morrison," in *Specifying* is one of the early discussions on funk. Willis argues that "'funk' is really nothing more than the intrusion of the past into the present" (108).

4 In *Workings of the Spirit*, Houston Baker uses "funk" as a trope for what African American scholars do: "Confronted by such a choice—a choice that mandates rigorous, engaged, theoretically informed critiques of black and white male and white women's hegemonic self-certainties—a Black Studies majority is likely to follow the course of those who prefer not to *theorize*. I don't think this refusal in the instance of Afro-American women scholars represents an act of bad faith so much as a faithful refusal to act 'bad': i.e., to figure forth and flesh out the funkiness that reveals a traditional and embodied history and historiography as the prison house of an inside containment" (18).

5 James Baldwin also discusses the aversion that pretentious middle-class black women have to funkiness in *If Beale Street Could Talk* (New York: The Dial Press, 1974). In scenes that merge sexuality and religion, Mr. Hunt uses notions of funk and erotica to devalue his wife who is a "Sanctified woman" (12).

6 Margaret Walker plays upon a racialized treatment in *Jubilee* where she has a dim-witted black male servant take responsibility for a southern belle's expulsion of gas.

7 Examples from a black community of self-deprecating folklore about black women can be found in Daryl Dance's *Shuckin' and Jiving*, a compilation of tales from informants in Virginia.

8 See Willis who aptly notes that "bodily orifices are in more than one instance related to the visage of colonialism" (281).

9 See Chapter 10 "Towards an Afrocentric Feminist Epistemology" in Collins's *Black Feminist Thought*.

10 Henry Louis Gates, Jr., discusses at length the concept of "double-voicedness" in African America literature. He argues that "the black tradition is double-voice" and that "signifyin(g) is the figure of the double-voiced. . . ." See *The Signifying Monkey*. M. Bakhtin distinguishes between single-voiced discourse and double-voice discourse in terms of poetic and prose tropes. See *The Dialogic Imagination*.

11 This folk expression means to disrespect someone by not recognizing how s/he wants to be called.

12 Miss Ann was the collective term given to symbolize the mistress of the plan-

tation. Her contemporary extension is any white woman who exercises her power by virtue of her partnership with patriarchy. The title, "Ms. Ann," implies that although now a feminist, Miss Ann exercises power analogous to that in earlier decades, demanding the same subservience from black women. Contemporary poet Lucille Clifton has a poem, "To Ms. Ann," which critiques global sisterhood on the basis of black women's memory of Miss Ann and mistrust that Ms. Ann is any different.

13　In *Song of Solomon*, Morrison describes the politics of acquiring names among the black characters in her work. Rather than receiving a nickname that is a diminutive of one's formal name, Morrison's characters have names that reflect an African influenced naming pattern: names "bear witness." They speak to one's experiences, character, or values. These are names earned from "yearnings, gestures, flaws, events, mistakes, weaknesses." These are names such as Jelly Roll, Guitar, Ice Man, and Milkman (330).

14　Anaya's Ultima is an example of a prophetic midwife. She knows that Tonio will appreciate the magic of language as he matures, for he selects pen and paper from her hands while he is yet a baby.

15　Compare Miranda's acceptance of the combination of the old and new in the CandleWalk ritual with her acceptance of the old and new with the quilt she is making: "Her needle fastens the satin trim of Peace's receiving blanket to Cocoa's baby jumper to a pocket from her own gardening apron" (137).

## CHAPTER THREE

1　Here, I use the subtitle of *Breaking Bread* by bell hooks and Cornel West. It brings together the engagement of mind and passion as a necessary combination and condition of black life.

2　Biblical scholars acknowledge that birthstools were used in Egypt. These stools usually consisted of two stones or stones laid in the shape of a horseshoe. A common Egyptian expression was "to sit on the bricks" or to give birth. Long after other American midwives had stopped using their version of birthstools, many grannies were still hiding their collapsible ones in their bags.

3　Genesis 35:16–20 tells the story of Rachel whose baby was in a breech position and her midwife who gave her the assurance that she would give birth to a boy. It was a hard labor and Rachel died. The son, Benjamin, lived; Genesis 38: 28–29 tells the story of Tamar whose midwife helps her to deliver twins. The midwife placed a scarlet thread on the hand, which is protruding out of the womb. This twin draws back his hand and in the interim, his twin brother leaves the birth canal. The midwife sees this upheaval as a "breech." Several births in the Bible have highly dramatic scenarios. When Rebekah gives birth to twin sons who struggle in her womb, one son, Jacob, upon entering the world, grabs the heel of his twin brother, Esau. Biblical midwives saw much adventure.

4 Even though there were, of course, women in Anglo cultures who conceived of their midwifery skills as a "calling from God," the grannies were most known for couching their vocation in a culturally specific theological framework and continued to do so throughout their practices.

5 Saul was on his way to Damascus to persecute Christians when a bright light from heaven knocked him to the ground. Saul heard a voice saying, "Saul, Saul, why persecutest thou me?" Saul's famous answer to the question was, "Lord, what wilt thou have me to do?" After three sightless days, a prophet restores Saul's sight. Because of his new mission to spread the gospel of Jesus Christ, Saul becomes Paul after the Damascus experience. See Acts 9:1–19.

6 See Molly Dougherty, "Southern Midwifery and Organized Health Care Systems in Conflict." Also see the various *Lessons for Midwives* manuals produced by different states. These manuals usually print the prayer, the creed, and the midwives' song, invariably a hymn.

7 In several videos that feature grannies, their singing of hymns can be heard in the background. For example, in "Delivered with Love" the grannies sing "Go Tell it on the Mountain" and "Like a Tree Planted By the Water." Hymns frame so many of their interviews.

8 Here, I am deliberately drawing upon Mae Henderson's work on testimonial discourse and the double-entendre of speaking in tongues as a religious phenomenon and as a trope. See "Speaking in Tongues."

9 Here, I am speaking in response to feminist theologian Rosemary Radford Ruether who suggests that Christianity, as quoted in Lepow, is "'the heir of both classical Neo-Platonism and apocalyptic Judaism'" and as such "embodies a dualistic world view that leads to authoritarianism and sexism (363). Ruether notes that classical Christianity associates "the psychic traits of intellectuality, transcendent spirit, and autonomous will" with the masculine. The grannies' brand of Christianity was as far from "classical Christianity" as slave Christianity was from master Christianity.

10 In Claudia Tate's interview with Morrison, Morrison speaks of black women as both harbor and ship (122).

11 Collins discusses the concept of both/and throughout *Black Feminist Thought*, and Barbara Christian does so in her article, "The Highs and Lows of Black Feminist Criticism."

12 This idea was explained in a workshop, "Crafting Anti-Racist and Feminist Practice in the U.S. Academy," Ohio State University, April 7, 1994; see also "On Race and Voice: Challenges for Liberal Education in the 1990s, *Cultural Critique* 14, 1989–90.

13  Although used in another context, I am indebted to Chandra Mohanty for conceptualizing the matter in this way.

14  See Walker, *In Search of Our Mothers' Gardens*, 231–43; to be a black woman and an artist/thinker is to have "contrary instincts." Similarly, Darlene Clark Hine defines "culture of dissemblance" as "the behavior and attitude of Black women that created the appearance of openness and disclosure but actually shields the truth of their inner lives and selves from their oppressors." See *Unequal Sisters: A Multi-Cultural Reader, in US Women's History*.

15  This is a reference to Audre Lorde's, "The Master's Tools Will Never Dismantle the Master's House."

CHAPTER FOUR

1  Cuban novelist Alejo Carpentier popularized this term in the late 1940s. Most often associated with Latin-American and South American writers, "magical realism" refers to a curious blend of the fabulous and the realistic.

2  Although Morrison acknowledges the tie between what she does and how magical realism functions, she is careful to point out that "she was well into *Song of Solomon* before she discovered Gabriel Marquez"(Caldwell Interview 242). For all of the similarities, she distinguishes differences. The magical realism of Latin American male writers was "so readily available to them— that mixture of Indian and Spanish. Whereas I felt the preachers, the story-telling, the folklore, the music was very accessible to me, but I felt almost alone. It wasn't only mine, but I didn't have any literary precedent for what I was trying to do with the magic. So I thought, boy, those guys—they've got it. Everybody understood the sources of their magic right away. Whereas mine was discredited, because it was held by discredited people. 'Folklorists!' Now its's sort of a little subject in the academy, but it did not have any currency . . . it's perceived of as illiterate"(Caldwell Interview).

3  Jessie Mae Newsome's sister, Arnetter Pool, also is well known in the area for her natural remedies.

4  In early interviews with several local journalists, Jessie Mae Newsome speaks of making the mark on a door, but she showed me a tree.

5  The community's interest in relationships was one of the reasons midwives had to come to the home where they were expected to do all kinds of work, staying for many days to manage the whole household. Thus, the granny had to have a bedside manner, a kitchen-table manner, a front-porch manner, . . .

6  To protect their confidentiality, I am using pseudonyms for those grannies whose registration files I discuss in the following paragraphs. These registration records can be found in The Georgia Department of Archives and History.

7 Several scholars have observed that much of African American fiction takes some of its conventions from slave narratives. See Robert Stepto, "Storytelling in Early Afro-American Fiction: Frederick Douglass's 'The Heroic Slave'" in *Black Literature and Literary Theory*, edited by Henry Louis Gates, Jr., 175–86.

8 The introduction to *The Slave's Narrative*, edited by Charles T. Davis and Henry Louis Gates, Jr, emphasizes that "the slave narrative represents the attempts of blacks to *write themselves into being*, (xxiii).

9 See Gayatri Spivak, "Reading the World: Literary Studies in the Eighties," *In Other Worlds: Essays in Cultural Politics*,102; c.f. Wall, *Changing Our Own Words*, 9.

10 Marion Wilson Starling lists these conventions in *The Slave Narrative*.

11 See scenes in Richard Wright's "Bright and Morning Star" in which a black mother, in the presence of evil white men, masks her intentions to put her son out of his misery *Uncle Tom's Children*. New York: Harper & Row, 1940. Of course, one hears echoes also of Paul Laurence Dunbar's "We Wear the Mask" and Ralph Ellison's early scene in *Invisible Man* where the grandfather confesses on his deathbed to having been a trickster all of his life (New York: Random House),1952.

12 Here I echo the death-bed curse from the end of the first chapter of *Invisible Man*.

13 Donald Bogle's *Toms, Coons, Mulattoes, Mammies, & Bucks* and *Black Women in America* are two useful sources for studying the lives of both Louise Beavers and Butterfly McQueen.

14 Paule Marshall, too, embeds the sense of an atavistic presence in the naming of her character, Avey, in *Praisesong for the Widow*.

15 See Otto Ernest Rayburn, "The 'Granny' Woman in the Ozarks."

16 As will be discussed in Chapter Five, *Mama Day* uses several of these birth omens. Little Caesar looks like a chicken because Miranda performed on his mother a chicken/egg cure.

17 For this insight I am indebted to Antonia MacDonald-Smythe who notes that in St. Lucia, a fruit tree is usually planted on the same site where the "navel string" has been buried. Folklore has it that the tree will always yield sweet fruit.

CHAPTER FIVE

1 Primordial mud mother is a term from *The Salt Eaters* and refers to the strength and wisdom gained and passed on from generation to generation of black women. It also alludes to a motherhood rooted in Africa.

2 Neither Morrison nor Naylor chooses for their women to give birth to seven daughters, although seven sisters are a part of conjure lore also. Loudell Snow

writes of how The Seven Sisters of New Orleans "were (are) reputedly great conjure women and healers" (52).

3  See Martha Ann Tyree Moussatos's article, "McTeer: Root Doctor."

4  Here I echo a line often repeated in Leslie Silko's *Ceremony*. "From time immemorial" captures the sense of on-going continuity, which *Mama Day* also has.

5  Morrison's *The Bluest Eye* begins this way by purporting to keep a secret: "Quiet as it's kept . . . (9).

6  Patricia Williams in *The Alchemy of Race and Rights* (1991) uses "polar bears" as an hieroglyph much like Naylor uses 18 & 23. I am indebted to Kate Husband for this insight.

7  See Laura Mulvey's "Visual Pleasure and Narrative Cinema" in *Visual and Other Pleasures*.

8  See Linda Alcoff, "The Problem of Speaking for Others."

9  See Maria Lugones's "Playfulness, 'World' — Travelling, and Loving Perception."

10  See Edward Bruner's assertion in *The Anthropology of Experience*.

11  Started as a memory aid for spelling Mississippi, this folk rhyme uses "crooked letter" to refer to each "s" in Mississippi and "hump-back" to refer to each "p."

12  There was also a Zula of Pulaski. So many of the names in Linda Stingily's family resonate with names of characters in literature: Balzoria/Zenobia; Zula/Sula; Odessa/Dessa.

13  In the television show, "The Beverly Hillbillies," Jed Clampitt was the hill-billy head of a family that overnight becomes rich because of finding oil on their property. They leave their small town and drive off to Beverly Hills. Although limited by their rural naivete, the family members were neverthe-less astute and resourceful.

14  Various family members remember events differently. For example Linda Stingily's mother, Mrs. Hattye D. Parker Stingily remembers holding up baby Odessa while the granny midwife tied the sixth finger with quilting thread.

15  Mary Stingily's father, Linda's uncle, chose to spell "Stingily" differently.

16  I debate mentioning one specific facility at Parker's Paradise because far too many scholars love to give those details that substantiate their informants as "the folks." Therefore, I give the next detail, not to separate my world from Carver's, but to speak to his sense of humor in reconstructing his land as Parker's Paradise. In a conscious redevelopment and critique of the pastoral, Carver has rebuilt the outhouse, constructing a fancy door, two fancy toilets, and two face basins with gold fixtures. It lacks a jacuzzi.

17  Quoted from *Nation and Narration*, 301.

18  Nanny tells Jany in *Their Eyes Were Watching God*, "Ah said Ah'd save de text for you" (32).

19 I am aware that there are discrepancies in times, dates, and ages in some of the stories. As elderly women, the grannies relied on memories that on some days were better than on other days.

20 Maude Callen was a well-known black nurse midwife who helped train many grannies in South Carolina. Very well respected by her contemporaries and clientele, Callen was often used as a contrast to the granny midwives as evidenced by this description of her in a photographic essay for *Life Magazine*, December 3, 1951: "Maude Callen is a member of a unique group, the nurse midwife. Although there are perhaps 20,000 common midwives practicing, trained nurse midwives are rare. There are only nine in South Carolina, 300 in the nation. Their education includes the full course required of all registered nurses, training in public health and at least six months' classes in obstetrics. As professionals they are far ahead of the common midwife, as far removed from the granny as aureomycin is from asafetida" ("Nurse Midwife Maude Callen Eases Pain of Birth, Life and Death" 135).

21 Both the Twain and Foucault quotes are taken from the epigraph to *Magic Eye: How to See 3D*. This book also uses Matthew 6:22 and a quote from a physician and a eye specialist to frame its discussion on the ability to see.

# BIBLIOGRAPHY

Abrahams, Roger. "Folklore and Literature as Performance." *Journal of the Folklore Institute*. 9 (1972): 75–94.

Achterberg, Jeanne. *Woman As Healer*. Boston: Shambhala Publications, 1990.

Alcoff, Linda. "The Problem of Speaking for Others." *Cultural Critique*. Winter 91–92: 5–32.

Anaya, Rudolfo. *Bless Me Ultima*. Berkeley: Tonatiuh International Inc., 1972.

Anzaldúa, Gloria, ed. *Making Face, Making Soul: Haciendo Caras. Creative and Critical Perspectives by Women of Color*, edited by Gloria Anzaldua. San Francisco: Aunt Lute Books, 1990.

Ansa, Tina McElroy. *Baby of the Family*. San Diego: Harcourt Brace Jovanovich, 1989.

Appiah, Kwame Anthony. *In My Father's House: Africa in the Philosophy of Culture*. New York: Oxford University Press, 1992.

Bakhtin, M. M. *The Dialogic Imagination*, edited by Michael Holquist. Austin: University of Texas Press, 1981.

Bair, Barbara, and Susan E. Cayleff, ed. *Wings of Gauze: Women of Color and the Experience of Health and Illness*. Detroit: Wayne State University Press, 1993.

Baker, Houston A. Jr. *Blues, Ideology, and Afro-American Literature*. Chicago: University of Chicago Press, 1984.

— — —. *Workings in the Spirit: The Poetics of Afro-American Women's Writing*. Chicago: University of Chicago Press, 1991.

Bambara, Toni Cade. *Salt Eaters*. New York: Random House, 1988.

Bascom, William. "Gullah Folk Beliefs Concerning Childbirth." rpt. *Sea Island Roots*, edited by Mary A. Twining and Keith E. Baird. Trenton, NJ: Africa World Press, 1991.

Behar, Ruth. *Translated Woman: Crossing the Border with Esperanza's Story*. Boston: Beacon Press, 1993.

— — —. "The Body in The Woman, The Story in the Woman: A Book Review and Personal Essay. *The Female Body: Figures, Styles, Speculations*, edited by Laurence Goldstein, Ann Arbor: University of Michigan Press, 1991.

Bhabha, Homi. *Nation and Narration*. New York: Routledge, 1990.

Blake, Susan L. "Folklore and Community in *Song of Solomon*." *MELUS* 7.3 (Fall 1980): 77–82.

Blum, Linda. "Mothers, Babies, and Breastfeeding in Late Capitalist America: The Shifting Context of Feminist Theory." *Feminist Studies* 19:2 (1993): 291–311.

Bogdan, Janet Carlisle. "Childbirth in America, 1650 to 1990." *Women, Health, and Medicine in America: A Historical Handbook*, edited by Rima Apple. New York: Garland Publishing, Inc., 1990.

Bogle, Donald. *Toms, Coons, Mulattoes, Mammies, and Bucks: An Interpretive History of Blacks in American Films.* New York: Continuum, 1973. Reprint with new preface, 1994.

Bordo, Susan. "'Material Girl': The Effacements of Postmodern Culture." *The Female Body: Figures, Styles, Speculations*, edited by Laurence Goldstein, Ann Arbor: University of Michigan Press, 1991.

Bowers, Susan. "*Beloved* and the New Apocalypse." *The Journal of Ethnic Studies.* 18.1 (1990): 59–77.

Bredesen, Norman B. "The Granny Midwife: Her Training, Licensure, and Practice in Georgia, Louisiana, and Texas." Hyattsville, MD: National Center for Health Services Research, 1970.

Brewer, Rose M. "Theorizing Race, Class and Gender: The New Scholarship of Black Feminist Intellectuals and Black Women's Labor." *Theorizing Black Feminisms: The Visionary Pragmatism of Black Women*, edited by Stanlie M. James and Abena P. A. Busia. London: Routledge, 1993.

Brooks, Gwendolyn. "Maud Martha." *The World of Gwendolyn Brooks.* New York: Harper & Row Publishers, 1971.

— — —. *Primer for Blacks.* Chicago: Third World Press, 1980.

Brown, David T. "Conjure/Doctors: An Exploration of a Black discourse in America, Antebellum to 1940." *Folklore Forum* 1990. 23: 1–2.

Brown, Elsa Barkley. "African-American Women's Quilting: A framework for conceptualizing and teaching African-American history." *Signs.* 14:4 (Summer 1989).

— — —. Polyrhythms and Improvisation: Lessons for Women's History." *History Workshop*, 31 (Spring 1991).

Bruner, Edward M. and Victor W. Turner, eds. *The Anthropology of Experience.* Urbana: University of Illinois Press, 1986.

Busia, Abena P. A. "What Is Your Nation?: Reconnecting Africa and Her Diaspora through Paule Marshall's *Praisesong for the Widow*." *Changing Our Own Words*, edited by Cheryl A. Wall. New Brunswick, NJ: Rutgers University Press, 1989.

— — —. "Words Whispered Over Voids: A Context for Black Women's Rebellious Voices in the Novel of the African Diaspora." *Black Feminist Criticism and Critical Theory*, edited by Joe Weixlman and Houston Baker. Greenwood, FL: The Penkevill Publishing Company, 1988.

Buss, Fran Leper. *La Partera: Story of a Midwife.* Ann Arbor: University of Michigan Press, 1990.

Butler-Evans, Elliott. *Race, Gender, and Desire: Narrative Strategies in the Fiction of Toni Cade Bambara, Toni Morrison, Alice Walker.* Philadelphia: Temple University, 1989.

Caldwell, Gail. "Author Toni Morrison Discusses Her Latest Novel *Beloved.*" *Conversations with Toni Morrison,* edited by Danill Taylor-Guthrie. Jackson: University Press of Mississippi, 1994.

Campbell, Marie. *Folks Do Get Born.* New York: Garland Publishing, 1984.

Carby, Hazel. "Introduction." *Iola Leroy or Shadows Uplifted.* Frances Harper. Boston: Beacon Press, 1893. Reprint 1987.

———. *Reconstructing Womanhood: The Emergence of the Afro-American Woman Novelist.* New York: Oxford University Press, 1987.

Chestnut, Charles. *Conjure Woman.* Ann Arbor: University Of Michigan Press, 1969.

Christian, Barbara, ed. *"Everyday Use": Alice Walker.* New Brunswick: Rutgers University Press, 1994.

———. "The Highs and the Lows of Black Feminist Criticism." *Reading Black, Reading Feminist,* edited by Henry Louis Gates, Jr. New York: Meridian, 1990.

———. "The Race for Theory." *Making Face, Making Soul / Haciendo Caras: Creative and Critical Perspectives by Women of Color,* edited by Gloria Anzaldua. San Francisco: Aunt Lute Foundation, 1990.

Clifford, James. "On Ethnographic Allegory." *Writing Culture: The Poetics and Politics of Ethnography,* edited by James Clifford and George E. Marcus. Berkeley: University of California Press, 1986.

Clifton, Lucille. *Two-headed Woman.* Amherst: University of Massachusetts Press, 1980.

Cobb, Ann Kuckelman. "Incorporation and Change: The Case of the Midwife in the United States." *Medical Anthropology* 5 (Winter 1981): 73–88.

Collier, Eugenia. "The Closing of the Circle: Movement from Division to Wholeness in Paule Marshall's Fiction." *Black Women Writers (1950–1980): A Critical Evaluation,* edited by Mari Evans. Garden City: Anchor-Doubleday, 1984.

Collins, Patricia Hill. *Black Feminist Thought: Knowledges, Consciousness and the Politics of Empowerment.* London: Harper Collins Academic, 1990.

Daise, Ronald. "Mary had a baby. Sing Hallelu!" *Reminiscences of Sea Island Heritage: Legacy of St. Helena Island.* Orangeburg, South Carolina: Sandlapper Publishing Company, 1986.

Dance, Daryl. *Shuckin' and Jivin'.* Bloomington: Indiana University Press, 1978.

Dash, Julie. *Daughters of the Dust: The Making of an African-American Film.* New York: The New Press, 1992.

Davies, Carol Boyce. *Black Women, Writing and Identity.* New York: Routledge, 1994.

———. "Mothering and Healing in Recent Black Women's Fiction." *Sage* 2.1 (1985): 41–43.

Davis, Angela. *Women Race and Class.* New York: Vintage, 1981.

———. "Reflections on the Black Woman's Role in The Community of Slave." *The Black Scholar* 3.4 (December 1971): 3–15.

Davis Charles T. and Henry Louis Gates, Jr. eds. *The Slave's Narrative*. New York: Oxford University Press, 1985.

Davis-Floyd, Robbie. "The Technocratic Model of Birth." *Feminist Theory and the Study of Folklore*, edited by Susan Hollis, Linda Pershing, and M. Jane Young. Urbana: University of Illinois Press, 1993.

Davis, Mary Kemp. "Everybody Knows Her Name: The Recovery of the Past in Sherley Anne Williams's *Dessa Rose*." *Callaloo* 12.3 (Summer 1989): 544–558.

Davis, Sheila P., and Cora A. Ingram. "Empowered Caretakers: A Historical Perspective on the Roles of Granny Midwives in Rural Alabama." *Wings of Gauze*, edited by Barbara Bair and Susan E. Cayleff. Detroit: Wayne State University Press, 1993.

"Delivered With Love." John F. Ott and W. Scott Lineburger, producers and eds., South Carolina Education Television, SCETV Communications, 1991.

Dent, Gina, ed. *Black Popular Culture*. A Project by Michele Wallace. Seattle: Bay Press, 1992.

Devitt, Neal. "The Statistical Case for Elimination of the Midwife: Fact versus Prejudice, 1890–1935 (Part 1)." *Women and Health* 4:1 (Spring 1979).

———. "The Statistical Case for Elimination of the Midwife: Fact versus Prejudice, 1980–1935." (Part 2) *Women and Health* 4:2 (Summer 1979).

de Weever, Jacqueline. "Toni Morrison's Use of Fairy Tale, Folk Tale, and Myth in *The Song of Solomon*." *Southern Folklore Quarterly* 44 (1980): 131–144.

Dingledine, Donald. "Woman Can Walk on Water: Island, Myth, and Community in Kate Chopin's *The Awakening* and Paule Marshall's *Praisesong for the Widow*." *Women's Studies* 22 (2): 197–216.

Donegan, Jane B. *Women and Men Midwives: Medicine, Morality and Misogyny in Early America*. London: Greenwood Press, 1978.

Donnison, Jean. *Midwives and Medical Men: A History of Inter-professional Rivalries and Women's Rights*. London: Heinemann, 1977.

Dougherty, Molly C. "Southern Midwifery and Organized Health Care: Systems in Conflict." *Medical Anthropology* 6:2 (Spring 1982): 113–125.

———. "Southern Lay Midwives as Ritual Specialists." *The American Way of Birth*. Philadelphia: Temple University Press, 1986.

Du Bois, W. E. B. *The Souls of Black Folks*. New York: New American Library, 1969.

duFort, Brian M., and Ismael H. Abdalla, eds. "African Healing Strategies." *Conch Magazine, Ltd*, 1985.

Dula, Annette, and Sara Goering, eds. *"It Just Ain't Fair": The Ethics of Health Care for African Americans*. Westport, CT: Praeger, 1994.

Dundes, Alan, ed. *Mother Wit from the Laughing Barrel.* Englewood Cliffs, NJ: Prentice-Hall, Inc., 1973.

Eaton, Evelyn. *The Shaman and The Medicine Wheel.* Wheaton, IL: Theosophical Publishing House, 1982.

Ehrenreich, Barbara, and Deidre English. *For Her Own Good: 150 Years of the Experts' Advice to Women.* Garden City, NY: Anchor Press, 1979.

— — —. *Witches, Midwives, and Nurses: A History of Women Healers.* New York: The Feminist Press, 1973.

Fahey, Valerie. "Shopping for a Midwife." *Health* 6, No.3 (May, June 1992): 58.

Ferguson, Russell, et al., ed. *Out There: Marginalization and Contemporary Cultures.* Cambridge, MA: The MIT Press, 1990.

Forbes, Thomas Rogers. *The Midwife and the Witch.* New Haven: Yale University Press, 1966.

Forster, E. M. *Howards End.* New York: Vintage Books, 1921.

Foster, Charles. *Conchtown U.S.A.: Bahamian Fisherfolk in Rivera Beach Florida.* Florida: Florida Atlantic Press, 1991.

Foucault, Michel. *The History of Sexuality, Volume 1.* New York: Pantheon, 1978.

Freedman, Alex S. "The Granny Midwife: An Example of Pariah Medicine." *Research Studies* (June 1974): 131–37.

— — —. "The Passing of the Arkansas Granny Midwife." *Kentucky Folklore Record* 20 (1974): 101–4.

Gaskin, Ina May. *Spiritual Midwifery.* Summertown, TN: The Book Publishing Company, 1980.

Gates, Henry Louis Jr. *Black Literature and Literary Theory.* New York: Methuen, 1984.

— — —. *Reading Black, Reading Feminist.* New York: Meridian, 1990.

— — —. *The Signifying Monkey.* New York: Oxford University Press, 1988.

Gilman, Sander. "Black Bodies, White Bodies: Toward and Iconography of Female Sexuality in Late Nineteenth-Century Art, Medicine, and Literature." *Critical Inquiry.* (Autumn 1985): 204–42.

Giovanni, Nikki. *Those Who Ride the Night Winds.* New York: William Morrow and Company, 1983.

Giroux, Henry. "Postmodernism and Border Pedagogy: Redefining the Boundaries of Race and Ethnicity." *Redrawing the Boundaries,* edited by Stephen Greenblatt and Giles Gunn. New York: Modern Language Association, 1992.

Goldenberg, Robert L., M.D. et al. "Neonatal Deaths in Alabama." *American Journal of Obstetrics and Gynecology.* 147.6 (November 1983): 687–93.

Goldman, Anne. E. "'I Made the Ink'": (Literary) Production and Reproduction in *Dessa Rose* and *Beloved.*" *Feminist Studies* 16.2 (Summer 1990): 313–30.

"Granny Woman: Mrs. Sarah Maddux." Broadside T. V. and Video Maker. Johnson City, Tenn, 1988.

Green, Rayna. "'It's Okay Once You Get It Past the Teeth' and Other Feminist Paradigms for Folklore Studies." *Feminist Theory and the Study of Folklore*, edited by Susan Tower Hollis, Linda Pershing, and M. Jane Young. Urbana: University of Illinois Press, 1993.

Grewal, Inderpal, and Caren Kaplan, eds. *Scattered Hegemonies: Postmodernity and Transnational Feminist Practices*. Minneapolis: University of Minnesota Press, 1994.

Griffin, Katherine. "Gladys Delivers." *Health* 6, No.3 (May, June 1992): 54–63.

Hale, Thomas A. *Scribe, Griot, and Novelist*. Gainesville: University Presses of Florida, 1990.

Hall, Julien. "Notes and Queries." *Journal of American Folklore*. 10.XXXVIII (July–September, 1897): 24–25.

Hand, Wayland D. "Magical Medicine: An Alternative to 'Alternative Medicine.'" *Western Folklore* 44 (1985): 240–51.

Harley, George Way. *Native African Medicine*. London: Frank Cass & Co. Ltd., 1970.

Haraway, Donna. *Simians, Cyborgs, and Women: The Reinvention of Nature*. New York: Routledge, 1991.

Harris, Trudier. *Fiction and Folklore: The Novels of Toni Morrison*. Knoxville: University of Tennessee Press, 1993.

— — — . "Of Mother Love and Demons." *Callaloo*. 2.II (Spring 1988): 387–389.

Henderson, Mae Gwendolyn. "Speaking in Tongues: Dialogics, Dialectics, and the Black Woman Writer's Literary Tradition." *Changing our Own Words: Essays on Criticism, Theory, and Writing by Black Women*, edited by Cheryl Wall. New Brunswick: Rutgers University Press, 1991.

Hersey, Thomas. *Sex, Marriage and Society*. New York: Arno Press, 1974.

Hine, Darlene Clark. *Black Women in America*. New York: Carlson Publishing Inc., 1993.

— — — . *Black Women in White: Racial Conflict and Cooperation in the Nursing Profession, 1890–1950*. Bloomington: Indiana University Press, 1989.

Hock-Smith, Judith, and Anita Spring. *Women in Ritual and Symbolic Roles*. New York: Plenum Press, 1978.

Holland, Endesha Ida Mae. "Granny Midwives: Portrait of a Timeless Profession." *Ms*. (June 1987): 48–51, 73.

Hollis, Susan Tower and Linda Pershing and M. Jane Young. *Feminist Theory and the Study of Folklore*. Urbana: University of Illinois Press, 1993.

Holloway, Karla. "*Beloved*: A Spiritual." *Callaloo* 13 (1990): 516–25.

— — — . *Moorings and Metaphors: Figures of Culture and Gender in Black Women's Literature*. New Brunswick: Rutgers University Press, 1992.

Holmes, Linda. "The Insurance Crisis." *Ms.* (June 1987): 74.

—— ——. "Medical History: Alabama Granny Midwife." *The Journal of the Medical Society of New Jersey.* 81.5 (May 1984): 389–91.

—— ——. "African American Midwives in the South." *The American Way of Birth.* Philadelphia: Temple University Press, 1986.

hooks, bell, and Cornell West. *Breaking Bread: Insurgent Black Intellectual Life.* Boston: South End Press, 1991.

—— ——. *Sisters of The Yam.* Boston: South End Press, 1993.

—— ——. *Yearning: Race, Gender and Cultural Politics.* Boston: South End Press, 1990.

Hufford, David. "Contemporary Folk Medicine." *Other Healers: Unorthodox Medicine in America,* edited by Norman Gevitz. Baltimore: Johns Hopkins University Press, 1988.

—— ——. "Folk Healers." *Handbook of American Folklore,* edited by Richard M. Dorson. Bloomington: Indiana University Press, 1983.

Hull, Gloria T. "'What It Is I Think She's Doing Anyhow': A Reading of Toni Cade Bambara's *The Salt Eaters.*" In *Conjuring,* edited by Marjorie Pryse and Hortense Spillers. Bloomington: Indiana University Press, 1985.

Hurston, Zora Neale. *Dust Tracks on a Road.* J.B. Lippincott Company, 1942. Reprint with an Introduction by Larry Neal. Philadelphia: J.B. Lippincott Company, 1971.

—— ——. *Their Eyes Were Watching God.* J.B. Lippincott Company, 1937. Reprint Urbana: University Illinois Press, 1978.

—— ——. *Mules and Men.* J.B. Lippincott, 1935.

Hyatt, Harry Middleton. *Hoodoo Conjuration and Witchcraft, Volume II.* Hannibal, MO: Western Publication Company, 1970.

Imperato, Pascal James. *African Folk Medicine: Practices and Beliefs of the Bambara and other People.* Baltimore: York Press Inc., 1977.

James, Stanlie M., and Abena P.A. Busia, eds. *Theorizing Black Feminisms: The Visionary Pragmatism of Black Women.* New York: Routledge, 1993.

Johnson, Georgia Douglass. "Plumes." *Black Female Playwrights: An Anthology of Plays Before 1950,* edited by Kathy Perkins. Bloomington: Indiana University Press, 1989.

Jones, Gayl. *Liberating Voices: Oral Tradition in African-American Literature.* Cambridge: Harvard University Press, 1991.

King, Deborah. "Multiple Jeopardy, Multiple Consciousness: The Context of a Black Feminist Ideology." *Signs.* 14.1 (August 1988): 42–72.

Kirkland, James, Holly F. Mathews, C.W. Sullivan III, and Karen Baldwin. *Herbal and Magical Medicine.* Durham: Duke University Press, 1992.

Kitzinger, Sheila, ed. *The Midwife's Challenge.* London: Pandora, 1988.

Laguerre, Michael S. *Afro-Caribbean Folk Medicine.* South Hadley, MA: Bergin and Garvey Publishers, 1987.

Larsen, Nella. *Quicksand and Passing.* New Brunswick NJ: Rutgers University Press, 1986.

Leavitt, Judith Walzer. "'Science' Enters the Birthing Room: Obstetrics in America Since the Eighteenth Century." *Journal of American History* 70.2 (1983): 281–304.

Lee, Carol. *Signifying as a Scaffold for Literary Interpretation: The Pedagogical Implications of an African American Discourse Genre.* Urbana: National Council of Teachers of English, 1993.

Lee, Dorothy H. "*Song of Solomon:* To Ride the Air." *Black American Literature Forum* 16.2 (1982): 64–70.

Lee, Valerie. "Testifying Theory: Womanist Intellectual Thought." *Women: A Cultural Review* 6.2 (1996): 200–06.

Lepow, Lauren. "Paradise Lost and Found: Dualism and Edenic Myth in Toni Morrison's *Tar Baby.*."*Contemporary Literature* 28.3 (1987): 363–77.

*Lessons for the Midwives.* South Carolina Board of Health, 1956.

Litoff, Judy Barret. *The American Midwife Debate: A Source Book on its Modern Origins.* New York: Greenwood Press, 1986.

———. *American Midwives: 1860 to the Present.* Westport, CT: Greenwood Press, 1978.

———. "The Midwife Through History." *Journal of Nurse Midwifery* 27.6 (November/December 1982): 3–11.

———. "Midwives in History." *Women, Health, and Medicine in America,* edited by Rima D. Apple. New York: Garland Publishing, Inc., 1990.

Logan, Onnie Lee as told to Katherine Clark. *Motherwit: An Alabama Midwife's Story.* New York: E.P. Dutton, 1989.

Lorde, Audre. *Sister Outsider.* Freedom, CA: The Crossing Press, 1984.

———. "The Master's Tools Will Never Dismantle the Master's House." *This Bridge Called My Back: Writings by Radical Women of Color,* edited by Gloria Anzaldua. Watertown, MA: Persephone, 1981.

Lubiano, Waheema. "Black Ladies, Welfare Queens, and State Minstrels: Ideological War by Narrative Means." *Race-ing Justice En-gendering Power: Essays on Anita Hill, Clarence Thomas, and the Construction of Social Reality.* Toni Morrison, ed. New York: Pantheon, 1992.

Lugones, Maria. "Playfulness, 'World'-Travelling, and Loving Perception." *Making Face, Making Soul: Haciendo Caras. Creative and Critical Perspectives by Women of Color,* edited by Gloria Anzaldua. San Francisco: Aunt Lute Books, 1990.

Malson, Micheline R. et al., ed. *Black Women in America: Social Science Perspectives.* Chicago: University of Chicago Press, 1988.

"Mama Lytton." author: Smith, Patricia, *Chicago Sun Times*, Sunday, May 10, 1987.

Marshall, Brenda. "The Gospel According to Pilate." *American Literature* 57.3 (October 1985): 486–49.

Marshall, Paule. "From the Poets in the Kitchen 1983." *Reena and Other Stories*. Old Westbury, NY: The Feminist Press, 1983.

— — —. *Praisesong for the Widow*. New York: Putnam, 1984.

Martin, Emily. *The Woman in the Body: A Cultural Analysis of Reproduction*. Boston: Beacon Press, 1987.

Martinez, Raymond Joseph. *Mysterious Marie Leveau, Voodoo Queen, and Folk Tales Along the Mississippi*. New Orleans: Hope Publications, 1956.

Mason, Theodore O. "The Novelist as Conservator: Stories and Comprehension in Toni Morrison's *Song of Solomon*." *Contemporary Literature* 29.4 (1988): 564–81.

Mathews, Holly. "Killing the Medical Self-Help Tradition Among African Americans: The Case of Lay Midwifery in North Carolina, 1912–1983." *African Americans in the South: Issues of Race, Class, and Gender*, edited by Hans A. Baer and Yvonne Jones. Athens: University of Georgia Press, 1992.

Mattox, Cheryl Warren. *Shake It to the One That You Love the Best: Play Songs and Lullabies from Black Musical Traditions*. Elsobrante, CA: Warren-Mattox Production, 1989.

Mbiti, John S. *African Religions and Philosophy*. New York: Praeger Publishers, 1969.

McClain, Carol Shepherd, ed. *Women as Healers: Cross-Cultural Perspectives*. New Brunswick: Rutgers University Press, 1989.

McFadden, Grace Jordan, Interviewer. "Sadie Nickpeay." Video, University of South Carolina, 1980.

McKay, Nellie. "An Interview with Toni Morrison." *Contemporary Literature* xxiv.4:413–29.

Mirikitani, Janice. "Prisons of Silence." *Making Face, Making Soul: Haciendo Caras. Creative and Critical Perspectives by Women of Color*, edited by Gloria Anzaldua. San Francisco: Aunt Lute Books, 1990.

Mohanty, Chandra. "On Race and Voice: Challenges for Liberal Education in the 1990s." *Cultural Critique*, 14 (1989–90).

Mongeau, Beatrice, Harvey L. Smith, and Ann C. Maney. "The 'Granny' Midwife: Changing Roles and Functions of a Folk Practitioner." *American Journal of Sociology*, 66 (1961): 487–505.

Morley, Peter, and Roy Wallis, eds. *Culture and Curing: Anthropological Perspectives on Traditional Medical Beliefs and Practices*. London: Peter Owen, 1978.

Morrison, Toni. *Beloved: A Novel*. New York: Knopf, 1987.

— — —. *The Bluest Eye*. New York: Pocket Books, 1970.

————. *Playing in the Dark: Whiteness and the Literary Imagination.* New York: Vintage, 1993.

————. *Race-ing Justice En-gendering Power: Essays on Anita Hill, Clarence Thomas, and the Construction of Social Reality.* New York: Pantheon, 1992.

————. *Song of Solomon.* New York: Knopf, 1977.

————. *Sula.* New York: Knopf, 1973.

————. *Tar Baby.* New York: Knopf, 1981.

Moussatos, Martha Ann Tyree. "J. E. McTeer: Root Doctor." *Sandlapper.* 31–32.

Mullen, Patrick B. *I Heard the Old Fishermen Say: Folklore of the Texas Gulf Coast.* Logan: Utah State University, 1978. Reprint 1994.

Mulvey, Laura. *Visual and Other Pleasures.* Bloomington: Indiana University Press, 1975.

Naylor, Gloria. *Mama Day.* New York: Ticknor and Fields, 1988.

————. *The Women of Brewster Place.* New York: Penguin Books, 1982.

Ngubane, Harriet. *Body and Mind in Zula Medicine: An Ethnography of Health and Disease in Nyusua-Zula Thought and Practice.* London: Academic Press, 1977.

Okpewho, Isidore. *African Oral Literature.* Bloomington: Indiana University Press, 1992.

Olney, James. "'I was Born': Slave Narratives, Their Status as Autobiography and as Literature." *The Slave's Narrative,* edited by Charles T. Davis and Henry Louis Gates, Jr. New York: Oxford University Press, 1985.

Paquet, Sandra Pouchet. "The Ancestor as Foundation in *Their Eyes Were Watching God* and *Tar Baby.*" *Callaloo* 13 (1990): 499–515.

Perrone, Bobette, and H. Henrietta Stockel, and Victoria Krueger. *Medicine Women, Curanderas, and Women Doctors.* Norman: University of Oklahoma, Press 1989.

Perry, Diana. S. "The Early Midwives of Missouri." *Journal of Nurse-Midwifery* 28.6 (November/December 1983): 15–22.

Pryse, Marjorie, and Hortense J. Spillers. *Conjuring: Black Women, Fiction and the Literary Tradition.* Bloomington: Indiana University Press, 1985.

Powell, Timothy B. "Toni Morrison: the Struggle to Depict the Black Figure on the White Page." *Black American Literature Forum.* 24:4 Winter 1990.

Puhr, Kathleen M. "Healers in Gloria Naylor's Fiction." *Twentieth Century Literature* 40.4 (Winter 1994): 518–27.

Radner, Joan Newlon, ed. *Feminist Messages: Coding in Women's Folk Culture.* Urbana: University of Illinois Press, 1993.

Rayburn, Otto Ernest. "The 'Granny Woman' in the Ozarks." *Midwest Folklore* 9 (1959): 145–48.

Reid, Margaret. "Sisterhood and Professionalization: A Case Study of the American Lay Midwife." *Women As Healers: Cross-Cultural Perspectives,* edited by

Carol Shepherd McClain. New Brunswick: Rutgers University Press, 1989.

Rich, Carroll. "Born With the Veil: Black Folklore in Louisiana." *Journal of American Folklore* 85 (1976): 328–31.

Rigney, Barbara Hill. *The Voices of Toni Morrison*. Columbus: Ohio State University Press, 1991.

Roberts, Diane. *The Myth of Aunt Jemima: Representations of Race and Region*. London: Routledge, 1994.

Roberts, Edna, and Rene M. Reeb. "Mississippi Public Health Nurses and Midwives: A Partnership That Worked." *Public Health Nursing* 2.1 (February 1994).

Roberts, John W. *From Trickster to Badman: The Black Folk Hero in Slavery and Freedom*. Philadelphia: University of Pennsylvania Press, 1989.

Robinson, Beverly J. *Aunt Phyllis*. Oakland: Regent Press, 1988.

Robinson, Sharon. "A Historical Development of Midwifery in the Black Community: 1600–1940." *Journal of Nurse-Midwifery* 29.4 (July/August 1984): 247–50.

Rosenberg, Charles and Carroll Smith Rosenberg, ed. *The Male Mid-wife and the Female Doctor: The Gynecology Controversy in Nineteenth Century America*. New York: Arno Press, 1974.

Sammons, Robert. "Parallels Between Magico-Religious Healing and Clinical Hypnosis Therapy." *Herbal and Magical Medicine*, edited by James Kirland et al. Durham: Duke University Press, 1992.

Santino, Jack. "On the Nature of Healing as a Folk Event." *Western Folklore* 49.3 (July 1985): 153–67.

Secundy, Marian Gray, ed. *Trials, Tribulations, and Celebrations: African-American Perspectives on Health, Illness, Aging and Loss*. Yarmouth, ME: Intercultural Press, 1992.

Shange, Ntozake. *sassafrass, cypress & indigo*. New York: St. Martins, 1983.

Silko, Leslie Marmon. *Ceremony*. New York: New American Library, 1977.

— — —. "The Man to Send Rain Clouds." *The Man To Send Rain Clouds: Contemporary Stories by American Indians*, edited by Kenneth Rosen. New York: Viking Press, 1974.

Smith, Claudine Curry in collaboration with Millie H. B. Roberson. *Memories of a Black Lay Midwife from Northern Neck Virginia*. Lisle, IL: Tucker Publications, 1994.

Smith, Theophus H. *Conjuring Culture: Biblical Formations of Black America*. New York: Oxford University Press, 1994.

Smith, W. Eugene. "Nurse Midwife: Maude Callen Eases Pain of Birth, Life and Death." *Life* 31, no.23 (December 3, 1951).

Snow, Loudell F. "Con Men and Consure Men: A Ghetto Image." *Literature and Medicine* (Fall 1983): 45–78.

Spivak, Gayatri. "Who Claims Alterity?" *Remaking History*, edited by Barbara Kruger and Philomena Mariana. Seattle: Dia Arts, Bay Press, 1989.

— — —. "Reading the World: Literary Studies in the Eighties." *In Other Worlds: Essays in Cultural Politics*. 1988.

Stallybrass, Peter and Allon White. *The Politics and Poetics of Transgression*. Ithaca, NY: Cornell Univerisity Press, 1986.

Starling, Marion Wilson. *The Slave Narrative, from 2nd edition*. Washington, D.C.: Howard University Press, 1988.

Stockell, Charles. "Resident Witch Doctor." *Beaufort Land of Isles*. The Beaufort County Chamber of Commerce, January, 1974.

Strandness, Jean. "Reclaiming Women's Language, Imagery, and Experience: Ntozake Shange's *sassafrass, cypress & indigo*." *Journal of American Culture* 10 (1987): 11–17.

Susie, Debra Anne. *In The Way of Our Grandmothers: A Cultural View of Twentieth Century Midwifery in Florida*. Athens: University of Georgia Press, 1988.

Tate, Claudia, ed. *Black Women Writers at Work*. New York: Continuum, 1983.

Taylor-Guthrie, Danille, ed. *Conversations with Toni Morrison*. Jackson: University Press of Mississippi, 1994.

Terry, Jennifer. "Theorizing Deviant Historiography." *differences: a Journal of Feminist Cultural Studies*. 3.2 (1991): 55–74.

Tesfagiorgis, Freida. "In Search of a Discourse and Critique/s That Center the Art of Black Women Artists." *Black Feminist Criticism and Critical Theory*, edited by Joe Weixlman and Houston Baker. Greenwood, FL: The PenKevill Publishing Company, 1988.

Thurer, Shari L. *The Myths of Motherhood: How Culture Reinvents The Good Mother*. New York: Penquin, 1994.

Thurman, Wallace. *The Blacker the Berry. . . .* New York: Macaulay Company, 1929.

Tom, Sally Austen. "The Evolution of Nurse-Midwifery: 1990–1960." Journal of Nurse-Midwifery. 27:4 (July/August 1982).

Towler, Jean and John Bramall. *Midwives in History and Society*. London: Croon Helm, 1986.

Turner, Lorenzo D. *Africanisms in The Gullah Dialect*. Chicago: University of Chicago Press, 1949.

Turner, Victor, and Edward Bruner, ed. *The Anthropology of Experience*. Urbana and Chicago: University of Illinois Press, 1986.

Twining, Mary A, and Keith E. Baird. *Sea Island Roots: African Presence in the Carolinas and Georgia*. Trenton, NJ: African World Press, 1991.

Ulrich, Laurel Thatcher. *The Midwife's Tale: The Life of Martha Ballard Based on Her Diary, 1785–1812*. New York: Vintage Books, 1991.

Vrettos, Athena. "Curative Domains: Women, Healing and History in Black

Women's Narratives." *Women's Studies* 16 (1989): 455–73.

Waite, Gloria. "Childbirth, Lay Institution Building, and Health Policy: The Traditional Childbearing Group, Inc., of Boston in a Historical Context." *Wings of Gauze: Women of Color and the Experience of Health and Illness*, edited by Barbara Bair and Susan E. Cayleff. Detroit: Wayne State University Press, 1993.

Walker, Alice. *In Search Of Our Mothers' Gardens*. New York: Harcourt Brace Jovanovich, 1983.

— — —. *In Love and Trouble*. New York: Harcourt Brace Jovanovich, 1974.

— — —. *The Color Purple*. New York: Washington Square Press, 1982.

Walker, Margaret. *Jubilee*. Boston: Houghton Mifflin, 1966.

Wall, Cheryl, A., ed. *Changing Our Own Words: Essays on Criticism, Theory, and Writing by Black Women*. New Brunswick, NJ: Rutgers University Press, 1991.

Wall, L. Lewis. *Hausa Medicine: Illness and Well-being in a West African Culture*. Durham: Duke University Press, 1988.

Wallace, Michele. "Variation on Negation and the Heresy of Black Feminist Creativity." *Reading Black, Reading Feminist*, edited by Henry Louis Gates, Jr. New York: Meridian, 1990.

Watkins, Mel. "Talk with Toni Morrison." *Conversations with Toni Morrison*, edited by Danielle Taylor-Guthrie. Jackson: University Press of Mississippi, 1994. Rpt. *New York Times Book Review* 7 (11 September 1977): 48–50.

Watson, Wilbur H., ed. *Black Folk Medicine: The Therapeutic Significance of Faith and Trust*. New Brunswick NJ: Transaction Books, 1984.

Wertz, Richard W and Dorothy C. Wertz. *Lying in: A History of Childbirth in America*. New York: The Free Press, 1977.

White, Deborah Gray. *Ain't I a Woman? Female Slaves in the Plantation South*. New York: W.W. Norton & Company, 1985.

White, Evelyn C., ed. *The Black Women's Health Book: Speaking for Ourselves*. Seattle, WA: Seal Press, 1990.

— — —, and Shafia Mawashi Monroe. "Interview: Lay Midwifery and the Traditional Childbearing Group." *"It Just Ain't Fair": The Ethics of Health Care for African Americans*, edited by Annette Dula and Sara Goering. Wesport, CT: Praeger, 1994.

Wilentz, Gay. "Civilizations Underneath: African Heritage as Cultural Discourse in Toni Morrison's *Song of Solomon*." *African American Review* 26.1 (1992): 61–74.

Williams, Patricia. *The Alchemy of Race and Rights: Diary of a Law Professor*. Cambridge: Harvard University Press, 1991.

Williams, Sherley Anne. "Some Implications of Womanist Theory." *Reading Black, Reading Feminist: A Critical Anthology*, edited by Henry Louis Gates, Jr. New York: Meridian, 1990.

— — —. *Dessa Rose* America. New York: Arno Press, 1974.

Willis, Susan. "I Shop Therefore I Am: Is There a Place for Afro-American Culture in Commodity Culture?." *Changing Our Own Words*, edited by Cheryl Wall. New Brunswick, New Jersey: Rutgers University Press, 1989.

———. *Specifying: Black Women Writing the American Experience*. Madison: University of Wisconsin Press, 1987.

Wollstonecraft, Mary. *A Vindication of the Rights of Woman*. 1792. Reprint edited by Miriam Brody. New York: Penguin Books, 1975.

Wyatt, Jean. "Giving Body to the Word: The Maternal Symbolic in Toni Morrison's *Beloved*." *PMLA* 108 (May 1993): 474–88.

Yellin, Jean Fagin. "Text and Contexts of Harriet Jacobs' *Incidents in the Life of a Slave Girl: Written by Herself*." *The Slave's Narrative*, edited by Charles T. Davis and Henry Louis Gates, Jr. New York: Oxford University Press, 1985.

# INDEX

Abrahams, Roger, 172n. 9

Adams, M.C., 144, 145, 155, 158, 160, 166–68

Africa, 37, 134

African: childbirth rituals, 33, 35, 75, 117, 120; diasporic traditions, 6, 9, 13, 14, 35, 37, 39, 49, 60, 77, 78, 112–20, 134, 181n. 1; epistemology, 10, 12, 47; healers, 33, 112, 113, 134, 175n. 10 proverbs, 11, 12, 33

African American women. See black women

African American women's literature: and breast-feeding 74–78; hygiene in, 52–55; narrative strategies of, 53,54; race relations in, 69–74

African American women's writers: as conjurers, 68, 103, 137, 138, 140; as culture bearers, 2, 171 n. 2; and empiricism 63–69; as ethnographers, 10; and folklore (see folklore); and grannies 2, 10, 18, 20, 46–49, 51–78, 89–93, 101; as healers, 2; as midwives, 8, 49; narratives of 19, 63–69; nineteenth century predecessors of, 89,94

*Alchemy of Race and Rights, The* (Williams), 97

Alcoff, Linda, 141

American Medical Association, 27, 30, 31

Anaya, Rudolfo (*Bless Me, Ultima*), 120

Ansa, Tina McElroy (*Baby of the Family*), 9, 122, 123

Aunt Jemima. *See* mammies

*Baby of the Family* (Ansa), 9, 122, 123

Baker, Houston, 13, 16, 94, 177n. 4

Bakhtin, Mikhail M., 38

Baldwin, James, *If Beale Street Could Talk*, 60

Bambara, Toni Cade, 9, 164; *See Salt Eaters, The*

Beavers, Louise, 111, 112

Behar, Ruth, 56, 169

*Beloved* (Morrison), 20,21, 54, 66, 76, 77;

Baby Suggs, 23, 52

birthing chambers, men in, 25–30; 174n. 2

binaries, resistance of, 20, 88, 90–92

black churches. *See* religion:in black churches

black feminist criticism. *See* womanist theory

black lay midwives. *See* granny midwives

black women: beauty aesthetic 55–63; bodies of 51–63, 66–68; and folklore 57, 58; and "funk" 53–55, 176nn. 3,4; hair of 61, 62; health movement, 9; and skin color 55–61, 112; and white women, 70–74

black women writers. *See* African American women writers

*Blacker the Berry, The* (Thurman), 56, 57, 61

Bless Me, Ultima (Anaya), 120

*Bluest Eye, The* (Morrison), 54, 58, 59, 74

breast-feeding, 74–78

Brooks, Gwendolyn: *Maud Martha*, 58; *Primer for Blacks*, 61

Brown, Elsa Barkley, 2

Bruner, Edward, 141

Callen, Maude, 161. 181n. 20

Carby, Hazel, 4, 56, 71, 96

cauls, significance of, 120–23

*Ceremony* (Silko), 116

Chestnutt, Charles, 13

childbirth, medicalization of, 17, 33, 42, 43; and natural stimulants, 44

childbirth metaphors: "brought to bed," 28, 29; "catching babies," 24, 36, 52, 84; "sit on the bricks," 178n. 2

Christian, Barbara, 53. 91, 92, 93, 138

class, politics of: and black/white relationships, 69–74; and "funk," 54; and health care, 27, 31, 47; and hospitals, 42; and life/death crises, 11, 47; and grannies' fees, 30, 84–86, 125, 126; and transportation, 45, 46; and women's bodies,